CELIA SANCHEZ:

THE LEGEND OF
CUBA'S
REVOLUTIONARY HEART

CELIA SANCHEZ:

THE LEGEND OF
CUBA'S
REVOLUTIONARY HEART

Richard Haney

Algora Publishing
New York

ISBN: 0-87586-395-7 (softcover)
ISBN: 0-87586-396-5 (hardcover)
ISBN: 0-87586-397-3 (ebook)

Library of Congress Cataloging-in-Publication Data —

Haney, Rich (Richard)
Celia Sanchez : Cuba's revolutionary heart / Rich Haney.
    p. cm.
Includes bibliographical references and index.
    ISBN 0-87586-395-7 (trade paper: alk. paper) — ISBN 0-87586-396-5
(hard cover: alk. paper) — ISBN 0-87586-397-3 (ebook)
    1. Sanchez Manduley, Celia, d. 1980. 2. Castro, Fidel, 1926—Friends and
associates. 3. Cuba—History—1933-1959. 4. Cuba—History—1959- 5. Women
revolutionaries—Cuba—Biography. 6. Revolutionaries—Cuba—Biography. I.
Title.

    F1788.22.S26H36 2005
    972.9106'4'092—dc22

                        2005015556

Front Cover. Top: Havana, 1977, courtesy of The Office of Historic Affairs,
Cuban Council of State.
    Bottom: Courtesy of The Osvaldo & Roberto Salas Collection/Office of
Historic Affairs, Cuban Council of State.

Printed in the United States

TABLE OF CONTENTS

INTRODUCTION

In the past two decades, I have studied the Cuban Revolution day and night, particularly in terms of how it relates to the United States. Along the way, I have come to believe that the historic event says more about America than anything that has transpired since World War II, including Vietnam and Iraq and even including the Cold War against the former Soviet Union.

For me, an all-consuming interest in Cuba began innocently enough. Throughout the 1970s I was Sports Director/Anchor of WTVR-TV, the CBS affiliate in Richmond, Virginia. After airing an interview with the "Brown Bomber," Joe Louis, I received a phone call from an elderly black woman named Nora Peters. A retired free-lance journalist and botanist, she knew Joe and asked if I could put her in touch with him. I did. Shortly thereafter, Tina Peters, Nora's daughter, called me and thanked me for being "kind and patient" with her seventy-two-year-old mother. Then Tina told me that Nora watched my nightly sports shows from her "remote cabin" and that she was "a recluse" but "she would love to meet you."

Eventually, I did rendezvous at a rural store in central Virginia with Tina who then drove me about forty miles to Nora's home, far up a rugged and winding sawmill road. It was well past midnight when we arrived, and after Tina introduced me to Nora, she lay down on the couch for a "short nap." It turned into a long nap. My first hour with Nora was at her kitchen table where she watched me consume a whole coconut cream pie and several glasses of sweet tea. We discussed various sports, including the three heavyweight title fights she had seen Joe Louis win. She then showed me her striking flower garden out

1

back, complete with a waterfall and outdoor lights. Back in the kitchen, I took deeper cognizance of three pictures that adorned a wall and depicted a youthful Nora on some tropical beach in the company of a beaming little white woman. When I glanced back at Nora, I noticed, to my surprise, that she was overcome with emotion. Her left hand nervously covered her mouth and tears flooded her eyes. Trying to lighten her load, I looked back at the photos and said, "What year was that? Where's this beach with the white sand? Who is the other lady?"

"That was 1973," she said. "It's at Varadero Beach in Cuba. The lady with me is my all-time dearest friend, Celia Sánchez. Umm. Fidel took those three pictures."

"Fidel...Castro?"

"Yes!" Nora laughed, a happy laugh that dashed away the tears. I just stared in incredulity. "Sit back at the table, Ritchie Wayne," she said. "You look flushed. Till Tina wakes up, would you like to hear how I ended up on Varadero Beach with Celia Sánchez and Fidel Castro?"

Thankfully, Tina didn't wake up till daylight.

In the ensuing four hours, my infatuation with Nora, and with Cuba, mounted. Nora showed me a collection of memorabilia from her eight visits to Cuba beginning in 1953. Five framed photographs on Nora's bedroom walls also featured the petite white woman, and I soon realized that Nora's bedroom was a shrine to Celia Sánchez — whom I had never heard of, prior to this visit. Nora then extracted two hat-size boxes from a glass cabinet and placed them on the bed. From the boxes, she pulled out more pictures of Celia as well as seventeen letters she had received from her over the years. The neat handwriting was in Spanish. The letters, totaling about eighty pages, intrigued me. "Tina told me you don't speak Spanish, Ritchie Wayne," Nora said. "But if you come back to visit me, I will have another fresh coconut cream pie for you and I'll have all those letters translated from Spanish to English. Would you like that?"

Nora, like members of my family, always called me "Ritchie Wayne." As we sat on her bed, enmeshed in her memories of Celia Sánchez, she explained why she was my "biggest fan" and had used "Joe Louis and Tina" to "facilitate" this visit: "I'm a central Virginia native, like you, Ritchie Wayne. I knew older members of your family because of their sawmill operations. But you were a baby when I went off to college and the big cities, and became a world traveler. But I often returned to Virginia to visit my grandparents. I heard about your polio when you were eight, paralyzing your right leg. Later, I heard you went off to Lynchburg College and then became a radio announcer. I listened to you when I could. Though we didn't know each other, we grew up on neighboring farms. I was a poor black girl in the rural South. You were a poor white boy crippled with polio. I was decades older, but I identified with you, asked about you. Then I watched you each night on WTVR television after I retired out here in the woods.

"A visit to Cuba in 1953 to study marine life changed me forever. The island's beauty enraptured me. So did the plight of the peasants in the Batista dictatorship. To prolong my stay in Cuba I became a volunteer nurse at a hospital in Santiago on Cuba's eastern tip. I met Celia there. It was quite a year on the island. Fidel and a few rebels attacked the Moncada Army Barracks on the edge of Santiago in July. They got shot to pieces and he got sentenced to fifteen years in prison. Later that year, a ten-year-old peasant girl whom Celia adored was kidnapped by Batista's Mafia thugs. The little girl, María Ochoa, was raped to death — and it wasn't even illegal. The Mafia ran the hotels and casinos, and they used children to entice rich gamblers and pedophiles from the States. Celia, a petite little doctor's daughter, declared war on Batista, knowing she was also declaring war on his two prime supporters, the US and the Mafia. In the Sierra Mountains and its foothills, turf she knew so well, she created, nurtured, and conducted the guerrilla warfare that history calls the Cuban Revolution. In other words, she did the impossible — and she did it while Fidel was in prison and before Che Guevara had ever set foot in Cuba. They joined her at the start of 1957 but they never forgot whose revolution it was or whose Cuba they were fighting for."

That soliloquy, which I remember (almost) word-for-word, gripped me. So did Nora's personality. She was one of the most intelligent and the most patriotic Americans I've ever known. In the last twelve years of her life, I shared her vivid memories of the one person she idolized — Cuba's revolutionary heroine Celia Sánchez. Nora carefully documented to me these intriguing facts:

• Celia was the primary creator, nurturer, and leader of the Cuban Revolution.

• After the triumph of the revolution on January 1, 1959, Celia was the prime decision-maker in Cuba from January of 1959 till her death from cancer in January of 1980.

• From 1980 till the present day, Fidel Castro, her most fervent acolyte, has ruled Cuba only as he perceives Celia would want him to rule it.

• As the elderly Fidel Castro anticipates and plans for "post-Castro Cuba," his prime focus in shaping the transition as much as he possibly can concerns precisely what he perceives Celia would want him to do, and his prime perception is that the last thing Celia would want is for the Florida-based Batistianos to regain control of Cuba.

The Cuban Revolution has had vast and ongoing repercussions for both Cuba and the United States over the course of the past half century, but the crucial role played by Ms. Sánchez is so generally overlooked that I had to convince myself how real she was. Utilizing the best sources in both countries, including declassified documents from both governments, I have concluded that Nora's insightful data pertaining to Celia and to Cuba is accurate and authentic. The documentation that led to that conclusion is contained in this book, which has been an unexpectedly long journey.

One afternoon during the long period while I was doing my research, I was in Morgantown, West Virginia, to broadcast a university football game. I was stopped at the hotel's front desk on the way to the stadium. In a phone call Tina informed me that, "Mama is dying, Ritchie Wayne. I hate to bother you but you need to know."

That Saturday afternoon I undoubtedly established a new record — for the worst play-by-play broadcast of a major collegiate football game in US history. Back in Richmond, I was tied down Saturday night and Sunday morning with the preparation and hosting of Coach Jim Tait's University of Richmond football highlights program. Thus it was mid-afternoon that Sunday when I arrived at Nora's home. Tina was sitting on the front porch. Inside, monitoring a sleeping Nora, was Dr. Patricia Anne Patterson.

I kissed Nora's cheek and then Tina escorted me to the kitchen. To my surprise, a fresh coconut cream pie and a glass of sweet tea awaited me on the table.

"Mama is not suffering," Tina said. "She's been asleep about six hours. When she wakes up, Pat will come get you. That's what mama instructed her to do."

Late that Sunday afternoon Dr. Patterson entered the living room and nodded at Tina, who then took me to Nora's bedroom. She was not only awake but also surprisingly alert, strong, and cheerful. Reaching for my hand and smiling broadly, she said, "Don't be sad for me, Ritchie Wayne. I'm not. Eighty-two years is a long time and this is something I equate to a trip to Cuba, to be with Celia." As I stood at Nora's bedside, Tina sat in a chair on the other side of the bed. Nora pointed to a table over by the window. "That box on the table," Nora said, "contains some things I want you to have. Mainly, it's those seventeen letters Celia wrote me from Cuba from 1953 till shortly before she died in 1980. On the back of each page I have translated her Spanish to English. I want you to use those letters and the other things I have given you to write a book about Celia and her Cuban Revolution. Use the letters and my notes as a guide but continue your research to corroborate each point with other reliable Cuban and American sources. And, most of all, somehow visit Cuba to finish your research. Will you do that, Ritchie Wayne...for me and for my Celia?"

Thus, my research on Celia Sánchez and the Cuban Revolution has been a labor of love and all-consuming. Many times prior to finalizing my biographical manuscript I tried to fulfill Nora's request that I visit Cuba to conclude the research. But the US government refused to grant me a visa to visit Cuba, maintaining that I was not a "legitimate author." After eight years of frustration, I hunkered down and wrote and published four books — *Chattahoochee, Sacajawea, Fawn,* and *Rosebud.* The first is a Civil War historic novel, the second a biography of the Indian girl famed for her Lewis & Clark exploits, and the final two are Western historic novels. Freshly minted copies of these titles plus a review from the *Denver Post* calling *Sacajawea* "the definitive book on America's most honored heroine" did the trick. The US Treasury finally admitted that I was a "legitimate author" and granted me a visa to visit Cuba to finish research on *Celia Sánchez, The Legend of Cuba's Revolutionary Heart.*

My legal and hard-earned trip to Cuba occurred in March of 2004. Prior to my visit, my intense research had included countless e-mail exchanges with Americans who possessed intimate knowledge of Cuba, such as my friend Tracey Eaton, head of the *Dallas Morning News* bureau in Havana.

Tracey met me at Havana's Victoria Hotel. He told me to contact Marta Rojas, a revolutionary heroine of the first order, a historian and Cuba's most honored writer and author. (Her book *Tania* was published in the US by Random House.) Marta wrote the front-page articles in the Cuban newspapers concerning the death of Celia Sánchez on January 11, 1980. She had known Celia intimately — and, said Tracey, Marta Rojas today has more influence on Fidel Castro than any other living person.

I now count Marta Rojas as a dear friend. I am deeply indebted to her for incalculable contributions to this book. Since my return to the US, I have exchanged many e-mails with Marta and consider her the greatest living expert on the revolution. In many of her e-mails, Marta included attachments of historical documents and scans of hand-written notes from Celia to Fidel and Fidel to Celia. I asked Marta if what Tracey Eaton told me was true: that she had more influence on Fidel Castro than any living person. She replied: "I reckon that's so.

But till the day he dies, Celia will have the most influence on him. Since she died, he has ruled Cuba only as he believes she would want him to rule it."

In the following pages I present the results of my research, hoping to convey an accurate portrayal of Celia Sánchez's remarkable life. I think the evidence shows that Cuban historian Pablo Alvarez Tabio got it right when he called Celia "the greatest maker of Cuban history."

Celia Sánchez was the prime factor in ejecting the brutal dictator Fulgencio Batista, the Mafia, and certain rapacious United States business interests out of Cuba on January 1, 1959. She remains the prime reason, after all these decades, that the powerful Florida-based Batistianos have not regained control of Cuba despite the continued fierce support of the US government. Moreover, her legacy will have more to say about "post-Castro Cuba" than all other competing factions, including Fidel Castro, the US President, and the Batistianos. University of Pittsburgh scholar Tiffany Thomas-Woodard called Celia "a woman of mythic proportions."

Most of the many edifices in Cuba named for Celia Sánchez, such as clinics and hospitals, reflect her unswerving and unselfish devotion to the Cuban peasants, especially the children and women. She fought to the end and always from the front lines for them and for what she called "*mi Cubita bella*," her "beautiful little Cuba."

Celia's childhood home in the town of Media Luna is now a shrine and a lovingly maintained tourist attraction. The sign fronting the most special home in Cuba states: "Native Home of Celia Sánchez, greatest and most outstanding clandestine and guerrilla fighter of the Cuban Revolution."

"Celia still lives in the people," states Tiffany Thomas-Woodard. "Celia is Cuban and is ours, like the mountains of the Sierra," writes Cuban poet Nancy Morejón. "Celia was Cuba's angel," Nora Peters said. "Even those who despised Fidel loved Celia," wrote Castro biographer Georgie Anne Geyer. "Celia made all the decisions for Cuba, the big ones and the small ones. We all knew no one could ever replace her," photographer Roberto Salas wrote in his 1998 book. Cubans on the island still have trouble accepting the fact that Celia died in 1980, and the poet Morejón constantly reminds them, "No one who lives in the people dies, or ever will die." In an e-mail dated January 3, 2005, Marta Rojas wrote: "We who knew her still think of Celia — every day, every hour."

Fidel Castro rates the ten most important people in the Cuban Revolution in this order: Celia Sánchez, Fidel Castro, Che Guevara, Camilo Cienfuegos, Haydée Santamaría, Raúl Castro, Frank País, Melba Hernández, Vilma Espín, and Juan Almeída. In that Big Ten, he separates Celia from all others, including himself, and when it comes to her he will only talk with close friends such as Marta Rojas, his brother Raúl, Juan, and Teté Puebla.

However, during an interview in March of 2004, he did say to me, "Thank you for understanding her, and loving her."

Celia Sánchez, above all others, still lives in the people on the island of Cuba. And that's why the Cuban Revolution still lives and, in any case, has left an indelible imprint on history, especially Cuban and US history.

Rich Haney

Prologue

Celia Sánchez Manduley was born on May 9, 1920, in the sleepy Cuban town of Media Luna. Her character was most shaped by her love for Cuba and by two special people — her father and little María Ochoa.

Celia virtually worshipped her father, Dr. Manuel Sánchez. He was head of the Cuban Medical Association — until he was ousted as a dissident. A wealthy man, he owned three farms. Celia came to sympathize with the farmhands and other rural folk, and she often assisted her father in caring for them. Celia's mother, Acacia Manduley, died in 1926 of a tropical fever relating to childbirth; her sister soon moved in with the family to help raise the nine children and look after the home, a nine-room house.

University-educated as a biologist and then trained at home as a nurse, Celia was profoundly attached to the country people and the country landscape, the "soothing and beautiful tones that flowed inside me like a tropical breeze from my little hometown of Media Luna," as she told Nora Peters in a letter dated February 17, 1977. Twice, Celia was about to be married but she abruptly broke off each engagement when her suitors insisted she move to big cities — Havana, in one case, Miami in the other.

A genteel doctor's daughter, she was in her early thirties when the crimes condoned by the Batista regime in 1953 revolted her and transformed her into a guerrilla fighter determined to overthrow the dictatorship.

In 1944, Celia assisted at the difficult birth of a peasant baby, María Ochoa. The little girl was sickly and three times the skilled Dr. Sánchez predicted she would "not survive the night" because of severe asthma attacks. Those nights,

Celia held María in her arms, not wanting her "to die alone in a crib." Each time, the baby simply refused to die, "blinking her brown eyes up at me each time it seemed nature tried to take her last breath away." By age five, María had outgrown her breathing problems and had become, as Celia told Nora, "the sweetest and most beautiful thing in beautiful Cuba."

María spent many of her days and nights with Celia until, at age ten, in 1953, she was kidnapped.

Dr. Sánchez and Celia were already distraught over the treatment of peasants and the "rape and robbery of Cuba" during the Batista reign. Celia attended underground dissident meetings and even crafted "a militia uniform and trained with a rifle in case a true revolution emerged." But Batista was too strong, and he was supported by both the Mafia and the US government. Two men — veteran politician Antonio Guiteras and young upstart Fidel Castro — had challenged Batista's treatment of the populace but Guiteras was murdered and Castro in 1953 was sentenced to fifteen years in prison. Celia was familiar with their stories, and she was aware that no peasant rebellion anywhere in the Caribbean or Latin America had come close to success. US-backed dictators were strong. But, for Celia, the fate of little María Ochoa was the last straw. She told her father she now had to at least try to "do something." She did. She went to the Sierra Maestra Mountains on the eastern tip of Cuba to fashion a peasant revolution that would take on Batista, the Mafia, and the United States of America. This was the revolution that Fidel Castro and Che Guevara joined in late December, 1956, after their perilous journey from Mexico.

Celia and her father both were fervent Cuban patriots, and they both were great lovers of nature. As a girl, Celia had enjoyed fishing, hiking, and camping excursions with her father. Their favorite getaways were in the Sierra Maestra Mountains, and she knew the trails well. The highest point in Cuba is the Sierra's Turquino Peak, which is 6,477 feet above sea level. Celia climbed to the summit of Turquino Peak many times. In 1952, Dr. Sánchez and his then 32-year-old daughter teamed up to transport a sculpture of Cuban patriot Jose Martí to the summit of Turquino Peak, and it remains there to this day. That adventure resulted in articles on the front pages of two Santiago de Cuba newspapers, constituting the second public notation of the shy Celia in Santiago. (The first came four years earlier, when she earned newspaper coverage as a biologist who devised a means by which swamp water was used to irrigate nearby family farms.) In 1957, after Celia had gained fame as a revolutionary, Dr. Sánchez told Herbert L. Matthews, "Beginning as a little girl, Celia knew the mountains and swamps of the Sierra like she knew the back of her hand, and she was more at home in those mountains and swamps than she was in her own bedroom."

Those were the mountains and swamps that Celia Sánchez utilized so brilliantly as a guerrilla fighter against anything and everything Batista sent to defeat her. The historian Tabio, for example, recounts that "the first tanks Batista sent after her ended up under swamp water because of guerrilla strikes and retreats she led" and "the first good weapons she secured were taken from befuddled Batista armies she maneuvered into swampy clearings." All the while Celia meticulously defended the nine clearings at the foothills of the mountains, protecting her base camps that were tightly hidden high up in the dense crevices of the Sierra mountains that she knew so well. And all the while Celia continued her daunting recruitment of rebel fighters from the peasant towns so familiar to her — Media Luna, Pilon, Santo Domingo y Las Mercedes, Niquero, Campechuela, Manzanillo. Tabio wrote: "If Batista or the US had managed to kill Celia anytime between 1954 and 1957 there would have been no viable Cuban Revolution, and no revolution for Fidel and Che to join."

In a 1973 letter to Nora Peters, Celia wrote:

> I was not a born guerrilla or revolutionary, for sure. But I knew all the nuances of the Sierra and I knew the enemy didn't. And I knew the Cuban peasants loved me and would follow me if they felt we had a chance against Batista. I had to show them we had a chance.
>
> As for the guerrilla tactics and the revolutionary stuff, that was purely a step-by-step process. I improvised all the way, reacting to each threat from the enemy. I guess a guerrilla fights defensively to survive while inflicting as much damage as possible, with the goal of getting strong enough to one day go on the offensive. By the summer of 1957 we were on the offensive and by the summer of 1958 we were winning big battles. Nora, I went to the Sierra knowing there was no blueprint to follow because no dictator supported by the U.S. had ever been really threatened by a peasant uprising.
>
> In the Sierra I knew Batista would come after me harshly and I knew he could overmatch me. To survive, we had to out-fight and out-smart them. We did, as we got stronger. And then we still had to out-fight and out-smart them, and we did that too. But I told Mr. Matthews when he came up into the Sierra not to rave that we were guerrilla saints or revolutionary icons. We were just peasant fighters doing what we had to do.
>
> In February, 1957, the first real meeting I had with Fidel, Che, Raul, Camilo, and Juan — after they joined us from Mexico — I told them the message we had sent to Havana was that we would fight to the death and I questioned whether the rich enemy leaders would do that when the going got really tough. Now I could write a text on guerrilla fighting and revolutionary tactics but back then, Nora, believe me when I say I was making it up as I went along. The governance of Cuba is similar because we still have the same powerful enemies. And all along the way I've only

wanted to be the little girl and the little woman no one ever heard of, just a lover of Cuba and all the beautiful things beneath our Cuban rainbows. But loving Cuba as I do took me to the Sierra to fight and then to Havana to protect what I fought for. I didn't plan it that way and I didn't want it to be that way. It just happened.

Her legacy and her role in enhancing life in Cuba are still highly honored. Celia created and funded a children's asthma clinic in 1959; on May 11, 2005, Fidel Castro, noting that the economy had sharply improved thanks to new commercial contracts with Venezuela, China, and Canada, stated that the welfare stipends for all Cubans would be doubled and that funding would be increased two-fold for the Celia Sánchez Asthma Clinic for Children.

As the transition to "post-Castro Cuba" nears, the significance of Celia Sánchez will be greatly amplified as the various factions in the US and Cuba try to reshape the island nation.

Chapter 1. Cuba

Cuba, the fifteenth largest island in the world, is truly beautiful. Shaped like an alligator just a hundred or so miles south of Florida, the tropical paradise extends 750 miles and overall is about the size of the state of Pennsylvania. The warmest month is July, with temperatures about eighty-six degrees and the coolest month is January, when it's usually about seventy degrees under clear, blue skies.

Cuba is rimmed by some 210 bays and 290 sun-drenched beaches. Primary ports include Havana, Cienfuegos, Manzanillo, Mariel, Matanzas, and Santiago de Cuba. There are no lethal plants or animals in Cuba, not even poisonous snakes. The national flower is the butterfly jasmine, the national tree is the royal palm and the national bird is a colorful beauty called the tocororo, which is a climbing bird that has red, white, and blue plumage. The flag of Cuba is also red, white, and blue and was designed in 1850 when Cuban peasants were seeking independence from Spain. There are now 11,300,000 Cubans. Spanish is the primary language, but French and English are also widely spoken.

Even more than its political history, even more than the proximity to the United States, Cuba's beauty is a prime reason so many people are fascinated by what it is — and by what happens there. And much has happened there since the first humans arrived in 3500 BC and, particularly, since Columbus caught sight of the gorgeous island in 1492 when he discovered the Americas. Other explorers, including Sebastián de Ocampo and Diego Velázquez, had also mapped out Cuba by 1512. Seven large settlements were established in Cuba by

1514 and, within the next year, Santiago de Cuba became the capital. The great city of Havana emerged in 1519.

From its first sighting by Columbus until the present day, Cuba's greatest assets — its beauty, its location, its climate, its size — have also constituted its biggest weaknesses, because the world's powers wanted to exploit it and, taking turns, many of them have done so. The exploitation began in earnest in 1522 when the first Africans were shipped to Cuba as slaves, setting up an unending tug-of-war from outsiders. French pirates attacked Havana in 1555; Spanish pirates sacked Havana in 1556.

By 1564, ships were transporting Cuban treasures back to their home ports. Foreigners viewed Cuba as both a playpen and a piggy bank. Sadly, that is a lure that true Cubans have never really been able to dispel.

To protect as much of Cuba's bounty as possible, Havana and Santiago became fortifications protected by sea walls and soldiers. The capital was moved from Santiago to Havana in 1607, the very same year that America got its first permanent English settlement at Jamestown, Virginia.

In 1674, construction of massive protective walls around Havana began; they were then reinforced by the various outside powers that alternated control of what many called "Treasure Island." Havana became the jewel of Cuba, but the whole island was the Pearl of the Caribbean. By 1700, tobacco had become the primary Cuban export, and in 1728 the University of Havana was founded. Not surprisingly, the expansive British Empire cast its covetous eyes on Cuba. In 1762, a powerful British army captured Havana, then all of Cuba. But England soon came to see Cuba primarily as a gateway to America; thus, in 1763, England literally traded Cuba to Spain for Florida!

From 1765 till 1790, Spain engaged in vast commerce in Cuba by exploiting the lush island as grossly as had all the other imperialists. By 1790, Spain was sending thousands of African slaves to Cuba, and by 1800 sugar had replaced tobacco as Cuba's primary export. By 1819, Spain was using Cuba as a base from which to conduct commerce with all other countries of the world.

In 1820, Spain tried without much success to abolish further importation of African slaves. Cuba as well as most of Latin America was thriving in the first half of the nineteenth century, and a will for independence permeated most of the islands. Cuba's first railroad was opened in 1837.

The United States in 1848 made a powerful but unsuccessful attempt to purchase Cuba from Spain. On the island itself, aspirations toward independence were crystallized when a band of patriots led by Narciso López created and raised a Cuban flag. In 1854, the US again tried to buy Cuba from Spain.

In 1865, the year the American Civil War ended, Cuba, mainly at the behest of Cubans such as Narciso López, ended the importation of slaves.

From 1868 to 1878, Cuba underwent its First War of Independence, which was partially successful and resulted in its slaves now being called "apprentices."

A Second War of Independence took place from 1895 till 1898, whetting America's appetite to exploit the chaotic situation. On April 22, 1898, the first shot of the Spanish-American War rang out when the USS Nashville captured a Spanish merchant ship near Key West, Florida. On July 1, 1898, future president Theodore Roosevelt and his "Rough Riders" waged a victorious assault on Cuba's San Juan Hill. Sixteen days later, Spain surrendered to the United States in Santiago de Cuba.

The US military controlled Cuba from 1898 till 1902 when a pervasive undercurrent of Cuban nationalism gained a measure of independence for the embattled island, which had tired of being a pawn contested by world powers.

Cuba became an independent republic in 1902 and elected Tomas Palma as president. However, a peasant uprising ousted Palma in 1906 and the US military installed Charles Magoon as governor from 1906 till 1909. José Miguel Gómez was elected President of Cuba in 1909, but he was corrupt, incompetent and racist. In 1912, Afro-Cubans in Oriente Province protested their brutal treatment, resulting in 3000 of them being murdered in one day by Cuban soldiers. That same year, US soldiers prevented another slaughter of former African slaves in Pinar del Rio province. In 1917, US soldiers were patrolling Cuba to make sure that sugar exports flowed freely.

The first Communist Party in Cuba was founded in 1925 in response to the fact that US businessmen owned two-thirds of Cuban farmland and most of the productive mines. Cuba's sugar industry flourished throughout the 1920s but so did whiskey, beer, gambling, and prostitution. Cuba had become a haven for the rich and powerful but a hellhole for the exploited peasants, who were kept in line by leaders who employed terror against them while catering to the wealthy Cubans as well as foreign interlopers — including American businessmen and the Mafia.

In 1933, a peasant revolt and general strike ousted Cuban President Gerardo Machado. A new revolutionary government — led by two men, Ramón Grau San Martín and Antonio Guiteras — took over and immediately engineered radical changes in Cuban society. They established a Department of

Labor to benefit the peasants, opened universities to the poor, gave women the right to vote and provided land to the peasants. But Sumner Welles, a key advisor to U. S. President Franklin Roosevelt, referred to the massive changes under Martín-Guiteras as "both communistic and irresponsible." Of course, what Welles meant was that Martín and Guiteras were too devoted to Cuba's six million peasants and not sufficiently interested in preserving Cuba's wealth for the US businessmen and the Mafia. The US refused to recognize the Martín-Guiteras government, which Cuba's own people adored.

FULGENCIO BATISTA

The chaos provoked by Sumner Welles and others who took that stance paved the way for an army sergeant named Fulgencio Batista to assume power in a coup on September 4, 1933. Batista, like many other Cuban leaders, was both corrupt and incompetent.

But the army sergeant was precisely the man that Washington wanted in charge of Cuba; Batista would dance to Washington's tune.

Batista and Sumner Welles decided to leave the peasant-loving Guiteras as titular head of the government for appearances' sake. But on January 14, 1934, Guiteras announced the nationalization of the US-owned Electric Bond and Share Company. That would be his last governmental act. On May 8, 1935, after again speaking out on behalf of the Cuban peasants, Guiteras was murdered by Batista's American-armed soldiers.

In the 1940s, Cubans such as Eduardo Chibas tried in vain to rid their country of the rampant corruption and racism.

In 1944, a student about to enter a Jesuit high school in Havana was named the best high school athlete in Cuba. That student's name was Fidel Castro.

In 1946, the Mafia — already closely tied to Fulgencio Batista — began holding its summits in Havana. One such Mafia summit at the Hotel Nacional featured all of the leading Mafia gangsters — like Meyer Lansky, Lucky Luciano, Frank Costello, Tommy Lucchese, Vito Genovese, Joe Bonanno, Santo Traficante, and Moe Dalitz. From the Hotel Nacional, Luciano famously ordered the murder of Bugsy Siegel, a Mafia associate in Las Vegas. Also in 1946, Frank Sinatra, a great friend of the Mafia kingpins, made his debut at the Hotel Nacional.

On August 4, 1951, Cuba's most popular radio commentator, Eddy Chibas, lamented on air what had happened in Cuba; immediately after that broadcast, Chibas was found dead, an apparent suicide.

In October, 1951, Dr. Augusto Fernández Conde — the former president of the Cuban Medical Association — strongly denounced "the atrocities of the Batista dictatorship" at the World Medical Association meeting in Istanbul, Turkey. In 1951, a respected Latin weekly magazine, *Revista Carteles*, reported that Batista and twenty of his cronies each had numbered Swiss bank accounts with deposits of more than $1 million each!

While lining his pockets from the Cuban treasury (along with his Mafia and their capitalist partners), Batista could not find enough money to buy the military supplies that ruthlessly kept him in power. The US government robustly provided free of charge all of Batista's arms — including airplanes, tanks, ships, and ammunition. Also, Batista's army was trained in joint missions by the three branches of the US armed forces. In the 1950s, US businesses owned 90% of Cuba's mines, 80% of its public utilities, 50% of its railways, 40% of its sugar production, and 25% of its bank deposits. Of course, the Mafia controlled the lush casinos and hotels in the capital city of Havana. As Guiteras rested in his grave, the uncouth Batista was wined and dined, both at the White House and at his Havana mansion.

Top officials of the United States government never failed to hail Batista as a "great leader" and as "a great friend of the United States." The American citizens whose tax money paid for the bullets that killed Antonio Guiteras and who were now paying for the bullets that were keeping Fulgencio Batista in power never uttered a word of dissent.

America certainly had good reasons to support Batista as Cuba's military dictator, as did the small cadre of Cuban cronies who merrily overlooked the harsh treatment rendered to the peasants. Batista shared the spoils of a brutal, corrupt dictatorship, and his associates didn't mind that he was selling the rest of Cuba, piece by piece, to foreigners.

Batista's best friend (for a thirty-year stretch) was the murderous Meyer Lansky, whose headquarters was a luxurious mansion in nearby southern Florida. From the very outset of the Batista dictatorship, the Mafia was America's partner in the rape and robbery of Cuba. That partnership, easily glossed over to an ill-informed American public, was destined to continue to this day.

Batista's ruthless, exploitative dictatorship became entrenched in Cuba as the US government and its unmatched military force solidly backed him up.

Fidel Castro, Cuba's high-school athlete of the year, was able to go on to the University of Havana because his father was of the elite class, a plantation owner. Fidel, while still a student, inherited $80,000 on his way to picking up a law degree.

Never particularly interested in money, the youthful Fidel gave his fortune away in bundles to Cuban peasants, especially poor women. Safely positioned to enjoy life among the privileged, even as a University of Havana student, Fidel began to speak out against Batista's treatment of the peasants. Physically imposing at six feet four inches tall, he also had a quick mind and a near photographic memory that enthralled his professors.

A voracious reader and a charismatic, spellbinding speaker, he was a natural-born leader with a penchant for polemics, especially in regard to anything political. He was also uncommonly, recklessly brave. Huge crowds gathered as he viciously denounced Batista. Batista began to notice.

Fidel took a trip to Colombia to side with that nation's peasants against what he termed "US imperialism that is stripping you of what little you have."

The young Fidel also expressed his concern for the rural workers of the Dominican Republic, which was governed by another US-backed dictator, Rafael Leónidas Trujillo Molina.

Trujillo had overseen the murder of so many peasants that respected journalists, later confirmed by top historians, were writing that the waters off the Dominican Republic contained "the best-fed sharks in the world." Hearing that Trujillo's personal yacht was sailing off the coast of Cuba, Castro rounded up a few friends from the university, rented a boat and, incredibly, took off after Trujillo. Like pirates, they boarded that yacht and took command of it, searching for the powerful ruler. As it happened, the dictator was not aboard that day, so Fidel left the captain with these legendary words: "My name is Fidel Castro! Tell Trujillo he one day will answer to me for his murdering thousands of his peasants!"

But, of course, the young Fidel was most concerned about what was now happening in his own homeland. After graduating from Jesuit elementary and high schools, Belén College, and the University of Havana Law School, Fidel practiced law, defending peasants free of charge.

In 1948, he married Mirta Díaz-Balart and they had a son whom they named Fidel. In 1952, Castro tried to enter politics and became a candidate for the Cuban Congress, but Batista canceled the elections.

Fidel and his younger brother Raúl then pooled their money to purchase guns and ammunition, believing the time had come to overthrow Batista. Fidel and Raúl led about a hundred young Cuban men and women in an attack on Batista's Moncada Army Barracks in Santiago de Cuba on July 26, 1953. They were shot to pieces, and the Castro brothers were captured. At his trial, closely guarded by one hundred Batista soldiers, Fidel defended himself, closing his defense with the words: "History will absolve me." He was sentenced to fifteen years in prison.

Cuban insiders as well as Castro's supporters knew that Batista would have Fidel murdered in prison. However, the young rebel now had a huge following, especially among Cuba's women, both rich and poor. They closely monitored the prison, making sure that Batista realized that US news outlets, including the *New York Times*, were also observing the fate of the audacious young rebel. This kept Fidel alive, though under tight security. His supporters, not so closely monitored, were routinely tortured and murdered.

On the University of Havana campus, Castro's friend José Echeverría was machine-gunned to death; another prime Castro supporter, 23-year-old teacher Frank País, was tortured to death on a street in Santiago by Colonel José Salas Canizares, Batista's most feared murderer. País was publicly kicked, stomped, and then shot in the back.

Suspected female supporters of Fidel were arrested, raped, tortured, and murdered. The fate of some Cuban women was even worse, as delineated by the nationally syndicated columnist Georgie Anne Geyer in her seminal book, *Guerrilla Prince*. One woman, blindfolded and tied to a chair, anticipated being raped, tortured, and murdered when a Batista thug began removing her blindfold. He dangled before her face a newly extracted human eye and said, "This is your little brother's left eye. Tell me what I want to know, or I will bring you his right eye."

Such atrocities to women and children were well known to the US government, which protested only when the incidents began to appear in the American media. Once the word got out, the public was quickly informed that "such rumors will be strongly investigated." The US government had nothing to investigate; they were actually training the soldiers in special torture methods, on US soil. This sort of program was an everyday thing at the Army School of the

Americas at Fort Benning, Georgia. Reams of newly declassified US documents also provide chilling evidence.

THE BROKEN CHAIN

Among the visitors who monitored the imprisoned Fidel Castro and helped ensure his longevity was a lovely black Cuban journalist, barely 21 years old, named Marta Rojas. Some members of the US media were also involved, especially Herbert L. Matthews of the *New York Times*. Rojas, whose credentials as a journalist afforded her access to Castro, risked her life once a week by hiding in her bra notes he had addressed to underground associates and then hand-delivering them herself, providing a vital communication link to the outside world.

With the powerful veteran politician Antonio Guiteras safely dead and the young firebrand Fidel Castro imprisoned, there were no challenges to the Batista dictatorship. The former army sergeant maintained a very powerful police force and he was supported by the United States.

Additionally, Batista was already tightly aligned with the Mafia and he had reinstituted the Communist Party of Cuba. In this milieu, in the mid-1950s, all the major cities in Cuba, especially Havana on the western tip, barely a hundred miles from the US, and Santiago on the southeastern edge of the island, were rife with gambling, crime and prostitution — orchestrated by Meyer Lansky.

Cuba's capital city, Havana, by the mid-1950s had replaced New York City, Chicago, and even Las Vegas as the Mafia's favorite playpen and piggy bank. The flood of tourists from the nearby US included everything from carefree college students to sex addicts and pedophiles. The island nation was not only exempt from US laws but, amazingly, this debauchery was supported by the omnipotent United States government because rich US capitalists got a share of the profits.

The US was supporting other dictators throughout the Caribbean and Latin America; but Batista in Cuba in the mid-1950s was considered the quintessential US-friendly dictator. He was the most powerful and the most secure, which also meant that the Cuban peasants were the most mistreated and the most besieged. Like a fisherman's net cast out from the big cities, a blanket of shame and a canopy of fear covered the whole island, amid varied pockets of covert dissent that — with Guiteras and Castro gone — did not alarm the overlords in Havana and Washington one iota.

Rural areas between Havana and Santiago began losing girls and young women to kidnappers — Mafia-directed bands of Batista's Police Force. Whole families were killed to facilitate the kidnapping of prized girls or young women, with impunity. Pre-teen girls were kidnapped in the countryside to lure rich US pedophiles. All of Cuba knew about this, and so did the US government.

In the small town of Media Luna, one petite young woman with big Spanish eyes was assisting her father, a highly-regarded provincial doctor, as he cared for an elderly patient. The young woman's name was Celia Sánchez. Suddenly, someone knocked on the door and pushed it open. Standing in the doorway was Celia's nineteen-year-old friend Felipe Mateo, a University of Havana student who worked as a janitor at a ritzy hotel and casino.

Felipe looked distraught. "Celia," he said, "I borrowed a car, because you had to know: I found the little girl you told me about."

"María! María Ochoa?"

He could hardly bring himself to tell her the details. A wealthy gambler from New Orleans had requested a "young girl," and the Mafiosi were only too willing to pluck one from the countryside for their free-spending patron. And a sultry-looking ten-year-old was sacrificed in the night. Her dead body now lay in the basement of the casino, used up and thrown away.

This stunned Celia to the core. It took her several minutes to begin the recovery that she already knew would never end. When she began to compose herself, she asked Felipe if his car had enough gas to get them to Havana before daylight. He thought it did.

Celia then hurried past her father's office to his bedroom. She removed a .38-caliber pistol from a drawer, along with two boxes of cartridges. Then she dashed to her own room, stuck a few essentials into a sack, and reached for the pistol.

"Celia...?"

She looked toward the door. It was her father. He stepped to the bed, reaching down to gently take the pistol from Celia's hand.

"Don't stop me, Papa," she said, softly but firmly. "Felipe found María's body. I don't know what I'm going to do but I'm going to do something. Please, Papa! Don't stop me." Those daunting eyes also pleaded.

Gradually, Dr. Sánchez, gave in. "I won't stop you," he said.

During the hasty drive to Havana, the pensive Celia held the sack in her lap. She just stared straight ahead. She had one weapon, a .38 pistol; and one soldier, Felipe Mateo. She contemplated how miniscule she was as she tried, without much success, to formulate a plan. The pedophile, Felipe informed her, had checked out of the hotel and headed back to New Orleans. But, apart from him, Celia had already determined who were her prime enemies — Batista, the Mafia, and the US government. Silently, she declared war on that troika, hopeless as it was. But from that moment on, she would be undeterred. The troika, she believed, would maintain firm control of the island but, to do so, they would now have to kill her. With that affirmation, as she closed in on Havana, Celia's mind focused on the body of ten-year-old María Ochoa lying on that hard basement floor.

The Studebaker pulled into Havana just prior to midnight. The city was still ablaze with nightlife, which Celia and Felipe tried to steer clear of.

They had a little time to kill on a secluded and sparsely traveled street. They had decided that 3:00 A.M. would be the safest time to execute the first key phase of her plan — stealing María's body. Felipe, in his role as nighttime janitor, would not arouse suspicion even in the company of Celia, who — wearing pants and with a nondescript gray scarf around her head — looked not unlike a janitor's helper. After a brief encounter with one of Felipe's fellow janitors in a stairwell, they were alone in the dark basement. In the hotel and casino overhead, the crowd was still buzzing.

Felipe gathered up the items they had discussed: a shovel, nails, planks, an ax, and a hammer; and Celia sat on the cold floor, cradling the precious body of María. Eyes closed and rocking gently back and forth, Celia waited for Felipe to make two trips to the car and then return to check the route from the basement back to the car before he signaled for her to stand, with the blanket-wrapped María in her arms.

A half-hour later the Studebaker had shed the neon lights of Havana to embrace the star-studded Cuban night on a lonely dirt road in Pinar del Río province west of the capital city. At daylight, "thirty-five miles from nowhere," as Celia would later tell Nora Peters, Celia and Felipe were digging a grave on a little rise up from a creek that was densely covered, almost hidden, by foliage. When the grave was completed, Felipe began taking rocks from the creek and its banks while Celia used a knife, hatchet, and some nails to fashion a cross. As Felipe lined the grave with rocks, Celia meticulously carved the cross with the words: "María Ochoa...10 years old...Forever Young."

Then came the hardest part — putting María into the hole and covering it with soil and stones. Celia procrastinated. She sat beside the blanket, opening it up. She stared at the bruised little face, seeing the beauty but also reading the dire trauma that now became a part of Celia's soul. The little girl's hands were at her sides. Celia moved them gently to María's chest. In the child's right hand something was still held tight. Celia slowly pried open the hand, which held a gold cross and a broken chain.

The broken chain suggested to Celia that María, just before she died, had grasped the cross and held it for dear life. Seeing it as a metaphor for a little girl that she knew to have been tenderly beautiful, thoroughly sweet, and deeply religious, Celia's first instinct was to put it back into María's hand. But then, that thought faded. Celia stared down at the dangling chain and felt the first surge, the first vibration of something that she had not known she possessed — a revolutionary heart!

Still holding the cross and the broken chain, Celia looked lovingly and longingly into María's face, aware of Felipe now standing patiently beside her. "My darling," Celia said aloud, "I will keep your cross and the broken chain and carry it with me where I must go. I will make them pay for what they did to you and for what they are doing to Cuba. Then I will get your broken chain repaired so I can wear it around my neck to honor you forever."

Then they buried María. Before they walked away, Celia forced a smile and then spoke these words aloud: "Vamos a ganar, María. Vamos a ganar." ("We will win, María. We will win.")

Finally, Celia Sánchez allowed Felipe Mateo to lead her away from the sacrosanct grave. Of course, keeping the sacred promises she had made to the precious little girl would be impossible.

However, over the course of the next five bloody years, doing the impossible would enshrine Celia Sánchez not only as a Cuban legend but also as the greatest female revolutionary of all time. The "broken chain" saga and the graveside words were later depicted by Celia in historic letters to Nora Peters and also corroborated by historian Pedro Alvarez Tabío in his interviews with her soldier, Felipe Mateo.

CHAPTER 2. THE REVOLUTION BEGINS

With Felipe Mateo as her chauffeur, Celia reluctantly put María's grave behind her.

All paved roads led to Havana, so they stuck to dirt roads as they circled southeastwardly around the capital city. Her revolutionary heart now ruled her being. She did not minimize the daunting task that lay ahead. The mistakes made by the dead Antonio Guiteras, José Echeverría, and Frank País, as well as the locked-up Fidel Castro, Raúl Castro, and their two staunch female warriors Haydée Santamaría and Melba Hernández, would not be replicated by the more pragmatic Celia. The other would-be revolutionaries had all been swatted aside like flies.

First, they would have to avoid Batista's prime bastions of power until, if ever, they had a force sufficient to go on the offensive. Celia's first order of business was to begin building that force. For now, they set course for Santa Clara, a mid-sized city seventy-five miles east of Havana.

Even a born revolutionary has to formulate plans step by step. While time was of the essence, she realized that patience and perseverance would have to meld with tactical brilliance, stealth, guts, and determination...fierce determination...if she had one chance in a million of succeeding. Despite the overwhelming odds against her, she planned to succeed. She owed that, she believed, to María and to Cuba.

Felipe and Celia ate at a small café in the heart of Santa Clara and filled the gas tank. Then they headed east, discussing how they might start enrolling volunteers. Celia knew the terrain in the foothills of the Sierras northeast of Santiago, and that was just perfect — it would enable them to get a start, far from Havana.

On the eastern edge of Santa Clara, Felipe turned onto the coastal highway headed toward Holguín, a city in southeastern Cuba almost within shouting distance of other towns and cities familiar to Celia — such as Camagüey, Guardalavaca, Nuevitas, Baracoa, Bayamo, Santiago de Cuba, and Manzanillo.

Just after sunset, they made two stops in Holguín at homes familiar to Celia, and she commenced her recruiting, lining up two lieutenants — a young man and a young woman — that she would depend on. Soldiers, supplies, weapons, ammunition, medicine, money...each new lieutenant would be told precisely what Celia wanted and how to become a part of the communication links she would set up. Into the night, they made two more recruiting stops in Nuevitas and one in Bayamo. It was well after midnight when they pulled into the sleepy little hamlet of Manzanillo, a peasant bastion where Celia knew she could knock on any of a hundred doors and be warmly received. From 3:00 A.M. till just after daylight, Celia and Felipe got some badly needed sleep, courtesy of some good friends. Celia had a dream — about María Ochoa, a María Ochoa who was alive and imbued with the joy of youth.

The Celia Sánchez Shrine now located in her hometown of Media Luna displays a letter she is said to have written this very day to her father, detailing the harrowing events surrounding María's burial and ending with these words: "I do not want you involved, Papa, but from this day on I will try to build a peasant revolution to fight Batista, the Mafia, and America. I will forever be thinking of you, and I know you will pray for me and for Cuba. Love always, Celia."

Within the next four weeks a tireless Celia, always in the company of her dedicated "first soldier" Felipe, crisscrossed the rural towns and farms in the foothills of the Sierra Mountain range, recruiting supplies as well as a myriad of young men and women ready and willing to fight the Batista tyranny. Utilizing Manzanillo as a base, Celia gradually built her force, even after her informers began to caution that Batista's garrison in Santiago had dispatched a police force targeting her. A meticulous planner and note-taker, she selected 143 young men and 47 young women to form the initial fulcrum of her army, ordering them to begin movements that would result in a rendezvous at a specific spot north of Pico Turquino near the base of the Sierras. There, they were to wait for her.

Aware that Batista's men were after her, Celia darted from one safe house to another as she went on recruiting. She found another fifty more men and women who would transport the bulk of the weapons and supplies that she had managed to procure to the 190 rebels that would be waiting at Pico Turquino. Using trucks and cars as well as horse- and mule-drawn wagons and carts, and two new jeeps, the supply convoys got underway from various directions north, northeast, and northwest of Pico Turquino. The two new jeeps were an accidental blessing. She secured them from four Batista soldiers whom she had been dodging for several days on her recruitment missions but then, miffed that they were slowing her operation, she, Felipe, and two young female rebels ambushed them on a dirt road outside Bayamo, killing the four soldiers and then collecting their booty — the two jeeps, extra gasoline, four rifles, five pistols, and two ammunition crates.

Celia herself drove one of the big supply-laden US-made jeeps to Pico Turquino and from then on she had a fetish for jeeps, and made plans to procure more from the huge supplies that she knew the US taxpayers were providing Batista. The cache from the four unfortunate Batista soldiers reminded Celia that tactical guerrilla strikes could greatly add to her arsenal, and this was the first time she actually began to think of her campaign as guerrilla warfare.

Of the 190 rebels she had assigned to the rendezvous point, 183 were there when Celia arrived and the other seven, plus thirteen more they had recruited, caught up with them four days later. Celia sent out runners to maintain communication and recruiting links to the area but pointed her main force directly at the base of the Sierra Mountains. The highest peak in the Sierras, Turquino rises up 6,477 feet above sea level. Those dense mountains, fronted by menacing swamps, were where Celia decided to establish her mobile base camps. All the while she depended on the contacts she had established to send her more men and more supplies, including weapons, ammunition, money, medicine, and gasoline.

From the outset, given the swampy environs, Celia was cognizant of the need to vaccinate her rebels against tropical diseases, especially typhoid and typhus, and she diligently did so. Medical supplies were a priority, almost on a par with weapons and food.·

Even with a fighting force, Celia had no immediate plans for offensive strikes against the Batista soldiers; they policed the area but mostly avoided the often deadly swamps and foreboding mountains. Those swamps and those mountains were critical factors and they appealed to Celia's guerrilla instincts.

Celia established four base camps, each comprised of about fifty rebels and all within sight of the Pico Turquino.

At the foot of the mountains were the treacherous swamps. The group made sure not to leave visible paths or roads leading to the base camps. Increasing numbers of government soldiers might come after them, but first they would have to deal with the "briar patches." And, within those briar patches, the rebels would have the edge because of Celia's familiarity with the terrain that sheltered them. And Celia at all costs would maintain her mountain strongholds, keeping the high ground that looked out over the swamps and valleys. Batista had US-supplied tanks and warplanes; the swamps and mountain crevices would go a long way to negate those enemy advantages. Early on, perhaps a bit recklessly, she welcomed probes or even attacks from Batista's soldiers. She had a growing fondness for those modern jeeps and weapons.

At first, the probes and then the attacks fulfilled Celia's wishes. Her rebels defended their ground ferociously and picked their moments to slash back fiercely, often in thrusts that Celia herself led from the frontlines. Her links among the region's populace supplied her with camouflage uniforms — green shirts, jackets, and pants as well as black boots. Thus attired, Celia kept María's medallion and chain in her buttoned-down left shirt pocket.

Famously superstitious, she always wore a gold bracelet around her left ankle for good luck. As a planner, organizer, and strategist, Celia quickly became a guerrilla legend. As a front-line fighter with incomparable bravery and skill, she was soon worshipped not only by the men and women she commanded but also by the residents in the area who began hearing about her. This aided immensely in steadily increasing her rebel army and its supplies. Also, a well-publicized Batista bounty was put on her head, as increasingly stronger armies were sent after her.

Yet, incredibly, during this formative period, Celia would lead the fighting by day and then, under the cover of darkness, slip stealthily through the jungle-like mountainous terrain and murky swamps right past Batista soldiers to facilitate recruitment in the foothills or rendezvous with messengers. This earned Celia a nickname — La Paloma, "The Dove." Her mountain messengers, known to history as "Manzanilleras," were vital in keeping communication lines functioning.

Two of Celia's bravest and most famed Manzanilleras — Lidia Docé and Clodomira Acosta — were captured and gruesomely tortured to death by Batista's police, but neither Docé nor Acosta divulged one word of information that would harm Celia's operation or her own safety.

By June of 1954, Celia was the proud owner of seventeen US jeeps and, from her own procurements as well as captured Batista supplies, she had stock-piles of weapons, ammunition, medicine, gas, oil, and food at her base camps. Her growing reputation resulted in steady streams of new peasant recruits. The first bounty posted on Celia was $10,000 but that increased to $25,000, then $75,000.

Early one afternoon, after routing an elite Batista force numbering just over 200 soldiers in a tough early morning battle, Celia's unit converged at a campsite in the foothills below Turquino Peak. Celia had already eaten and was sitting on a stump smoking a cigarette as a medic re-bandaged her bloody right shoulder.

She had just glanced at one of the cardboard posters depicting the $75,000 bounty on her head, before casually tossing it aside.

Ada Martinez, one of her top aides and best fighters, walked over and handed Celia a batch of messages. "Read this one first," she said, giving Celia a hand-written note on a brown piece of paper. Celia held it in her left hand and began reading, as the medic worked on her injured right shoulder:

Dear Celia,

What you have done and are doing has thrilled and inspired me beyond any-thing I have ever imagined. I pray one day I will be free to join you. Till then I will be at your side in spirit each step of the way. I dream of the day I can touch you and be with you.

Fidel Castro

Chapter 3. Celia's Cuba

Early that afternoon, Celia and her top lieutenant, Ada Martinez, strolled around the temporary campsite in a clearing beneath Turquino Peak.

They were surveying the aftermath of that morning's tough but victorious battle down in the marshy valley. Celia's right arm was in a sling, but at the moment she was much more concerned with observing how diligently her medical staff was tending to the wounds suffered by about fifteen of her loyal young rebels. Ada, however, was much more focused on the shoulder injury of the leader, Celia.

Ada reported on an enemy force that was nudging its way along the north edge of the swamp. "About 250 strong. No tanks. Two artillery pieces being pulled by jeeps. About twelve jeeps in all, at least two with mounted machine guns. They are camped and awaiting word from scouts, two of which we captured as they crossed Anglo Creek. We have three units beyond this camp's perimeter monitoring that group. It's the only one to worry about at the moment but another troop train arrived in Santiago around noon yesterday."

Celia gave instructions for the next day's action, seeking to protect the clearings while taking full advantage of the swamps. "Make sure groups One and Two are ready to attack from Clearing #3 tomorrow."

"They're ready."

Celia and Ada continued their tour of the campsite. Shortly, they stopped to contemplate a group guarding some ten newly captured prisoners at the edge of a circular patch of palm trees down the hillside. Ada noted that they now had about seventy prisoners still being processed. This was a fast growing problem...guarding them, caring for them, or setting them free.

It was a risky guessing game, deciding whom to let go and whom to accept as new recruits. Some Batista soldiers were genuinely switching sides, but with a bounty on her head there were surely turncoat volunteers trying to slip into the units just so they could get close enough to kill Celia.

Even now, seven heavily-armed bodyguards — four men and three women — closely encircled both her and Ada. The devotion of her followers was inspirational. Indeed, after Celia was wounded in the morning, Ada had looked back to see Teté Puebla wipe a white cloth over the place where her blood had spilled. Folded up in her shirt pocket, it was now a precious talisman. The week before, Puebla had run to a machine-gun nest and destroyed it with a hand grenade, and used a pistol to shoot her way out. She was fifteen years old.

Ada turned the conversation to the letter from Castro. Did Celia think he would ever get out of prison? Would Batista or the US government ever permit that?

"I doubt it. He would be too much of a threat to Batista. Fidel would be dead now, if there weren't so many new people watching him..."

Later in the pivotal year of 1954, as Fidel Castro languished in prison, the imbroglio on the island of Cuba was easily defined. It pitted the immovable object, dictator Fulgencio Batista, against the irresistible force, Celia Sánchez — all ninety-nine pounds of her. At this point, Batista thought she was just a nuisance.

During this crucial period, Celia Sánchez was not only the creator and the leader of the Cuban Revolution; she *was* the Cuban Revolution. As the insightful witness Ada Martinez stated, the Cuban Revolution "would cease to exist" without Celia. As the eager but safely incarcerated young rebel Fidel Castro stated, she was his inspiration.

The best chronicler of Celia's astounding achievements and unrivaled fortitude during this time was historian Pedro Alvarez Tabio. After the dust had settled and the blood had dried in the Sierras, Tabio asked 300 of the Sierra rebels about their single most pertinent memory of the revolutionary struggle. "The answers were strikingly monotonous," Tabio wrote. "They could separate Fidel, Che, Camilo, Raúl...all the macho heroes...from the revolution but there was one heroine, it seems, they could not disconnect from the momentous event they had been a part of. Her name was Celia Sánchez, the greatest maker of

Cuban history and both the organizer and leader of the Cuban Revolution. After that monotonous reaction from my 300 participants, I chose fifty for whom I asked a follow-up question. What made her so special? I wondered. The fifty answers that came back were also monotonous. Each one, with amazingly little variation, described Celia in the same succinct manner: 'She was the bravest, smartest, and most focused person I have ever known. Only she could have done what the Cuban Revolution did.' And one more thing about Celia. Despite all of her accomplishments, she must have spent one-third of her time and energy deflecting credit away from herself to others — during the revolution when she was the supreme catalyst and after the revolution when she was the supreme decision-maker in Cuba, right up until her death from cancer on January 11, 1980. Her enemies cooperated fully in this endeavor because, while they could demonize flamboyant and macho men such as Fidel, they knew they could never demonize the sacrosanct, angelic Celia. So, they never tried, although during and after the revolution they tried to kill her above all others, even Fidel, and with good reason. She put the revolution together and she held it together. Unlike her phalanx of enemies, she never craved fame, power, or money — just what was best for the Cuban peasants. And against overwhelming and seemingly insurmountable odds all along the way, she succeeded to the highest degree possible, considering the unending obstacles she faced, mostly from omnipotent next-door neighbor America. From her hometown of Media Luna to the Sierra Maestra Mountains to the capital city of Havana, she did all she could as long as she could for the Cuban peasants she loved so passionately. And from above, she still loves them."

Tabio wrote the above words for the magazine *Bohemia* in May, 1990. They stand the test of time as confirmed by Nora Peters; and as confirmed to the author by three of Celia's still-living acolytes — Fidel Castro, Marta Rojas, and General Teté Puebla — during a research trip to Cuba in 2004. General Teté Puebla to this day treasures the white cloth stained with the first blood that Celia shed in the Sierra battles.

I was introduced to Marta Rojas, the legendary revolutionary heroine, by Tracey Eaton, head of the *Dallas Morning News* bureau in Havana. She is reckoned to be the person who has the most influence on Fidel Castro today. Rojas is now seventy-six years old and is still a vibrant and fine-looking lady, and is an internationally acclaimed author. Ms. Rojas sent me many email messages, four of them on December 19, 2004, reminiscing about Celia Sánchez much as Nora Peters reminisced with me face-to-face over the last twelve years of her life.

Marta sent me copies of actual correspondence between Fidel and Celia, which form an important basis for this book.

One such note came into play in 1954 in the Sierra Maestra Mountains of eastern Cuba, as Celia Sánchez was becoming what Tabio called "the greatest maker of Cuban history." The dialogue from the Sierra is derived largely from statements made to Tabío by participants such as Ada Martinez as he interviewed former rebels to capture the moods and backdrops of the rebel movement.

The hot, late-afternoon Caribbean sun penetrated down through the dense roof of foliage that protected and concealed the winding trail leading higher and higher into the mountains. Straggling up the tunnel-like path were 175 tired and bedraggled rebels who had just waged a hard but successful four-hour battle against 400 Batista soldiers in the foothills. At the head of the stretched-out procession, trudging wearily ever upward toward her prime base-camp, was Celia Sánchez. At her back, strapped over her right shoulder was her prized Belgium rifle; belted at her side was her fourteen-shot Italian Aziri pistol. An ammunition pouch dangled against her left hip, and muddied binoculars bounced against her chest at the end of a leather strap that was around her neck and now soaked in sweat.

She stopped, as did the procession behind her. In unison, they reached for the canteens that had been filled at a creek a mile back down the trail.

Celia slumped into a sitting position at the shady, leafy edge of the trail and her gesture was replicated in chain-reaction fashion on down the hillside. Ada now sat beside Celia, first taking another gulp of water from her canteen, and they discussed casualties.

"Seven dead and maybe three more in the swamp waters. Dante's patrol is searching. About twenty-five wounded, and the jeeps are taking them home along with the seven bodies by using the Number Five road. We estimate fifty enemy dead and eighty-five wounded till they retreated back from the edge of the Montoon Swamp and into the woods beyond clearing #9. Command Group Four will secure the area through the night under your orders to permit the fetching of their dead and wounded but not any penetrations this side of clearing #9. We'll send down ammunition, two machine guns, food, and water to Group Four. You also said to move two of the sharpshooters with the Browning long-range rifles to Group Four in case that reconnaissance helicopter comes back, and that order has been given."

Celia, her tired eyes blinking, pondered the initial battle report. Then she lay back till her head rested on the soft, leafy ground. The bend of her left arm covered her eyes. "Wake me in five minutes, Ada."

Celia actually had a ten-minute nap. The base-camp was still two miles away and ever upward through the dense mountains.

That night, alone in her tent, Celia periodically heard distant gunfire from the foothills but she was not otherwise disturbed. This meant that neither Group Four nor units on the perimeter were encountering major difficulty; just probes.

Celia's tent nudged against Ada's and both were surrounded throughout the night by twelve bodyguards. At the front of Celia's cot was a battery-operated radio that could receive and send messages, but it was silent this night.

Celia got seven hours of much-needed sleep, which was blessed with a dream about a fishing trip she took as a young girl with her father. It was a sad dream, upon reflection; she missed him terribly.

After breakfast the next morning, Celia spent a full hour at a conference table with five lieutenants, each of whom provided updates on the previous day's battle as well as the deployments of the various rebel units stationed below the base-camp that morning. Ada, Celia's aide-de-camp, stood and observed the session but, at its conclusion, spent fifteen minutes summarizing the new information with Celia. Then both women toured the site to check on the status of the now-revised number of twenty-nine rebels wounded the day before. One of the injured happened to be the feisty and lovely fifteen-year-old Teté Puebla, who had a bandaged head resulting from a tree limb that fell on her during the battle. Her right eye was also bruised and discolored. "But, Celia," Teté said, "this bandage is just for show. If my unit goes out today, I'm going!"

Celia pursed her lips and then tightly hugged the fearless teenager. She whispered, "We'll see, honey. We'll see. Get some rest."

At 2:00 P.M. that day, Celia attended the burials of nine of her troops killed the day before, including two bodies recovered overnight from the swamp.

At 4:00 P.M. Celia and Ada were briefed on the positions and movements of the three Batista armies in the area.

Concerned by the advance of one of those units toward Clearing #6, Celia told the three key officers of Command Group One to plan an ambush for the next morning and be prepared to discuss the strategy with her at 6:00 P.M., just after supper. Ada missed that session because she had gone to the south end of the dense campsite to fetch the latest communications delivered by mountain messengers.

This day there were four messages, which Ada passed to Celia as they sat at twilight in front of their tents. "Read that top one, first," Ada said.

Celia complied.

Celia:

As best I can, I monitor your activities as highlights of my days. Never to have seen you, never to have helped you, pains me so very much. Maybe...just maybe...that will change. I close my eyes and what I see is Celia's Cuba — not Batista's, not the Mafia's and not America's. One day I plan to help you make Celia's Cuba a reality.

Fidel Castro

Celia looked up from the note, pondering it as she stared straight ahead. It was a bold note, certainly; and it also hinted at a certain optimism. Did Castro have reason to think that he would be able to escape? If he did, and if he could join them, that would add fuel to their endeavor, in a big way.

Chapter 4. "Modesto"

In the early months of 1955, the young firebrand Fidel Castro was into his second year of imprisonment. So were the other three prime planners and key participants in the ill-fated July 26, 1953, attack on Batista's strong Moncada Army Barracks — his younger brother Raúl and two fiercely dedicated young women, Haydée Santamaría and Melba Hernández. The rape and robbery of Cuba continued unabated with Fulgencio Batista fully supported by the Mafia, the Communist Party of Cuba, and the United States. The capital cities of Havana and Washington were quite satisfied with how things were going.

Batista had both an army and a police force — trained and armed by the United States — that brutally and routinely tortured and murdered any and all peasants who displayed even a hint of dissent. One element of the torture methods employed by the dictatorship concerned what historians call "Batista's eye specialists." As warnings to others, peasants — men, women, and children — would be arrested, taken to a military hospital, and have one or two eyes removed before being dropped back off in their communities. Peasant girls and women were routinely kidnapped and raped by Batista henchmen as part of a program of intimidation and hedonism.

Innocent and harmless family members were often used to punish or to solicit information from arrested dissidents. Perhaps the best historical example of this relates to the imprisonment of Haydée Santamaría, the young woman who helped plan and then participated in the Moncada attack. Haydée was tied to a chair and blindfolded, and forced to listen as Batista's men tortured her fiancé, Reynaldo Boris Luis Santa Coloma, to death. Then her blindfold was removed and Reynaldo's cut-off testicles were rubbed over her face and chest. (Haydée would later get out of prison, join Celia in the Sierras, and become, next to Celia, the second most important female guerrilla fighter. After the triumph of the revolution, the brilliant Haydée wrote a famous book — "Rebel Lives" — and also created a notable museum with a branch in Paris, France. In 1980, shortly after the death of her idol Celia Sánchez, the beloved Haydée committed suicide).

The brutality of the Batista regime created fierce enemies the dictatorship would later have to confront.

Into 1955 — with the threat from the imprisoned Fidel, Haydée, Raúl, and Melba effectively cancelled — Havana and Washington also pretended there was no problem with the little uprising — Celia's revolution — that had sprung up in the Sierra Mountains. But the sharply increased US arms shipments to Batista, as well as the huge bounties put on Celia's head, indicated otherwise. The ninety-nine-pound daughter of a provincial doctor deserved that bounty. She was indeed a problem — the only one.

During this period, Marta Rojas was a twenty-two-year-old journalist in Havana. Her credentials gave her access to the imprisoned Fidel Castro. Some of the notes she secreted out made their way to Celia Sánchez, whom Fidel knew, at this point, was the only hope for overthrowing the brutal dictatorship.

In addition to the clandestine support of Cuba's young elite, such as Marta Rojas, Celia particularly had the support of Cuban peasant women all over the island — because they and their families suffered the most under the Batista tyranny. Also, because Celia was so admired and Batista was so fiendish, from time to time — via her mountain messengers and her radio hook-up — Celia received vital data and acute warnings from keenly informed sources highly positioned in both governments — Cuba's and America's. In that precise manner, Celia learned about the Army School of the Americas at Fort Benning, Georgia. This clandestine CIA-run operation trained soldiers and assassins from US-friendly dictatorships throughout the Caribbean and Latin America; trained them at the expense of the US taxpayers, particularly in the fine arts of murdering and/or torturing anyone identified as a dissident threat to those US-friendly dictators. From one source that turned out to be a top officer at Fort Benning, Celia learned that a particular assassin trained at Fort Benning was being sent to Cuba to kill her.

Such information gleaned from a variety of sources had first to be carefully analyzed. Celia was not one who could be easily tricked. Soon, she began to give credence to the data being provided by the Fort Benning officer. The assassin being sent to specifically target her was code named "Modesto." He was a handsome, black-haired native of Mexico with a California background, and soon Celia was provided a picture of him. She was advised that Modesto was unusually smart, "a ruthlessly calculating and effective killer."

A Cuban sympathizer at Fort Benning added: "He is currently the highest paid such US assassin." Killing Celia had become a CIA priority.

Celia and Ada Martinez took note. Daily threats from Batista soldiers coupled with the never-ending task of building, supplying, and leading her own force kept them busy. From Manzanillo, Yara, and Campecheula, they began hearing about a special army unit comprised of six uniformed soldiers who were moving swiftly in three huge US-made jeeps from town to town, garrison to garrison. Atrocities against peasant farm families were soon connected to that special unit. Moreover, the three-jeep convoy was led by Modesto.

Monitoring Modesto's gruesome trail, Celia saw that his strategy was to draw her from her strongholds — the mountains, swamps, and foothills of the Sierras — out into the open countryside where scattered peasant families resided. Indeed, brazenly now, Modesto began to leave his taunting calling cards. The body of a peasant girl, about fourteen years old, was found along an isolated dirt road. Her raped and mutilated body had a note attached to it by a pocketknife that pierced her chest: "Dear Celia: I'm going to continue to have fun until you come out and personally stop me. Modesto."

Two days later, a farmhouse outside Yara told a tragic tale. A ten-year-old girl, naked and mutilated, lay dead on the kitchen floor. Her parents were dead and still tied to chairs. They had been shot in the head after apparently being forced to watch the torture-murder of their daughter. Again, Modesto left a note taunting Celia: "Wow! This was fun. Modesto."

A furious Celia had sent out units to catch Modesto, but he was extremely mobile and one of the jeeps was armed with a machine-gun. Then Celia and Ada noted a pattern to his operation. There were two army garrisons outside Santiago separated by about fifteen miles. Modesto utilized both garrisons, one for supplies and the other for communications and lodging. That meant that every day or two he could be counted on to traverse the lone dirt road that connected the two garrisons. Celia knew the area well. About midway between the two garrisons the narrow, twisting, dusty dirt road had a sharp curve, skirting the edge of a cliff on one side and crowded by dense trees on the other. On two different days Modesto's three jeeps had been observed barreling at a high rate of speed around that curve. Those two occasions were once near daybreak and once near twilight; she excitedly scanned that data inside her candle-lit mobile tent.

It was time to strike.

With a force of 18 troops, Celia decided to set off to Clearing #3, then walk four kilometers to the dirt road. Ada had never seen Celia so intense, so heated, so red-faced. Ada would stay behind to monitor the radio. Ada handed Celia two high-powered walkie-talkies before they exited the tent.

The first leg of the mission took an hour and fifteen minutes. The five jeeps were left with Group Four after Celia got a briefing on the whereabouts of the Batista soldiers in the area. She would maintain radio hook-up with Group Four in case she needed a back-up. Between Clearing #3 and the dirt road was a tight forest with dense foliage. Strikingly petite but also strong and fit, Celia was weighted down with equipment that included her rifle, pistol, knife, three hand grenades, a flashlight, and a walkie-talkie. Fiercely motivated, she anxiously led the nineteen-person patrol into the dark forest. A vivid image of Modesto's smiling face, from one of his glossy photos, dominated her senses.

Tearing her way through the thick forest, using a flashlight to pierce the darkness and both hands to carve openings in the thorny maze, this was the quintessence of the transformed Celia: the doctor's daughter who emerged as a do-or-die guerrilla fighter because of the legal slaughter in Batista's Cuba of a ten-year-old peasant girl.

If Celia and Ada had studied Modesto, it is clear that he too had studied Celia. He knew precisely what would draw Celia out of her mountainous strong-holds — the torture-murders of innocent peasant girls. The initial phase of his plan had worked; her daunting and dangerous destination this night, the seldom-used dirt road that connected two of Batista's army garrisons, would mark the furthest west she had ventured since establishing her rebel bases on the island's eastern tip.

Modesto's intelligence profile also may have noted that she knew the eastern half of the island like the back of her hand. When she burst through the forested barrier onto the dirt road, she recognized she was about 250 yards west of the sharp curve that factored mightily into her strategy.

As her eighteen compatriots emerged onto the road, Celia used her flash-light to check her wristwatch. It was 2:39 A.M. She clicked off the flashlight and gestured for the others to do the same. On the clear and moonlit morning about three hours prior to sunup, the pitch-black forest had already been replaced by welcome hints of daylight. Celia took a deep breath, gulping in the fresher air.

Using hand signals, Celia instructed the others to spread out up and down the road to quietly monitor the area to make sure no army patrol had set up an ambush after possibly detecting her unit's march through the forest.

After about ten minutes of silently reconnoitering the area, Celia told her first lieutenant on this mission, a brilliant fighter named Imelda Santos, to regroup on the forested side of the road. There was nothing at all on the other side — just a sharp cliff that fell away, restricting Celia's prime worry to the narrow road itself.

Shortly, seventeen heavily armed rebels sat or knelt on the side of the road with the wall-like black forest at their back but an azure, brightening sky above the precipice before them. Celia and Imelda stood in front of the fighters, who anxiously awaited final instructions.

"The curve is 250 yards that way," Celia began, pointing with her left hand. "My radio reports indicate that Modesto is spending tonight at the garrison we have marked #1, in that direction." Celia's right hand pointed eastwardly down the road. "Mario and Sylvia, I want the two of you to take a walkie-talkie and go 200 yards down the road in that direction, and take up station there. You can see for miles toward the garrison, especially jeep lights. Stay in touch with me regarding anything you see. Berto, I want you to take a walkie-talkie and then station yourself 200 yards past the curve in the other direction. Stay in touch with me regarding anything you see. The other sixteen in this unit will now go to the curve.

"The reason we brought the saw and ax along is this: We will cut two big trees and lay them across the road, tree-line to cliff, about thirty yards into the curve, so the driver of the lead jeep will not see the barrier till it is too late to avoid crashing into it. Hopefully, the other two jeeps will crash into the first one."

Pacing back and forth in front of her troops as daylight began filtering through the palms, Celia continued to detail her instructions. "Eight of us will be on one side of the road and eight on the other, to provide a crossfire at the jeeps. When the firing commences, the three with the other walkie-talkies will race to join us. The crossfire will be slanted, as we have practiced, so as to avoid hitting each other. Imelda and I have six hand grenades between us, and they will be used. But all of us will commence firing with rifles and then switch to pistols as we close in. The firing must be quick and intense.

Celia continued. "I expect each jeep to have two men. If they do crash into the barrier, there are six men we have to kill quickly. If I have judged their pattern correctly, they will show up around daylight on their way out to terrorize the farmers. But remember, if things do not follow that pattern we will have to improvise. I do not expect any other traffic on this isolated road, even later during the day. But that could change. And Modesto might not show at daylight. If not, we'll maintain a vigil near the downed trees throughout the day, hoping he'll show up near nightfall on his return. If any other traffic shows up, like farmers, we'll stop them after we're alerted by the sentries with the walkie-talkies.

"If, for example," she continued, "a whole battalion of soldiers uses the road we'll have to fight them as guerrillas because the downed trees will have tipped them off to the ambush. So, be ready to improvise, but first concentrate on what we expect — that Modesto and the three jeeps will barrel around that curve right into the barrier. Understand? Do all of you understand?

"One final thing. I want Modesto real bad. I have the men and women I trust to accomplish that. Now, let's deploy."

The three sentries trotted to their stations. More orderly, Imelda ordered the other fourteen into a walking march up the road. Celia and Imelda followed behind them. Celia noticed something.

"Imelda," Celia said, "the young girl with the red bandana around her neck...that's Dani, isn't it?"

"Yes. She's the new girl, who said she was eighteen. We found out she's sixteen. But, Celia, she's been on two hard missions and passed with flying colors. You told me to line up our seventeen best. Dani is one of our very best." Celia still had reservations about including such a young and inexperienced fighter in this do-or-die mission, but it was too late to change that. They continued walking up the road toward the curve.

By 4:20 A.M. the ambush was ready and the waiting began.

Celia knelt on one knee at the head of seven rebels on the side of the road nearest the cliff; Imelda sat on the ground in front of seven other rebels across the road, near the tree-line. Directly in front of them were the two huge downed trees, closing the road in a "Y" fashion that would guide the speeding jeeps into the wall-like forest and not over the cliff — if all went well.

They waited. If the pattern held, the three jeeps would enter the curve at a high speed, almost bumper- to-bumper. Their nerves were on edge. Where was the dawn? Finally, at 5:18 A.M. a misty daylight began to seep into the sky. They waited.

At 6:11 A.M. the cool daylight had wiped away the long night's darkness. Celia arose from her one-knee crouch, her rifle in her left hand. The chirps of flighty, stirring birds sliced through the silence. Celia's right hand reached to her side for her canteen. She took a few gulps of water and then just stood staring through the leafy barrier. She was not nervous, just excited. "Celia, over!" barked the walkie-talkie.

"Mario, what's up?"

"Celia, here they come! About a mile away, coming your way, three big jeeps, six men! Fifty...sixty...miles an hour! Looks like bumper-to-bumper, joy ride! They'll be on you in seconds! The lead jeep sports a flag. The third jeep has a mounted machine-gun! Get ready! Over!"

"I heard you, Mario! You 'n Sylvia stay hidden, then join the fight!"

Celia notified Imelda. "The plan is working! Three jeeps! Six men! Seconds away! Be ready! Look first for flying debris from the jeeps! Then attack after I shoot first!"

Celia calmly placed her rifle on the ground and used both hands to unfasten the belt that held her flashlight and canteen. She tossed the belt into the road, and now heard the first rumblings from the approaching jeeps. Her left hand reached down to retrieve the rifle and instinctively as she stood her right hand reassuringly went to pat first her holstered pistol and then the three hand grenades.

In an instant the jeeps came crashing into view. A cacophony of noise and flying debris from the jeeps and the barrier shattered the air. Celia ducked down, rifle at the ready, and spotted human movement crawling against tree limbs that pushed hard against the pile-up of jeeps. She fired. Fifteen other rifles immediately joined in. A rifle and a pistol answered back. Celia moved forward, emptied her rifle and then dropped it, reaching both for a hand grenade and a pistol as the fusillade intensified amidst a swirl of dust. She underhanded a grenade at the front jeep and fired two pistol shots before her grenade — and another one tossed by Imelda — blasted off almost simultaneously. Squinting and ducking briefly, Celia then gripped her smoking pistol and peered into the pile-up.

The smoke assaulted her eyes and the searing heat shot out to her as Celia aimed her pistol, which she believed still held four of the original fourteen bullets. Her left hand grabbed a clip loaded with fourteen more. In that close-up stance, aiming her pistol and looking for something else to shoot at, Celia spotted something through a gap in the smoke and flames. She saw one of her rebels, the one wearing the red bandana around her neck, racing down the road in panic and then ducking into the woods! Oh, my. In the heat of battle, Dani was fleeing, and Celia's heart churned at having brought along such a young girl. But only for a split second. The business at hand, as the shooting tapered off and then ceased, now centered around all of the remaining eighteen rebels encircling the still flaming and smoky pile-up searching out any hint or movement from the six bandits.

The body count came up one short. Had one man got away? Minutes later, after some of the smoke had cleared, they still counted only five. Celia and Imelda backed out of the carnage and emerged shoulder-to-shoulder, pistols still at the ready, as the other rebels encircled the now flaming inferno.

"Any casualties, Imelda?"

"I don't think so."

"After it clears up a little more, I'll check to see if Modesto is one of the five bodies, but we don't have time to hunt for the sixth one. He probably crawled away early and got to the woods. He's had a head start toward one of the garrisons. The garrison to the east is just six or so miles away and the one to the west is no more then eight miles. Someone must have heard all this damn noise.

"We need to clean this up. Use the ropes to pull and push the first two jeeps and the trees over the cliff and they'll sink into the marsh. The five bodies, too. That one jeep that fell off to the side there, maybe we can start it. Then we'll need to smooth out the dirt with branches. Get that started. We don't have much time and if we get caught here we'll have to shoot our way out. I'm going to check those bodies to see if Modesto is one of the five dead."

Celia took a few steps when Gloria Espinosa, one of her rebels, ran up, panting. "Celia! Celia! Come with me! Just come with me!"

Celia and Imelda both followed Gloria as she trotted down the road. Soon, Gloria cut into an opening in the woods. They sliced their way through the thick growth. At the edge of a grassy clearing, Gloria stopped, and pointed. Imelda eased up beside Celia.

Before them now was a sight, a scene, none of them would ever forget. The sixteen-year-old Dani stood, very poised, pointing her pistol down at...Modesto! The handsome assassin was in a seated position leaning back, with his right arm resting on a log. His stomach was blood-soaked and more blood oozed out of his mouth, but his blinking eyes focused on Celia, whom he surely recognized. Celia glanced at a profile of Dani's face. The teenager was entirely focused on her task. Dani had not run away in the heat of battle.

Celia looked back down at the killer. She was speechless, but Modesto managed to emit an historic sentence: "I...reckon...you won...Celia."

"Yes, thanks to a sixteen-year-old girl. The Army School of the Americas didn't teach you as much as you thought.

"Your five men are dead. I don't hear shooting back there, so it looks like your back-up's not coming. I can wait a few minutes for you to die. If it takes longer, I'll kill you myself."

Finally, Modesto went limp; his head tilted and his body slipped to the right. He twitched once; then the career of America's highest paid assassin was over.

Celia turned her attention to Dani. "Sweetheart," Celia said, "I hope you know what a great thing you did today for Cuba. I will always love you, and always admire you. And by the way, I only know you by your nickname. What is your real name?"

Dani smiled proudly, and then hugged Celia. "My real name is Danielle," she said. "Danielle Ortiz."

CHAPTER 5. THE TOUCH, AT LAST

The Cuban Revolution was fueled and powered by brave young Cuban women, with the incomparable Celia Sánchez at the forefront. After the brilliant dispatch of Modesto — the heralded killer sent by America from Fort Benning, Georgia, to assassinate Celia — the fledgling revolution in Cuba's Sierra Maestra Mountains embraced another heroine, the sixteen-year-old Danielle "Dani" Ortiz. Many fiercely motivated teenage Cuban girls had joined Celia's cause and then emerged as legendary guerrilla fighters. The fifteen-year-old Teté Puebla, for example, was already firmly installed as a key officer with the "Maríana Grajales Brigade," an all-female guerrilla unit that time and again out-fought and also out-smarted larger and better-armed Batista forces.

(As of 2005, Teté is a general in the Cuban army; she is a prime reason the revolution was victorious and, forty-six-years later, she is a prime reason it has not been overturned. Dani, another worshipper of Celia Sánchez, continued to fight brilliantly. After the triumph of the revolution, Dani insisted on being Celia's primary bodyguard and, right up till Celia's death from cancer on January 11, 1980, no one ever had better protection, as countless would-be assassins from the CIA, the Mafia, and the transplanted Batistianos in southern Florida discovered. On January 11, 1981 — one year to the day after Celia's death — Dani swam out into the ocean and never returned. Earlier that morning she had told a priest, "I dreamed last night that the CIA was sending three assassins to heaven to kill Celia. I must save her.")

To know Celia Sánchez was to love her. In many instances, those who loved her were willing to die for her — such as the still legendary "mountain messengers" Lidia Docé and Clodímira Acosta. Danielle "Dani" Ortiz was not the only one who never recovered from Celia's death from cancer in 1980. As noted, Haydée Santamaría, the second most famous revolutionary heroine, committed suicide shortly after Celia died.

(In March of 2004, while I was in Cuba researching this book, I happened to stop off at a park on the edge of Havana. My driver Carlos and I struck up a conversation with a fourteen-year-old schoolgirl named Ada Contreras, who was sitting on a stone bench reading a book. Ada, fluent in Spanish and English, was a lovely girl, neatly attired in her school uniform. I noticed she also had nice rings on her ring fingers, a handsome watch on her left wrist, and a shiny silver bracelet on her right wrist. I said, "You must like jewelry." She smiled and said, "I usually don't wear any of this but today I just felt like it." Then she raised her left leg and turned down her white sock, revealing a tiny gold bracelet around her ankle. She said, "But I always wear this. Celia Sánchez, our revolutionary heroine, always wore a gold bracelet around her left ankle for good luck when she was fighting in the Sierras." Ada had no idea I was in Cuba to research this book about Celia Sánchez.)

Cuban women are not the only ones who idolized Celia Sánchez. Castro, stagnating in Batista's Isle of Pines prison in 1954 and 1955, became perhaps her greatest admirer when he learned about the revolution she had created and was leading in the Sierra Mountains. He wrote that he longed to "touch" her and to join her, to help her make Batista's Cuba "Celia's Cuba." And the historic day would indeed come when he would finally get to do just that.

All of his long life Fidel Castro has been most influenced by women and he has much preferred their company to any association with men. He has famously loved many women but he has worshipped only one — Celia Sánchez. It began with his beloved mother Lina; she was a peasant maid to his wealthy father Angel when they began their large family. It continued with Fidel's closeness to his sisters Angelita, Emma, Juanita, and Lidia. At the age of twenty-two, he married Mirta Díaz-Balart; they honeymooned in Miami where Fidel, who never thought much about money, went broke and had to borrow money for their return to Cuba. A University of Havana law student, Fidel inherited $80,000 and quickly gave most of it away to poor peasant women in Havana.

Physically imposing, athletic, Fidel also easily established new academic records at Belén College and the University of Havana. He also earned a repu-tation as a peasant-loving, fearless critic of despots, especially in Cuba and throughout the Caribbean and Latin America. At the University of Havana, Fidel became known for his fiery anti-Batista, anti-Mafia, and anti-US speeches, which gained him an increasing following from the rural classes. In addition, Cuban women, rich and poor, became his great admirers.

The focused and driven young Castro didn't have to devote much of his time to chasing young women. They chased him. Many historians are more fascinated with his women than his politics or his revolutionary fervor. In addition to Mirta, his litany of lovers included Naty Revuelta, Teté Casuso, Lucila Velasquez, Isabel Custodio, Dalia Soto Del Valle Jorgé, Gloria Gaitán, Marita Lorenz, and many more.

Fidel found women irresistible, especially redheads. In the early days of his triumphant revolutionary fame, some of America's richest, most famous, and most beautiful women shamelessly lusted for the flamboyant Cuban, including a notable array of Hollywood starlets, such as the redheaded Beverly Aadland, one of the stars of the 1958 classic "South Pacific." At the time, the seventeen-year-old Aadland was better known as the girlfriend of Errol Flynn. But Flynn, like many Hollywood types, was even more enchanted with Fidel Castro's 1959 revolutionary triumph in exotic Cuba, and especially with the young female guerrilla fighters that inundated Castro. Flynn's last movie was "Cuban Rebel Girls" and Beverly Aadland was one of the cinematic rebels. In real life, with Errol Flynn's cooperation, she was also Fidel Castro's lover.

But every one of the bevy of Castro lovers is fascinating — Marita Lorenz, for instance. She was a great-looking girl, half German and half American, all of seventeen years old, when she cast her green eyes at Fidel in February of 1959, just over a month after the revolutionary triumph. Marita, mesmerized by publicity about the teenage Cuban girls who had fought so heroically, found herself at a celebratory party that included Fidel — while Celia was burning the midnight oil, tending to state business back in the new revolutionary government's headquarters. Marita caught Fidel's eye; they became lovers.

Marita soon lived across the hall from Fidel and Celia's office in the Havana Libre Hotel. Amazingly, shortly thereafter, a CIA plot to assassinate Fidel and Celia connected Marita to the lead CIA agent, Frank Sturgis, who would later gain fame as one of the Watergate burglars. That ended Marita's affair with Fidel but marked the beginning of a life of intrigue. Lorenz apparently worked for the CIA, then the FBI. She had a child by the former President of Venezuela (shortly before he was arrested and deported to Spain), and later claimed to have known something about John F. Kennedy's assassination.

Fidel's multitude of love affairs will forever distract historians but they are relevant here because of how they impacted Celia Sánchez, who commented on them in six of her seventeen letters to her American friend Nora Peters between the years 1959 and 1979. I took Celia's letters to Cuba in 2004. Startlingly frank, written as one friend to another and not from an historic perspective, the letters discuss Fidel and his lovers but also significant events such as the Bay of Pigs attack, the Cuban Missile Crisis, the assassination of JFK, Celia's love of the American ideal of democracy and her bitter hatred of US capitalism, the Batistianos in southern Florida, the 1976 terrorist bombing of a Cuban airplane, and others. Celia even revealed to Nora the name of the JFK White House intimate who had called to warn her about the impending Bay of Pigs attack.

Celia's views and revelations about Castro's lovers are especially noteworthy since, as all historians know, from 1957 till her death in 1980, Celia was the woman at his side day and night, almost without fail. Historians have puzzled for decades about her "toleration" of his many lovers. She was the one person who commanded and dominated all aspects of his being, even including the access of lovers to him. As Georgie Anne Geyer described it, in Guerrilla Prince: "A river of devoted and devouring women was flowing like quicksilver through his life.... Meanwhile, Celia stood guard as valiantly as she could...shooing them out of Castro's bed and bedroom."

Celia in one letter to Nora mentioned teenage beauties Marita Lorenz and Beverly Aadland as Fidel's "toys." She described Teté Casuso, a brainy and striking secretary and publicist, as "smart enough and pretty enough to claim him had she not tired of his, our, politics." But through it all, Celia told Nora, "I have been jealous of only one woman in Fidel's life, and that is Naty. The bimbos didn't trouble me, but Naty did. I actually thought she was full-time worthy of him, if times permitted. And I loved her too, respected her so much. But I couldn't let him go. I love him but mostly I need him because Cuba needs him. As long as I live or as long as Fidel lives, the Batistianos and the Mafia and the capitalists will not reclaim Cuba. Aside from politics, I could survive losing him to Naty. But with the threat from the US, how could I cast politics aside? Oh, Nora! I didn't ask to be a revolutionary. I surely didn't ask to be a politician. All that was forced upon me."

In another letter to Nora, Celia wrote, "Fighting the Batistianos, the Mafia, and the US sometimes seems easy compared to balancing my love for Cuba and my love for Fidel. A woman who does not crave power or money, like me, should not be forced to be a revolutionary or a politician. That, I guess, is my dilemma."

That was the Celia Sánchez who referred to her native island as "mi Cubita bella." The historian Carlos Franqui asked her how in the world she did it — how in the world did she put together a peasant revolution that defeated the combined might of a powerful dictator, the most powerful nation in the world, and the strongest criminal organization in the world?

Celia replied: "They loved gluttony. I loved Cuba. I guess I loved Cuba more than they loved gluttony." She even loved Cuba more than she loved Fidel, and Fidel told Nora Peters, "I've always respected her love for Cuba."

All his life, Fidel has been famously private and noncommittal about women. In notable television interviews, ABC's Barbara Walters and CBS's Dan Rather both asked Castro if he would say anything at all about Celia Sánchez. Each time, he said not a word; he just raised his hands and shook his palms at them. To this day he only speaks of Celia with the most intimate friends they shared, especially Marta Rojas. The now seventy-six-year-old Marta today has more influence on Fidel than any other living person, according to Tracey Eaton, head of Havana's Dallas Morning News bureau.

I mentioned to Marta that Eaton had told me she was the person with the most influence on Fidel. She replied, "For people still living, perhaps I am. But till the day he dies, the person with the most influence on him will be Celia. He thinks of this island as Celia's Cuba."

Castro is a very private man. At the age of seventy-nine, in the year of 2005, he is married — yet very, very few Cubans are even aware of it.

In the mid-1950s, shut up in the Isle of Pines prison, Fidel was consumed with two things: (1) ending his 15-year sentence so he could join Celia Sánchez's anti-Batista revolution, and (2) writing torrid love letters to a woman who was not his wife Mirta.

Her name was Naty Revuelta. From November of 1953 till March of 1954, Fidel wrote Naty dozens of love letters from his prison cell. Naty was born in 1925 near the University of Havana. In the 1950s, Naty was considered the most beautiful woman in Havana and she was a much-photographed socialite; she lived in a mansion and was married to a doctor. She loved Cuba but hated the Batista dictatorship. In the anti-Batista underground, she met the young Fidel. She raided her savings and sold her jewels to help finance Fidel's ill-fated attack on Batista's Moncada Army Barracks on July 26, 1953. They fell madly in love.

Fidel's letters to Naty became a part of history in the 1990s when their out-of-wedlock daughter, Alina Fernández, defected to the US in 1993 and sold

Naty's letters from Fidel to the media. (Dr. Fernández divorced Naty in 1959 when he learned about the letters.)

One typical missive from Fidel was dated November 7, 1953:

Dear Naty,

An affectionate greeting from my prison, although it's been a while since I last heard from you. I keep, and will always keep, the tender letter you wrote to my mother. If you have had to suffer on my account for various reasons, think that I would gladly give my life for your honor and well-being. Outward appearances should not concern us; it's what's within our consciences that matters. Some things are lasting, despite life's woes. Some things are eternal, like the impressions I have of you, so indelible that I shall carry them to the grave.

Yours forever, Fidel

Another letter said,

My dearest Naty, You are woman. Woman is the most delicate of the world's creatures. No tribute made to a woman is proper or beautiful if it's made to the detriment of another; whoever makes it does not deserve the passion of any woman, although a woman who doesn't encourage it is no woman. You are bold; I like that. I am aglow. So, 'intimacy is a powerful foe that can raise walls and destroy bridges.' You're saying that to console me, right? Write to me, for I cannot live without your letters.

With much love, Fidel

The Fidel Castro who was writing those love letters from prison to Naty Revuelta was also writing ardent revolutionary notes to Celia Sánchez.

Naty's letters were being sent by regular mail; the notes to Celia were being smuggled out of prison by the young journalist Marta Rojas.

The letters to Naty were screened by prison officials, who diverted some of them to Fidel's wife Mirta, dooming the marriage.

Naty's love affair with Fidel resulted in the birth of Fidel Castro's only known daughter, Alina Hernández. She fled Cuba in 1993 and now regularly attacks her father on Miami radio. Naty remains devoted to Castro. Apparently, Fidel, Haydée Santamaría, and Melba Hernández met clandestinely in Naty's mansion to plot the 1953 attack on the Moncada Army Garrison; Haydée and Melba participated in the attack while Naty largely funded it.

Tad Szulc, a major Castro biographer, wrote: "Fidel's life has been predicated by an extraordinary contingent of beautiful and/or highly intelligent women who, in effect, dedicated their lives to him and his cause — and without whom he would not have succeeded."

Of all the women in Fidel Castro's life, there has been just one absolute superstar — Celia Sánchez. In Guerrilla Prince, Geyer revealed that in the

Sierras when Fidel craved a fountain pen, he asked Celia; when he wanted a dentist, he asked Celia. And Celia was the only one that could over-rule him.

Roberto Salas, a world-famed photographer and chronicler of the Cuban Revolution who is still alive and is still closely associated with Fidel, wrote, in his 1998 book, Fidel's Cuba; A Revolution In Pictures, "Celia (from 1959 till 1980) made all the decisions in Cuba, the big ones and the small ones. When she died of cancer in 1980, we all knew no one could ever replace her." To this day, Roberto's most prized possession is an engraved watch Celia gave him.

Since her death, Fidel has doggedly ruled Cuba as he perceives she would want him to rule it. He believes, for example, that Celia would want his young Foreign Minister Felipe Peréz Roque to be Cuba's next long-term leader, so he will try to make that happen.

When Celia began her Revolution, Fidel Castro was in prison and Che Guevara had never set foot in Cuba.Regarding this crucial and eclectic period in the history of Cuba, historian Pedro Alvarez Tabio concluded: "The two men with the guts and the capability to threaten Batista — veteran politician Antonio Guiteras and young upstart Fidel Castro — had been easily thwarted. Guiteras was killed and Castro was imprisoned. That left one person on the island with the guts and the capability to threaten Batista. Her name was Celia Sánchez. Had she been killed or imprisoned anytime between 1954 and 1957, there would have been no viable Cuban Revolution, and no revolution for Fidel Castro and Che Guevara to join."

***

Deep in the mountains of eastern Cuba, the resourceful and resilient Celia continued to build her revolution. In western Cuba's capital city, the impunity with which Batista's men brutalized the people began finally to garner more headlines in Caribbean and Latin American newspapers and magazines, influencing greater coverage by powerful US entities such as the New York Times.

The historic murders of the Giralt sisters and later, the gruesome torture-murders of fourteen-year-old Willie Soler and his three playmates made headlines and impelled more and more outraged family members to organize and lead protests.

And now, the media at last was watching. As long as such things were kept from the media, America didn't give a damn. But, finally embarrassed and concerned that the spotlight on Cuba might jeopardize its exploitation of Latin America overall, the US government at last exerted pressure on Batista, seeking to clip his wings.

It was common knowledge that the hero to the peasants was the imprisoned young rebel, Fidel Castro. Throughout the Caribbean and Latin America he was considered a "political prisoner." Indeed, he would have been murdered except for the publicity; and the twenty-two-year-old Havana journalist Marta Rojas was one who helped make sure that influential journalists such as Herbert L. Matthews of the *New York Times* remained interested in Fidel's incarceration.

In early 1955, to combat the media exposure of Batista's brutality toward the peasants, the US persuaded him to grant amnesty to some of its high-profile "political" prisoners, realizing the gesture would be meaningless unless the popular and celebrated Fidel Castro was included, along with his brother Raúl as well as the two young women — Haydée Santamaría and Melba Hernández — who had helped them plan and then participated in the ill-fated Moncada attack.

At this point, Celia controlled only her revolutionary niche in the Sierras, but she now also had three things going for her: (1) growing peasant support across the island; (2) an effective network of underground communication links that included the Isle of Pines prison; and (3) sympathy from sources within both the Batista and US governments. Thus, Celia was aware of the pressure on Batista from the US to grant amnesty to the Isle of Pines prisoners, including Fidel.

Moreover, she was tipped that, not surprisingly, a murder detail would be put on Fidel's trail the moment he exited the prison.

Celia was now factoring the fate of Fidel into her overall plans. Celia juggled her priorities judiciously. She now counted Fidel near the top of her list, given his courage and skill in defying Batista while he was a young polemicist at the University of Havana. Celia's exchange of notes reflected her determination never to neglect recruiting.

After tips from sympathizers within both the Batista and US governments regarding the rumored amnesty and the murder detail, Celia used her underground network to get the following note to Fidel. She now was using code names:

Alejandro,

If you are granted amnesty, a murder detail will be assigned to you immediately and it will be relentless. You must stay undercover in one safe house after another. I want you to "touch" me and "help" me but most of all I want you to stay alive. Anticipating your release, a second note from me will list the safe houses designed to help you get off the island, because to try to join me now is too dangerous. In the next note I will provide names, etc., of contacts in New York City and Mexico City. They will help you recruit (money, rebels) and then you will join me at a designated coastal site that I will communicate to you via the Mexican contact that knows how to contact me electronically.

Bless you; good luck.

Aly

On May 15, 1955, Castro and the other survivors of the 1953 Moncada attack were released in a unique general amnesty forced upon Batista by the US government. Batista viewed this as an opportunity to have Castro killed, but Fidel slipped the net.

One of the safe houses utilized by Fidel was owned by Natalia "Naty" Revuelta, the socialite who had been the recipient of his love letters. Described by historians as "the most beautiful woman in Havana in the 1950s," Naty risked her life to spend nights in safe houses with Fidel.

On June 24, 1955 — one month and nine days after getting out of prison — Fidel left Cuba, bound for New York City. There he met and stayed with Cuban-born Osvaldo Salas, who lived and worked right across from Madison Square Garden.

Salas, a favorite of Life and Look magazines as well as newspapers such as the New York Times, was one of America's most accomplished, best-known, and best-paid photographers in the 1950s. By the time he hosted Fidel Castro in 1955, he had taken some of history's most famous photographs of celebrities such as Joe DiMaggio, Rocky Marciano, and Marilyn Monroe. Osvaldo and his teenage son Roberto would later move back to Cuba and become the official photographers of Revolutionary Cuba, and thus intimates of both Fidel Castro and Celia Sánchez. In 1998, to honor his late father, Roberto Salas published a book entitled FIDEL CASTRO: A Pictorial History of the Cuban Revolution.

The book includes two of the famous Castro photographs from his excursion to New York City in 1955: (1) a full-page photograph of the suit-attired, clean-shaven Castro walking in Central Park, and (2) a photograph of Fidel sitting at a cash-strewn desk during one of his NYC recruiting missions.

The Salas book includes the two most famous photos of Celia Sánchez: (1) in uniform standing with a female soldier beside one of her beloved jeeps, and (2) a pensive pose, smoking a cigarette, with a photo of Che Guevara as a backdrop. In the captions Roberto notes that Celia, never one to seek publicity, would gently chastise but never scold him when he took her picture.

After New York, Fidel's recruiting mission took him to Mexico City, where Celia had also arranged contacts. Mexico would prove to be quite an adventure for Fidel, including a return to prison. Both Batista and the US had agents after him. At one point he and twenty-two of his associates spent three weeks in a Mexican jail for "illegally possessing arms," as Herbert L. Matthews points out in Revolution In Cuba.

In Mexico City, Fidel's brother Raúl met a young doctor from Argentina named Ernesto "Che" Guevara. Che's post-graduate travels through Latin America had already turned him into a pro-peasant revolutionary. Raúl Castro introduced Che to Fidel. One night-long session induced Che to agree to go to Cuba. In Reminiscences of the Cuban Revolutionary War, Che wrote, "I had been linked to him from the outset by a tie of romantic adventurous sympathy, and by the conviction that it would be worth dying on a foreign beach for such a pure ideal." In that manner, with that resolve, Che stepped onto the pages of history.

A telephone call from Celia in Bayamo, Cuba, to Fidel in Mexico City induced him to purchase a used boat that would take him and his new recruits from Mexico to a rendezvous with Celia at a specific spot on Cuba's south-eastern coast. Celia instructed Fidel to debark at the coastal town of Niguero in the province of Oriente and, once a follow-up call had confirmed the approximate day of his arrival, she would meet him there with a force that would protect them.

The yacht Fidel bought in Mexico City for the dangerous trip to Cuba had a soon-to-be-famous name stenciled on its side — "Granma." But Granma was a boat designed to accommodate twelve to seventeen vacationers, not eighty-two armed fighters. Yet, Fidel, Raúl, and Che crowded in a total of eighty-two, with a load of gas cans on the deck. Somehow, they eluded the US-Batista agents as well as the befuddled Mexican authorities, and snuck out of Mexico under the cover of fog and darkness. Fidel had advised Celia to be waiting for him at Niguero on November 30, 1956.

In the open sea, leery of being spotted by military planes or ships, the Granma never used lights, even at night or in dense fog, as it nudged closer and closer to Niguero, where Celia waited with rebels, trucks, jeeps, and supplies.

Off the southern coast of Cuba, the Granma was running low on fuel when one of the men was knocked overboard in the choppy seas. Time and fuel were short; they circled frantically but the search for the missing man seemed futile. Fidel was told they would have to go on. He adamantly refused. The circling and the search continued. Then Pichirilo Mejías, the yacht's helmsman, spotted their comrade. He was rescued. The journey resumed along the Cuban coast.

On December 2, 1956, Celia still waited at Niguero; the Granma was three days late. The radio transmitter on the boat was not working. The Granma began leaking, and it was spotted by one of Batista's reconnaissance helicopters.

The boat had to be beached near the coastal town of Las Coloradas, fifteen miles from Niguero. The eighty-two rebels scrambled ashore but the helicopter spotters had alerted a Batista army, which waited in ambush. The rebels were almost defenseless; they had to debark in the murky waters of a swamp, not a beach, at a spot called Alegría de Pío. The Batista soldiers opened fire, killing seventy of the eighty-two. The other twelve, as best they could, hid in the thick, thorny, and marshy undergrowth; most were wounded and only three had weapons. Celia, alerted by peasants in the area, raced to help them.

Celia managed to fight off the Batista soldiers as the twelve surviving rebels from Granma crawled deeper into the swamp. They scattered. Celia sent rebels and peasants to find them and give them food and water, knowing that most of them had been killed.

One of the first survivors discovered in the swamp was bleeding from two rifle wounds and suffering an asthmatic attack. Celia had ample medicine, bandages, and even asthma remedies. Thus, Che Guevara — the baby-faced doctor from Argentina — survived to fight another day.

Where was Fidel? Raúl? Were they among the survivors? For four days, Celia didn't know. Then she got word from her battery of rescuers that the Castro brothers were alive. The twelve Granma survivors were: Fidel Castro, Raúl Castro, Che Guevara, Camilo Cienfuegos, Juan Almeida, Efigenio Amejeiras, Ciro Redondo, Julio Díaz, Calixto García, Luis Crespo, José Poncé, and Universo Sánchez. On December 18, 1956, the twelve survivors were all accounted for and were being nursed back to health, individually or in groups of three or four. And still, Celia had yet to see Fidel.

Celia herself had cared for Che Guevara and four others. But scattered as they were in the dense and swampy environs, other medics from her unit had administered to Fidel as Celia the nurse also had to be Celia the guerrilla leader to keep Batista soldiers still in the area at bay. She got word that Fidel had one "irksome" wound but that he was fine. Also, she was told that he was "anxious" to see her. Ada Martinez was the rebel leader who delivered that message to Celia. Ada would later describe that moment to Bohemia Magazine: "Celia covered her face with her hands. She cried, for the twelve she saved and for the other seventy."

The next morning, on the edge of a farm in the shadows of the Sierra Maestra Mountains, Celia Sánchez for the first time looked up into the face of Fidel Castro. Years later, in a letter to Nora Peters, Celia wrote: "Never had I been either emotional or overwhelmed in battle, Nora. But I was both when I looked up at Fidel for the first time, as his strong hands gripped my shoulders. I don't think I said anything. I don't think he did either. I think that's why Ada, and some others, moved us over to a table beneath a tree, so we would at least speak to each other. Fidel, famous for five-hour speeches, spoke one word. It was, I'll never forget, 'finally.' Then, Nora, I smiled rather broadly and lightened up. I said, 'Finally what? Finally, you get to touch me...and help me?' He still didn't say anything, just nodded. He...just nodded. And that was it, our first ever meeting."

***

The Granma, the little yacht that brought Fidel and Celia together, now has Cuba's main daily newspaper, and a whole province, named for it. In The Twelve, historian Carlos Franqui quotes Celia Sánchez as saying, "Just consider where the landing took place. If they had debarked right on the beach instead of at the swamp, they would have found trucks, jeeps, gasoline. It would have been a walkaway."

In Guerrilla Prince, Georgie Anne Geyer writes: "Later, when the world was different, she would reminisce romantically about those irreplaceable months in the Sierra. Sitting with Fidel and some American journalists on a farm on the Isle of Pines, she recalled in her husky, throbbing voice, 'Ah, but those were the best times, weren't they? We were all so very happy then, really. We will never be so happy again, will we? Never.'"

Celia Sánchez the guerrilla fighter, to the end of her days, relished the fighting in the Sierras as "the best times." That, I believe, helps explain why she was and is the greatest female revolutionary of all time. The triumph and the longevity of the Cuban Revolution, against all odds, stand as monuments to what she achieved, always carrying in her buttoned-down shirt pocket or around her neck the medallion left behind by María Ochoa.

But her visions of a post-Batista Cuba were still a long way off, even with Fidel Castro in the Sierras at last, to "touch" her and "help" her.

Courtesy: *The Osvaldo &
Roberto Salas Collections/
Office of Historic Affairs,
Cuban Council of State.*

Photo taken in 1958 on an armed march in
the Sierra Maestra

Photo taken in 1960, the year after
the victory of the revolution, as
she waved good-bye to VIPs at
the Havana Airport.

Photo taken in 1958. On the right, Fidel Castro.

Nancy Pavón at the age fifteen on October 12, 1971. She is lying in a hospital bed after her right foot was blown away in a terrorist attack on her coastal cabin, Boca de Samá, by two speed boats.

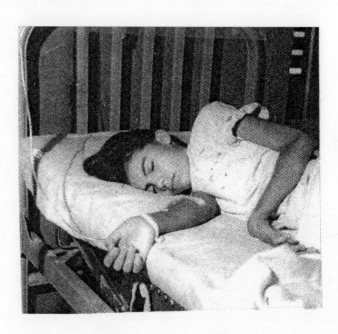

Chapter 6. Beating Batista

Celia's eclectic band of rebels — ranging from teenage girls like Teté Puebla and Danielle Ortiz to the tough-as-nails thirty-year-old Ada Martinez — all marched to the cadence of her drum, or the beat of her revolutionary heart. That was the heartbeat that constructed the revolution that finally threatened the venomous dictatorship of Fulgencio Batista and eventually alarmed the US, which feared losing the opportunity to siphon off the wealth and resources of Cuba that could have otherwise benefited the Cuban people.

The unchecked greed of the Mafia and the capitalists was revealed to all, including Celia, during the twenty-five tumultuous years that the US government fought to keep Fulgencio Batista at the head of Cuba. Celia, growing up in the little town of Media Luna, was quite aware that the US had installed Batista-type dictators all over the Caribbean and Latin America. Corporations such as the United Fruit Company furnished kickbacks to those ruthless dictators in exchange for a free hand in exploiting the nation's wealth. Key owners of the United Fruit Company included the US Secretary of State John Foster Dulles and CIA Director Allen Dulles.

Fidel Castro's own father, Don Angel Castro, had a contract with the US-owned United Fruit Company that helped him get rich in Batista's Cuba. He owned 36,000 acres of land. With the triumph of the revolution, the very first property that the new government nationalized was Don Angel Castro's huge farm. Fidel Castro famously issued that order, which stood because Celia Sánchez approved it. Shortly, Fidel, the peasant-lover who was bitterly resentful of his father's deal with the United Fruit Company, issued a second order — to flood the entire Castro property, including the home-place — to provide irrigation for the peasant farms in the area. History records that Fidel's irrigation order was overturned by the only person capable of overturning it — Celia Sánchez.

Another privileged young man who sided with the poor was the Argentine doctor Che Guevara, who also had a visceral hatred of the United Fruit Company. Thus, on the first night Che met Fidel in Mexico City, their long discussion reached a crescendo when Fidel happened to mention the United Fruit Company. That was the moment when Che made the decision to join Fidel to hook up with Celia Sánchez's peasant revolution.

The US backed its dictators with the US military, the US treasury, and America's Central Intelligence Agency, which was formed shortly after World War II to meet the growing threat from its war ally, the Soviet Union. Like most things American, the CIA was apparently created by decent leaders for a decent purpose — securing intelligence to protect America from enemies.

But like some things American, the CIA soon evolved into an unchecked and powerfully funded covert operation on a par with and closely equivalent to the Soviet Union's notorious KGB. From sending assassins to put down (or foment) revolutions in other people's countries to torturing men and women captured during a war in their own country, the US continues to act in ways that are so heinous that most Americans simply refuse to believe the evidence.

The more she learned about the CIA, the more Celia realized that Cuba's experience was typical of democratic America's undemocratic tracks all over Latin America, and beyond. The CIA-orchestrated murder of Patrice Lumumba in the Congo, for example, made way for the thief/killer Mobutu. She also knew why the US favored killer-thiefs rather than "peasant-lovers." Those who spent resources helping the local people left too little for international capitalists to rake off the top. Where, she wondered, were the average US citizens whose taxes paid for all the atrocities but who never saw a penny of the spoils?

Now, Castro had indeed come and he helped with the planning and the fighting each day, and soothed Celia with touches each night. In an e-mail dated 12-19-04, Marta Rojas told me, "From Day One, Fidel always, without fail, treated Celia like the angel she was. I will sometimes accept criticism of him on all other subjects, and criticize him myself, but not when it comes to Celia. Absolutely never when it came to Celia!"

Here is the way Celia, in a November 19, 1979, letter to Nora Peters, described that union with Fidel in the Sierras: "From the first moment I looked into his eyes, Nora, I knew that he was in awe of me, maybe worshipful. In retrospect, I guess I felt the same about him. I knew all about him before I ever saw him in the Sierra. I knew I wanted him, needed him. Now it's two decades later. We remain in awe of each other, worshipful of each other. I am proud of that. In all this time, against overwhelming odds all along the way, he has at least given me the chance to keep all those promises I made so long ago to María Ochoa. Despite all, I kept them."

(That was the letter in which Celia for the first time told Nora that she had been diagnosed with cancer. Nora made her eighth and final trip to Cuba to be with her friend, and she later confirmed that María Ochoa's repaired broken chain and the medallion of Christ was around Celia's neck when she died and when she was buried.)

In 1957, six of the twelve Granma survivors became key point commanders for Celia. Those six were Fidel Castro, Che Guevara, Camilo Cienfuegos, Raúl Castro, Juan Almeida, and Calixto García. Celia and Fidel were the leaders of Command Group One. They fought side by side by day and slept side by side at night, regardless of the circumstances.

Celia's revolutionary heart was now blessed with the man she loved, a man who also happened to be a fearless and brilliant point commander. "After two battles," Celia later told Nora Peters, "I knew he was my choice to be Cuba's future leader."

***

After interviewing the twelve survivors, Celia held a conference with the six she had chosen to be point commanders. Her aide Ada Martinez was the only other person in attendance. Celia and Ada remained standing as the six men hovered over the map. With a stick pointer, Celia tapped the location of the base camp. "Here we are, gentlemen, about 2500 feet elevated and surrounded by dense forest, especially on both sides and at our back. You may have noticed there are no discernible roads leading up here, and the jeeps, gas cans, and so forth are down near the base. I allow some smoking and some fires for food by day but not at night. They scout us with both reconnaissance helicopters and small planes, two of which we have shot down with Browning rifles. They've tried heavy bombers but they can't see this main camp and if they dip down they draw heavy small arms fire and then have trouble elevating over the peaks. One of their bombers crashed into the trees about 500 feet below the peak, but it's so dense up there I haven't sent a unit to check it out."

Celia now tapped nine specific spots on the map.

"These nine places bordered in red," she continued, "are the nine clearings down below us that are the logical means to get up here. Otherwise, the forest itself protects the other three sides. And the spots bordered in yellow are the swamps amidst the clearings that are sufficient to protect those areas."

Celia's initial instructional session to her notable new commanders is documented by at least three good sources: her letters to Nora Peters, the post-revolutionary writings of Che Guevara, and the painstaking interviews done by historian Pedro Alvarez Tabío with Ada Martinez and others.

"On the map," she continued, "you'll see swamps and deep water that, in places, includes sinkholes and quicksand. We must know those places by memory but I've indicated them with little notes on the map. The enemy doesn't know these spots till they encounter them, and we've induced tanks into those spots by baiting and retreating. You'll see some tanks sticking partly out of the swamp water, and there are more beneath the water out of sight. We maintain ten separate guerrilla units that are assigned to monitor and protect the nine clearings, attacking and retreating when necessary. Never do I want a major unit in one place, but with radio and walkie-talkie contact all units stay in touch and, when necessary, can converge to assist each other, always with the intent of striking hard and quick but ready to retreat to the mountains and the swamps. But the nine clearings are our primary focus. We cannot, for example, allow tanks to take up positions in or on the edges of those clearings or they would be able to fire randomly into our sanctuaries. To prevent that, if necessary, we go on the offensive to engage them more on our turf, which I consider to be the swamps and the forested foothills leading toward the mountains. We have good intelligence on their shipments of troops and supplies, and we have ventured out to derail two of their trains, then scoop up the leftovers. The plan, gentlemen, is to stay solvent as guerrilla fighters and to inflict as much damage as possible to the forces sent to eliminate us."

Celia then walked around in front of the table.

"But guerrilla warfare is not the long-range plan, gentlemen," she added. "We only fight as guerrillas on our chosen turf as we build an army that will one day soon go on the attack all the way to Havana! Any questions?"

Camilo Cienfuegos, sporting a coal black beard, gazed up. "How many rebels do you have now and how many do you need...to go on the attack?"

"I'm using only 212 as my main fighters, much less than the enemy believes I'm using. That's how many I can adequately arm and trust. I have more arms coming, and more rebels. So, we puff up like a bullfrog to make them think we're bigger and stronger than we actually are. But we have to screen new recruits because assassins, spies, and more and more saboteurs are trying to infiltrate. Those bounty posters you've seen are just one of the collateral off-springs of all that. So, to answer your first question, I have 212 prime guerrilla fighters."

She grinned, then said, "I know 212 doesn't sound like much but believe me, as guerrilla fighters they are like thousands. I have them spread out in ten units to protect the nine clearings. Fidel, your Moncada raid lacked sufficient attacking force, as you know. From where we are now, we will build a sufficient force to attack any stronghold, including the Moncada garrison outside Santiago and Camp Colombia on the edge of Havana. We have screened 250 more rebels that we'll outfit as soon as we get the arms and equipment now heading here as a convoy circles Manzanillo."

Fidel raised a point. "Batista is counting on two things to wear you down — a war of attrition and cutting your supplies because he has the numbers and arms advantage. And he can keep building."

"Yes, but so can we. I'm not short of peasant volunteers, it's just the screening process that slows us down and the arms, plus supplies such as gas, are racing ahead of that procedure. About one-third of our arms have been extracted from the enemy, including all those jeeps down yonder. We will now escalate that tactic. We have good communication lines from here to Havana, both electronic and foot messengers, and massive peasant support that is growing by the hour. Attrition will not beat me, Fidel. I have 325 non-combatants just stashing supplies, and all of them want to join the fighting."

Che Guevara inquired what she meant by appointing them as point commanders. Were they to wait till she had an attack army?

"No. The six of you, starting later today, will each take over units down at the clearings. I was a bit pompous when I said Fidel and I will lead Command Unit One. Like you other five, Fidel and I will be guerrilla fighters leading up to units like Command Group One, Command Group Two, and so forth that will go on the attack. I want that to be soon, a matter of months, because Batista will more and more be supplied by the US. So, when we go on the attack we must surprise them, we must win, and we must keep pressing the attacks relentlessly. And we also must be patient as we get to that stage. But starting now, I want you new commanders to start working with the rebels around the clearings."

With that, the six men and two women began milling around the table. Raúl Castro inquired about the social tensions that must arise in a camp full of energetic young men and women.

"Yes, problems do come up, but we handle them. I've stressed that I will not tolerate wrong-doing. And I will not tolerate even consensual sex. That's not why we are here. There have been infractions. We have booted eight...maybe ten...out of here for mere distractions. And one man, Raúl, had gagged a girl, dragged her up into the forest, beat her, and raped her. We executed him by firing squad after a trial and by unanimous consensus."

***

The sagacious Celia had chosen well. Her six new point commanders, Fidel, Che, Camilo, Raúl, Juan (a black Cuban), and Calixto all proved to be sound fighters and sterling leaders. They adapted quickly although at times she had to temper their enthusiasm for going on the offensive. Shortly after the revolutionary victory, Camilo wrote a column in the newspaper Granma explaining "how most quickly we new commanders adapted to Celia's guerrilla style that pointed the way to the success we achieved." That three-page column, entitled "Fast Start," is still in the Cuban archives.

Patient and pragmatic, Celia continued building and supplying her overall force while her ten pockets of guerrilla fighters staved off one excursion after another from the increasingly stronger Batista armies. Her instant pairing with Fidel, including their sleeping arrangements, caused a few early murmurs but soon its uniqueness was generally accepted. Asked about it later by Herbert L. Matthews, Raúl Castro replied: "Celia was not in those mountains to party. She was there to beat Batista. She and Fidel were the decision-makers. All-night sessions consumed them. They weren't partying. They were deciding how best to beat Batista."

Celia Sánchez and Fidel Castro were in a lean-to tent at the edge of a clearing two miles from the mouth of the La Plata River in eastern Cuba. A light but steady tropical rain rhythmically echoed from the tent's roof. Mist seeped in from the two-foot opening above ground level. Celia was lying back on a folding cot, covered by a wool blanket. Her left arm curled over her tired eyes.

For three hours she had sat beside Fidel at a little wooden desk with a slanted top, in flickering candlelight, going over battle plans that would be employed at sunup. He was still there, crafting last-minute notes or underlining old ones. They were both anxious and a bit nervous. Except for some guerrilla retaliatory strikes forced upon their defensive posture, this would be the rebel army's very first offensive thrust at Batista. The target five miles away at the mouth of the La Plata River was an army garrison. Intelligence reports had indicated the garrison had been freshly supplied three days earlier, apparently in readiness to receive an army that was newly arrived on the edge of Santiago. At the moment, about fifty soldiers guarded the garrison. Celia and Fidel were surrounded by eighty-five rebels from their Command Group One. The plan within the hour was to take eleven jeeps and two trucks to move one mile closer to the garrison, then march another mile through a forested cove before launching an all-out attack at daylight.

They believed the garrison was now well-stocked with modern US-made weapons, ammunition, and supplies they sorely needed. But, the attack and getaway would have to be executed quickly, before the new army unit in Santiago reached the area. To get back to their eleven jeeps and two trucks, they counted on using captured garrison vehicles. There were no roads leading directly through the forest to the garrison, so a circuitous route lined out on a map would be used to get back to their stashed vehicles.

She opened her eyes and checked her wristwatch. It was 2:39 A.M., January 17, 1957. Fidel stood up, still looking down pensively at the map and the pages of notes. Finally, he lay down beside her and held her in his arms for the last half hour of the night.

The blistering daybreak attack at the mouth of the La Plata River is recorded as a glittering success, the sheer audacity of it catching the garrison by surprise. And it is registered as the Cuban Revolution's first offensive thrust at Batista. About thirty of his soldiers were killed; about twenty more were captured and left alive, unarmed, and locked in a storage shed at the garrison.

The rebels lost two men and seven more were wounded. Nine jeeps and three trucks were confiscated, and the booty included a cache of weapons and supplies, plus two tanks loaded with cannon-caliber ammunition. Fifty-two of the rebels marched back through the forest to their vacated vehicles. Fidel and Celia drove the lead jeep in this hastily organized but disciplined convoy as they made the circuitous route outlined on the map to the other side of the forest.

***

The rebel victory quickly drew attention in Havana and Washington. They too recorded it as the beginning of the rebel offensive. Havana and Washington would now send larger and stronger armies to the Sierras. Once underway, the rebel offensive would have to continue and it would have to be relentless. It was!

Batista sent two armies to the Sierras, led by two of his best young officers — Lt. Angel Sánches Mosquera and Major Joaquín Casillas. The rebels responded with a successful ambush against Mosquera on January 22, 1957, at Arroyo del Infierno. On February 9, at Altos de Espinosa, a larger Batista army led by Casillas severely pounded but did not defeat a rebel contingent that included units of Fidel's Group One and Che Guevara's Group Two. Celia decided to regroup, dispersing her forces and conferring with her point commanders. She vowed to stay on the attack and she didn't want to get bogged down in a war of attrition. Raúl's Group Three and Camilo's Group Four were assigned to assist Fidel and Che in the next confrontation with Casillas.

Meanwhile, in February of 1957, one of Celia's non-combatant stratagems came to fruition and she deemed it important enough to pursue even amidst the now intense fighting. Always seeking good publicity for her revolution, Celia had tried to arrange for well-known US newspapermen to come to the Sierras and report on the uprising against Batista. Lo and behold, on February 14, 1957, Celia was called away from a war council to read a note from a mountain messenger: Herbert L. Matthews, a famous reporter for the New York Times, had arrived and was awaiting safe escort to the battlefront!

This startling development returned Celia to her famed La Poloma ("The Dove") posture. She and the equally fearless Haydée Santamaría slipped past hostile forces to rendezvous with Matthews at a railhead in the foothills, notwithstanding the bounty on her head. Celia and Haydée then escorted Matthews to the base camp in the Sierras.

Always downplaying her role in the revolution, Celia chose to put Fidel front-and-center. Herbert L. Matthews authored a series of glowing articles in the New York Times about Fidel and his gritty band of peasant rebels fighting in the Sierras against the powerful dictatorship of the US-backed Batista. The articles were picked up by other newspapers all across the US, making heroes out of "the determined but out-manned and out-gunned rebels." Now, the American people knew about the revolution and they had someone to root for — "The young, fearless, bearded leader named Fidel Castro," as Herbert L. Matthews put it.

As the printed articles originating in the New York Times under the respected Matthews byline filtered back to Celia in the Sierras, she resumed her orchestration of the intensified war. So did a more angered Batista, who bolstered his army and increased his collateral brutality. Frank País, a twenty-three-old teacher who had been a vital recruiter for the rebels, was captured on

March 11, 1957, and then tortured to death on a public street in Santiago. Two days later, a student rebel leader, Fidel's good friend José Echeverría, was gunned down on the University of Havana campus. On April 20, 1957, Batista ordered Captain Esteban Ventura to murder four other student leaders; the gruesome slaughter took place in an apartment on Humboldt Street in Havana and it is now known as "The 7 Humboldt Street Massacre."

All the while, Batista was holding news conferences at gaudy press functions to tell the media that there "is no problem at all in the Sierras." On March 30, 1957, Batista opened the new Shell oil refinery in Havana. On April 6, he hosted a highly publicized "Mafia party" at the Havana Hilton.

Historian J. A. Sierra may be America's best expert on Cuba and the Cuban Revolution. To show what Celia was up against, here is J.A. Sierra's appraisal in the "History of Cuba Timetable":

> In 1934 Fulgencio Batista took over the Cuban government in what became known as 'The Revolt of the Sergeants.' For the next twenty-five years he ruled Cuba with an iron fist, and the full blessing and endorsement of the United States. Batista established lasting relationships with organized crime, and under his guardianship Havana became known as "the Latin Las Vegas." Meyer Lansky and other prominent gangsters were heavily invested in Havana, and politicians from Batista on down took their cuts.
>
> Through Lansky, the Mafia knew they had a friend in Cuba. A summit at Havana's Hotel Nacional, with mobsters such as Frank Costello, Vito Genovese, Santo Traficante Jr., Moe Dalitz and others, confirmed Meyer Lansky's and Lucky Luciano's authority over the US mob, and coincided with Frank Sinatra's 1946 singing debut in Havana. It was here that Lansky gave permission to kill Bugsy Siegel. Many of Batista's enemies faced the same fate as Siegel. Nobody seemed to mention the many brutal human rights abuses that were a regular feature of Batista's private police force.

Celia Sánchez, even as she waged her fight against Batista, the Mafia, and the US, believed it was important "to mention" what was happening in her homeland. Guided by her patriotic father, the provincial doctor who also was president of the Cuban Medical Association, Celia grew up admiring America's democracy, geographically so close yet seemingly so unattainable. She believed that the US citizens would be appalled if they knew what their government was doing in Cuba. And when Herbert L. Matthews came to the Sierras to report on her revolution, as he did, in extravagant detail, she kept up the momentum by working her communications pipeline to get CBS-TV, America's top television news organization, to come.

"La Paloma" ("The Dove") once again risked her life, as did Haydée Santamaría, to escort CBS television newsman Robert Taber and his film crew to the

Sierras. Taber filed his first report back to the US on April 23, 1957. Primed by Herbert L. Matthews and Robert Taber, other key news outlets in the US finally started covering the story as well. Fidel Castro, whom both Matthews and Taber portrayed as "the brave and charismatic rebel leader," became a hero in the US. This fulfilled Celia's quest to get the American public on her side and start to get them to think more critically about their government's Cuban venture.

Celia shrewdly had made Fidel the face of the revolution but, with his admiration and approval, she continued to call the shots in the Sierras.

On May 14, 1957, the US, stung by the fresh US news reports about the Batista brutalities in Cuba and by the popularity of the anti-Batista movement, named Earl Smith as the new US Ambassador to Cuba, replacing Batista's friend and apologist Arthur Gardner.

On May 18, 1957, Celia's supply pipeline successfully delivered a huge stash of new automatic rifles and crates of fresh ammunition.

On May 28, 1957, Che Guevara led an attack on Batista's supposedly impregnable garrison at El Uvero in the southern range of the Sierra Maestra.

Che would always believe that the victory at El Uvero was a turning point in the revolution and to him it was "a truly major battle of the war for us. We had gone from defensive to offensive warfare, learning how to beat the enemy."

On May 30, 1957, two days after that victory, a still euphoric Che Guevara wrote in his diary: "The inspiration to win at El Uvero welled up in me from Celia Sánchez. I walked around this campsite tonight. We can't wait for the next battle! Every rebel fighter in these mountains is beginning to believe we will win this thing. It's because of Celia, our constant reminder that the angels are on our side. It makes it better...to have one angel...in this bloody fight."

On June 4, 1957, United Press International (UPI) reported in newspapers across America that "800 US-trained and equipped Cuban troops are being sent back to Cuba to fight against the Rebel Army in the Sierra Maestra region."

On July 21, 1957, Fidel Castro, on Celia Sánchez's orders, officially named Che Guevara "Commander of the Second Rebel Army." Later that night, Celia and Fidel settled in for an all-night session to outline tentative plans for the next two offensive strikes against Batista armies — at Mar Verde and El Salto.

Fidel asked why Celia thought Mar Verde and El Salto should be the next two targets. "I believe, Fidel," she said, "we need to press on, with even more audacity. We now need to capture garrisons and hold them, and capture towns and hold them. That leads up to capturing cities like Santiago and Santa Clara, and holding them. Then we attack Havana! But this is a new phase, and it has to start at some time and some place. I want it to start now, with Mar Verde and El Salto. You, Camilo, and I will lead the attack on Mar Verde. Che, Raúl, Juan, and Calixto will lead the attack on El Salto. They will be simultaneous. After we take them, we must hold them...while continuing this phase all the way to Havana."

"Celia," he said, "you've seen the numbers here — 300 defenders at Mar Verde, five posted machine guns. It would be quite a challenge to attack it."

"Everything about this revolution is quite a challenge, Fidel. But, we're not here to play games. We are here to prepare for the day when we can attack and hold our ground. And then attack somewhere else and hold that ground. It has to start at a certain time and place. The time is now. The two places are Mar Verde and El Salto, simultaneously."

"Celia ... has anything ever scared you?"

She stared hard back at him now, surprised."Yes," she said sternly. "I've been scared once in my life. That was when I buried María Ochoa. It scared me to have to put that precious little girl into that deep hole, and cover it up. My first soldier, Felipe Matéo, was there that day. He will tell you, that scared me. I haven't been scared since!"

Now a more solemn Fidel Castro stared in awed silence at the tiny warrior, Celia Sánchez. This was the Celia Sánchez he had come to worship.

CHAPTER 7. THE BIG BATTLES

Celia's audacious plans for the attacks at Mar Verde and El Salto had to be postponed. In the summer of 1957, two units of Cuban soldiers trained and armed in the US returned to the island to augment the already very strong garrisons at Mar Verde and El Salto. Celia, studying the reports, decided she would have to fight her way to those two outposts.

On August 20, 1957, in eastern Cuba's Las Cuevas region, a rebel force attacked a strong Batista army at Palma Mocha. In the battle, Celia and Fidel each received several slight wounds and Celia lost her good luck charm, the small gold bracelet she wore around her left ankle. The fierce battle ended with hand-to-hand combat, but the rebels won. The losing commander, set free by the rebels, sent a message to Havana, a message that was left behind when Batista fled the capital city. It ended with this sentence: "We didn't win because he wouldn't lose."

"He" was Fidel Castro. After the battle, "he" somehow procured another gold bracelet for Celia, and personally attached it around her left ankle.

On September 5, 1957, a rebel army led by Che Guevara attacked and defeated Batista's proud "Rural Guards" outside the important naval port of Cienfuegos.

Throughout September of 1957, Celia's audaciously brilliant new point commanders — Fidel, Che, Camilo, Raúl, Juan, and Calixto — won a series of skirmishes against bewildered Batista forces. Celia would later describe the month of September 1957, with these words: "Batista still out-manned and out-gunned us. But now I knew our fighters out-matched, with guts and intelligence, anything Batista threw at us."

Into the fall of 1957, as her offensive victories began to pile up for the first time, Celia never lost sight of the need to keep "cheerleading" to her vital peasant supporters on the island. Che's diaries told her that the Argentine doctor was a prolific and excellent writer, in addition to being a courageous guerrilla fighter. She admired his intellect and his keen memory, which enabled him to recite long classical poems to her by the campfire at night.

One night, as they parted, she told Che, "I will provide the wherewithal if you will agree to publish a newspaper that will be called El Cubano Libre ("The Free Cuban"). I want it to be the newspaper of the Rebel Army. Think about it and let me know in the morning."

On November 4, 1957, "El Cubano Libre" was published in the Sierras for the first time. Che Guevara was listed as the "Editor and Publisher." The Cuban peasants, newly inspired, giddily spread the newspaper all across the island, much to the dismay of their enemies.

That a petite and gentle young woman should have led such warriors, such forceful men as Fidel Castro, Che Guevara, and Camilo Cienfuegos, is mind-boggling. In fact, Fidel, Che, and Camilo became her three greatest disciples, embellishing her control of the anti-Batista forces in the Sierras and then later in revolutionary Cuba when she herself devised the pecking order — #1 Fidel, #2 Che, and #3 Camilo — in the new Cuban government. Celia was always the front-line operative in the Sierras and then, in Revolutionary Cuba from 1959 till 1980, she was clearly the behind-the-scenes primary decision-maker, pitting her resolve against that of the world's most powerful men.

Celia had resolved that the Batistianos, still partnered with the Mafia and US capitalists, would never again reclaim Cuba. The US just as adamantly resolved to quickly overthrow the new revolutionary government in Cuba and reinstall the Batistianos and all their friends. That effort has been ongoing for forty-six years.

Oh, yes! In the Sierras and in revolutionary Cuba, there were indeed power struggles among the leadership's top echelon. But through it all, one thing remained constant — Celia Sánchez's dominant role. And that is precisely why Fidel Castro holds the record as today's longest-surviving leader.

There is, for sure, one other prime reason why Fidel Castro has been the leader of Cuba for forty-six years despite daily efforts by the US to take him out, and that is the unfathomable policy of the Batistiano-directed US government.

The leaders in the US in 1953 failed to acknowledge or apologize to the Cuban people for the wave of terror that had been unleashed, and that fed a nationwide outrage that gave the revolutionaries support.

And ever since the triumph of the revolution, the US has yet to apologize to the Cuban people for the killings of children, the torture and murder of women, and the slaughter that includes the terrorist bombing of a Cuban airplane full of young athletes on October 6, 1976. Such overt lack of compassion, such callous lack of concern for "the people" has given Fidel Castro the power to remain as Cuba's leader all these decades. Vilified as he has been and as he is, in the eyes of many Cubans there is a stark contrast between Celia Sánchez's Fidel and America's Batista.

Celia Sánchez, from the very beginning of her revolution, recognized the Achilles heel of America's occupation of Cuba. She explained it this way in a 1977 letter to Nora Peters:

> Even if the majority of Americans don't realize it, Nora, the wanton murder of innocent children by thieves and terrorists is considered to be abhorrent by the decent people in this world. If the US had merely displayed a touch of remorse about the Batista/Mafia murders of Cuban children, the US would still be robbing Cuba blind to this day. When I went to the Sierra to start my very long-shot revolution, I knew the vast majority of the peasants on the island agreed with my perception that the US, Batista's main backer, sanctioned the murders of María Ochoa and other Cuban children. And that's why I got the do-or-die support of the peasants. I'm not superwoman and Fidel is not superman. If the US, at any point from 1957 to 1977, had the intelligence to denounce the Batista murders of children like María and Willie Soler or the Batistiano murders of the children on the Cuban airplane last year, the US would have had this little island back long ago. That stupidity on the part of the US government accounts for the success and longevity of the Cuban Revolution, Nora. As long as I live, or as long as Fidel lives, the US will not reclaim Cuba! After I die, and after he dies, the US will still not have a picnic, unless it gains some sense and apologizes for Batista, the Mafia, and the Batistianos who not only robbed Cuba blind but murdered our children. Draw the distinction, Nora, between Batista's Cuba and our Cuba. Little girls were legally murdered in Batista's Cuba. That ended on January 1, 1959. Since then, the US has tried to destroy us and isolate us and starve us...and we're still here. The revolution not only protects little girls but guarantees them excellent free educations, excellent free health care, and guarantees them shelter. We always will, at least until and if thieves like the Batistianos in Florida and the US capitalists recapture this island. The American people seem to have a problem deciding whether it's best to murder little girls or to protect and care for them in a proper way. Well, Nora, I've never had that problem.

> That distinction should explain to the American people why we won the revolutionary war and why the revolution, not America, still rules Cuba. María Ochoa was and will always be the inspiration for the Cuban Revolution, at least as long as it has my stamp of approval. Had the US, while it was robbing Cuba blind, shown just a little respect for her, the US would still be the dominant force on this island. But the US, Nora, didn't have that respect nor has it had the intelligence to even

pretend that it did. Fidel respects little Cuban girls or, at least, he is intelligent enough to pretend and to act like he does. By comparison, your US leaders are idiots, Nora. Somewhere in the past quarter century regarding Cuba, I expected the US government to at least pretend it has a modicum of respect for little peasant girls. But its support of first Batista and now the Batistianos is so purblind it doesn't even pretend to do so. It is sometimes hard for a little island to beat off continuous attacks from the world's very strongest nation. But displaying more intelligence and more guts is not hard at all.

I learned that lesson fighting in the Sierra. We now practice it daily. Greed and stupidity, Nora, negate the vast superiority in weapons, plus the fact that respect for the sanctity of little peasant girls motivates us more than their love of money and gluttony and power motivates them. Oh, yes, Nora. I hear all the excuses your media gives for the Batistianos not reclaiming Cuba. Excessive greed and stupidity are the reasons but are never mentioned, I notice. If the US government or people had sense enough to just apologize for the atrocities of its beloved dictators like Batista, they would have Cuba back by now. We rebels, Nora, get far too much credit for winning the revolution. Our enemies deserve most of the credit, for being greedy cowards and idiots.

***

Celia Sánchez not only survived but triumphed in the Sierras when she not only had far fewer rifles and pistols than her enemies but also when she had no artillery, tanks, or warplanes. So, how did the Cuban Revolution survive and triumph? Her explanation to Nora stands the test of time. When you're outgunned and out-manned to the mammoth degree she was, you had better be smarter and braver than your enemies! She was, as revealed by the years 1957 and 1958 when the most bloody and most decisive battles of the Cuban Revolution took place in the Sierra Maestra Mountains and its foothills. As you will see, one particular battle would always be considered by Celia (and most historians) as the decisive turning point in the war against Batista.

Here's how Celia depicted that battle years later, to Nora Peters: "It was a touch-and-go ten-day battle in July of 1958, Nora. Each side thought numerous times their side had won. The two leaders — who knew each other from law school — led their armies brilliantly and fiercely, sometimes in hand-to-hand combat. Our leader was Fidel. What I saw in those ten days convinced me that no warrior in history had ever displayed more guts or more intelligence than Fidel did, and that's why we won. Had we lost that ten-day battle, we would have lost the war. But when it was over, I knew two things: (1) We were headed to Havana, and (2) I wanted Fidel to be the next leader of Cuba."

But to get to that ten-day battle in July of 1958, Celia first had to get through 1957 and its daunting series of bloody battles.

1958 was the turning point in the Cuban Revolution, but 1957 was just as significant because it crystallized Celia's courage, ingenuity, ardor, and resilience. She was, after all, the heart and soul of the revolution, the inspiration for all the others. Forged in the crucible of her indomitable soul was the unwavering will to win. And 1957 provided numerous opportunities to lose; but she wouldn't lose.

Che Guevara wrote for posterity that his startling victory at El Uvero on May 28, 1957 turned the tide in the bloody revolutionary fight. "It was a victory that meant our guerrillas had reached full maturity. We now had the key to the secret of how to beat the enemy."

But many more bloody battles would follow, as he knew they would. It wasn't until November 26, 1957, that Celia finally ordered the rebel attack on Mar Verde. It was a victory but a costly one. A young rebel captain named Ciro Redondo was among the dead. The next day a tearful Celia promoted Ciro Redondo posthumously to commander. On December 6, 1957, Celia finally ordered the attack on El Salto, another hard-earned victory, which Celia credited to "the brave and tactical brilliance" of Lt. Lalo Sardiñas.

By the last month of 1957, Batista was losing a lot of soldiers and a lot of military hardware to the rebels, but far to the west, in Havana, he pretended it wasn't happening. On December 10, 1957, Batista opened the $14 million Hotel Riviera, a personal gift to his best friend, the Mafia's Meyer Lansky. The Hotel Riviera opening was a lavish event massively covered by the US media; Ginger Rogers headlined that night. Lansky was quoted in the US press as saying, "Ginger can wiggle her ass but she can't sing a goddamn note."

Meanwhile, the Rebel Army in the Sierras was beginning to kick Batista's and Lansky's asses. While the goons in Havana were partying lavishly, Celia was orchestrating their demise in the Sierras.

In December of 1957, the top Latin American magazine, Revista Carteles, reported that the top twenty Batista officials each had Swiss bank accounts in excess of $1 million, and that was only one place they stashed their loot. Most of it was stashed in southern Florida. Meyer Lansky and Santo Traficante each had lavish mansions in southern Florida as well as in Havana. The US corporations also made out like the bandits they were, owning — according to Revista Carteles and other historical accounts — "90% of Cuba's mineral wealth, 80% of its public utilities, 50% of its railways, and 25% of its banking institutions."

In January and February of 1958, the US government — on behalf of the corporations — sent Batista additional millions of dollars worth of military equipment.

Meanwhile, Che Guevara's rebel army newspaper, *El Cubano Libre*, was very successful. Why not try for a radio station? Captured towns in eastern Cuba provided radio equipment as well as engineers. In February of 1958, Radio Rebelde ("Rebel Radio") went on the air from what Celia called "the free territory of Cuba." And, the most ubiquitous voice on early Radio Rebelde broadcasts was that of Celia Sánchez. She loved to taunt Batista: "You can't stop the Rebel Army in the Sierra and soon I will be in Havana for what I hope will be the pleasure of looking into your murdering eyes! Then it will all be over for you! You want me real bad. I want you much worse!"

Next to Celia, a feisty rebel named Violeta Casel was the most feminine voice over Radio Rebelde. Violeta had been a dear friend of Lidia Docé and Clodomira Acosta, two martyred rebels. The passion that had drawn them to fight gave them an indomitable will. Ordinary soldiers with ordinary weapons were at a disadvantage against them.

In early March of 1958, Raúl Castro and Juan Almeída commanded a small army (seventy fighters) that conducted a series of very successful strikes in the mountainous Sierra Cristal region, due north of Santiago. This created a crucial diversion allowing the main rebel forces to strike elsewhere throughout March and April of 1958.

In May of 1958, Batista sent an army of 10,000 to launch his biggest offensive yet in the heart of the Sierra Maestra Mountains and its foothills. Two main rebel armies — commanded by Celia Sánchez, Fidel Castro, Che Guevara, and Camilo Cienfuegos — were ready with punishing guerrilla strikes that stunned the larger and better-armed Batista armies.

Those guerrilla strikes skillfully maneuvered Batista armies onto Sierra turf that the rebels, especially Celia, knew so well; this stratagem almost always went like clockwork. In a December 19, 2004, e-mail, Celia's friend and fellow revolutionary heroine Marta Rojas told me, "Celia knew the Sierra like she knew the back of her hand — the mountains, the swamps, the foothills. I still hear about the time she shot at three approaching tanks with her pistol, retreating and hiding behind trees till she led the three tanks directly into marshy quicksand, where they just disappeared from the war."

In the first week of June, 1958, amidst intense fighting in the Sierras, a mountain messenger delivered an important note for Celia. Ada Martinez asked

Fidel to present it to her personally. He did, with deep sadness, asking her to sit down and read it in the privacy of their tent. The note from a provincial doctor informed Celia that her father, Dr. Manual Sánchez Silveira, was dying and had "no more than ten days to live." Celia's mother, Acacia Manduley, had died when Celia was a little girl. All her life, Celia had worshipped her father.

The note, of course, devastated her. She pressed it to her chest and closed her eyes, as tears streamed down her face. Fidel moved over to sit beside her, his right arm embracing her as he tried to shelter her from the pain.

"I told Ada," Fidel said, "we will break off the war. I will take you home, with full security, so you can be with your father. We won't resume the war till after the funeral."

Shortly, Celia's eyes opened. She placed the note on the slanted wooden table and used a white cloth to wipe the tears from her face.

Then she took a deep breath, composing herself, before looking around at Fidel. "Nooooo," she said. "We can't break off the war, not now. I must stay here. That's what Papa would want me to do. Fidel, what I must do is write him a note and make sure the messengers get it to him before he dies. Go tell Ada. By the time you get back, I will have the note written."

Dr. Manuel Sánchez died on June 24, 1958. On his chest when he died, they say, was this note, clutched in the fingers of both hands, from his precious daughter:

Dear Papa,

I need not tell of my love for you that I have cherished each day of my life. You know all of that. Now, know I will love and cherish you every step I take every day more. I have felt you with me during each advance of this revolution, with each step along the way. What I do is for Cuba, the little Cuban children. I got that from you, as I watched you save little María during her childhood sicknesses. You taught me that she and all the Cuban children were worth saving — no matter the cost. So, I pay the cost, such as not being with you now. I know you want me here, for the children. Thank you for being my father. I want you proud of me and knowing that you are means everything. Till, one sunny day, we meet again, my love goes with you.

Celia Esther

(Esther was Celia's middle name. Her childhood home in Media Luna is now a Cuban shrine and tourist attraction. A plaque says: "Native house of Celia Sánchez Manduley, the greatest clandestine and guerrilla fighter of the Cuban Revolution." The above letter is one of 234 personal items on display at the shrine; a typed citation attached to the letter states: "The letter above in Celia's handwriting was on Dr. Sánchez's chest when he died.").

On June 28, 1958, Celia received a written report of her father's burial on a day when she was in the Santo Domingo region of the Sierras planning a bold attack on a 10,000-man Batista army. The attack took place the next morning.

At Santo Domingo Celia's rebels gave her a stunning victory, capturing over 800 prisoners along with vast arrays of arms and supplies. All the prisoners were released. Celia, as usual, just told them to "go home." Fidel, as usual, told them, "If you don't go home, tell Batista to send another army, and we'll be waiting."

Batista then sent a larger and still better-equipped army, 14,000 men. This led to what turned out to be the longest and bloodiest revolutionary battle, the battle that Celia Sánchez labeled "the turning point in the war" and the one that made her say, "For me, when it was over, I knew that I wanted Fidel to be Cuba's future leader."

THE BATTLE OF JIGÜE

Terrence Cannon used these words in his book Revolutionary Cuba: "The Battle of Jigüe, which lasted ten days in mid-July of 1958, was probably the most important and certainly one of the most interesting, revealing the complex nature of the war. During it, some letters were exchanged, troops on opposite sides shared their food, and a commander changed his allegiance."

The Batista army set up headquarters at the fork where a creek emptied into the Jigüe River very close to the rebel stronghold in the Sierras. Celia thought this was impudent, given that she prided herself on her reputation for audacity. So, she convinced a skeptical Fidel to attack. He did, scattering the Batista soldiers on July 14, 1958.

By nightfall, the rebels had gained the territory around the fork of the river; but the retreating Batista soldiers had regrouped by the next morning and they launched a furious and punishing counterattack.

Here is the way Fidel later described that counterattack over Radio Rebelde: "On the morning of the fifteenth, the air force appeared. The aerial attack against our positions, with machine-gun strafing and 500-pound explosive bombs as well as napalm, lasted uninterrupted from six in the morning until one in the afternoon. The pasture and forest were left scorched, but not one of the rebel combatants moved from his position."

A tape recording of that Radio Rebelde broadcast is still available and it has rendered for historians like Terrence Cannon the exact transcribed words of Fidel, which paralleled all other accounts of that counterattack in the Battle of Jigüe.

Despite the aerial and ground bombardment, Fidel rallied his troops and they never retreated an inch, but they were forced to fight defensively throughout the second day. On the third day, the Cuban army (Battalion 18, Batista's very best) launched a massive ground attack. The fighting was so intense and close up that both sides tossed down empty rifles and used pistols and/or knives. Fidel, leading the rebels from the front line, was close enough to get a good look at the face of the commander of Battalion 18. It was José Quevedo, his old friend from law school!

In the heat of battle on the third day, José recognized Fidel, too. They actually shouted at each other, using first names. But the fighting raged on, evolving into bloody standoffs by day with each side regrouping and caring for its wounded at night.

Amazingly, and reminiscent of America's Civil War in the 1860s, at nighttime the opposing soldiers in the Battle of Jigüe conversed and even tossed food and tobacco to each other. But the next day they fought furiously against each other from sunup to dusk.

On the fourth day of the battle, Celia was knocked to the ground when a rifle shot tore away the right side of her left boot. On her side, as the boot filled with blood, Celia reached to her ankle to make sure her good luck charm was still there. It was. She then reached for her rifle. Fidel helped her to her feet, asking, "Are you all right? Do you need...?"

"No! I'm fine! I just need a new boot! Let's go!" (This anecdote is mentioned in a June 1993 article written by historian Pablo Alvarez Tabío in Bohemia Magazine). Celia limped just slightly as Fidel led her to a clump of downed palm trees, their front line in the marshy terrain.

The fierce fighting continued into a fifth, sixth, and seventh day. Each side, at various junctures, got the upper hand. Fidel and José began to use couriers to send notes to each other, with each man asking the other "to surrender."

Neither did. The fighting raged on with first one side and then the other gaining "ever so slight edges," as Celia would later tell historian Carlos Franqui.

Throughout the afternoon of the seventh day of fighting, the rebels got the edge and pushed Battalion 18 back to a tree-line by nightfall. That night Fidel

81

used a courier under a white flag to get a hand-written surrender message to José.

That message was retained for posterity and it has been used in many historical accounts of the pivotal battle. Word for word, it stated:

> Jose,
>
> With great sorrow I have learned that you are in command of the surrounded troops. We know that you are a learned and honorable military officer of the Academy, with a law degree. You know that the cause for which your soldiers, as well as yourself, sacrifice and die is an unjust cause. I offer you a dignified and honorable surrender. Accept this offer and you will not surrender to an enemy of the fatherland but to a sincere revolutionary, a man who fights for the welfare of all Cubans, including that of the soldiers who fight us. You will surrender to a university classmate who wants the same things you want for Cuba.
>
> Fidel

José refused.

Battalion 18 was reinforced the next day and again furiously attacked. Fidel held his ground on July 18 and on the 19th he led a scathing attack of his own. By nightfall on July 19, 1958, José's Battalion 18 was beaten.

The next morning, Fidel ordered a cease-fire from 6:00 A.M. till 10:00 A.M. José used the time to think it over. He surrendered, believing that Fidel would have him and his other officers shot immediately. Instead, Fidel had his rebels give the prisoners water, food, and cigarettes. This gesture was later confirmed by both sides. Also, the rebel medics tended to the wounds of the prisoners.

Fidel personally told José, "Go home now, and I hope you don't come back because you are a helluva leader. You did not surrender after my last note but what I said still stands."

Major José Quevedo, the leader of Batista's defeated Battalion 18, did not "go home." He spent that night in deep discussion with Fidel and Celia.

The next morning José Quevedo "changed sides," as Terrence Cannon wrote in Revolutionary Cuba. From that moment till the end of the war, José Quevedo and many of his men fought very valiantly for the Cuban Revolution against Fulgencio Batista.

Yes, the bloody ten-day Battle of Jigüe in July of 1958 was the turning point of the Cuban Revolutionary War in the Sierra Maestra Mountains.

And, yes, the Battle of Jigüe was what convinced Celia Sánchez, once and for all, that she wanted Fidel to be the future leader of Cuba. The fact that — in January of 1959 — it would be her decision to make is what makes that pivotal battle so very significant. She later told her friend, Nora: "No warrior was ever braver or more brilliant than Fidel was during the ten days of the Battle of Jigüe. But I also observed how very honorable he was to José. So did José. That's why José and many of his men fought the rest of the war with us and not against us. I knew then, Nora, that we were on our way to Havana! The little revolution had grown big."

CHAPTER 8. ON TO HAVANA

The ten-day Battle of Jigüe in July of 1958 changed the dynamics of the Revolutionary War in the Sierra. Not only had the rebels defeated Batista's best 14,000-man army but his prized young commander and many of his soldiers had switched sides. Havana and Washington took keen notice. Also, Celia's campaign to "win the hearts and the minds of the American people" began to irritate the US government.

The New York Times articles were widely syndicated, and the CBS-TV reports painted both a righteous and romantic portrait of the rebel cause. And Washington was now taking cognizance of the increased fervor among the Cuban peasants to oust Batista. Surely, the news of the battlefield victories by the rebels gave them hope. And so did the two propaganda organs Celia had implausibly created in the Sierras — the brash rebel newspaper and radio station.

In the Caribbean and throughout Latin America, there was now burgeoning interest in the Cuban Revolution. After all, the peasants in those countries were also living under the yoke of US-backed dictators. Could a peasant revolution overthrow such rulers?

At long last, the US government sent this coded message to Batista: "The climate is not conducive to further military or diplomatic assistance at this time."

Now, he was essentially on his own.

Batista's reaction was to try to buy time, to let things cool off, in the hope that the US government would resume its broad support. After all, it was the US corporations who were getting all the cream.

On July 28, 1958, the Rebel Army in the Sierra got word that a couple of Batista's men in Santiago wanted to meet with the "rebel leaders" under a flag of truce for the purpose of "discussing an end to hostilities."

After two days of haggling, with a Jesuit priest in Santiago acting as the intermediary, the tension-filled session took place at the edge of what was called "Clearing #9" on the rebel map. Fidel Castro, with Celia at his back, sat at a table across from Batista's two messengers. Their proposal: If the Rebel Army would lay down its arms, its leaders would be incorporated into the Batista government and, if the rebels responded positively to that overture, Batista would then send a peace commission to iron out the details within five days.

A stoic Fidel pondered the proposal in silence for about a half minute, a non-committal expression dominating his countenance. He stood up, gestured with his index finger to the two Batista messengers, and then walked Celia about thirty yards away from the table in the tall grass.

"What do you think?" he asked, looking softly down at her.

"I think Batista is a thief, killer, and a liar.... I don't want stooges like that back here in five days. In five days, I expect to be in another battle."

Fidel nodded, without blinking an eye and without altering his demeanor. He just walked Celia back to the table. Then his demeanor changed. Brusquely and firmly, without sitting back down, he verbally assaulted Batista's two unhappy messengers, closing with these words: "Tell Batista to send soldiers, not negotiators! I'll only negotiate his surrender or his death!"

***

The open-air session in Clearing #9 on July 30, 1958, was destined to be replicated thousands of times over in the course of the next twenty-two years, with Celia at Fidel's side, day and night. In the luminous presence of US media people at countless news conferences, Fidel held court as Celia stood beside him. And it was the same at vital sessions with important people, such as Soviet Deputy Premier Anastas Mikoyan, who nicknamed Celia "Spanish Eyes."

If Fidel was to render a major decision, without fail it would be proffered or fully approved by Celia. Then, regardless of Fidel's opinion, he would back that stance with all the vast energy and power of his considerable stature.

This was the diminutive Celia Sánchez that Fidel's seminal biographer Georgie Anne Geyer said could and did over-rule Fidel whenever she chose; the Celia that Roberto Salas in his 1998 book said "made all the decisions for Cuba."

Marta Rojas, the revolutionary heroine who is Fidel's best friend to this day, said in an e-mail to the author dated 12-19-04: "As he has grown older, his memories and his dreams of Celia have become more and more prevalent. He needed her so much those twenty-three years from 1957 till her death in 1980. And today...he needs her more than ever."

The aftermath of the ten-day Battle of Jigüe in July of 1958, as well as the blistering rebel reaction to the Batista peace initiative in Clearing #9, reverberated around the capital cities of Havana and Washington far to the west of the Sierras.

Batista was taken aback by Fidel's definitive threat to negotiate only the dictator's "surrender or death." But both Batista and Mafia man Meyer Lansky realized they had to dance to Washington's tune because their Cuban dictatorship hinged solely on the support of the US government.

Pressured by Washington, Batista sent the Sierra rebels a written peace proposal on August 13, 1958; it was three typed copies of a more definitive peace overture than the one presented verbally in Clearing #9. The rebels were now essentially offered control of the eastern third of the island, everything southeast of the city of Camagüey. This meant that Havana would remain the capital of the western two-thirds of the island while Santiago, the second largest city and former capital, would be the rebel's capital on the eastern third of the island.

By now, the unofficial but readily apparent rebel hierarchy had evolved into a Big Five in this precise order: Celia Sánchez, Fidel Castro, Che Guevara, Camilo Cienfuegos, and Raúl Castro. There were at times fractious divisions between the four men but no one questioned the fact that Celia was "the supreme empirical authority," as Che would later term it. She wielded her power "succinctly and effortlessly" as Camilo told Herbert L. Matthews in 1959 in *Revolutionary Cuba*.

Celia's nature exuded "calmness, thoroughness, and modesty," Raúl Castro stated, on reflection, in 2002, in the presence of US news bureau heads in Havana. Raúl added, "She was saintly, not pushy. Our universal admiration of her, I really think, constituted her power. We all knew it was her revolution. Mine and Fidel's and Haydée's had essentially ended with the Moncada attack on July 26, 1953. She resurrected all three of us when we joined what she had created in the Sierras. If we ever forget that, we will have stolen her basic tenets of the revolution."

Over the decades, media sessions with Raúl have been rare, and usually concerned military matters. Thus, his philosophical views on the revolution in that 2002 session were notable, especially the significant connection he surprisingly applied to Celia Sánchez, who had been dead twenty-two years, and to modern Cuba. He concluded that session with these words, as reported by the Reuters news service in Havana: "When she had the power to take anything she wanted from Cuba, she took nothing — not a peso. As the two leaders of Cuba all those years, she and Fidel lived mostly in her small apartment on 11th Street in Havana but she put peasant families in the plush mansions left behind by the Batista and Mafia crowd. All she ever wanted, after she had the power to enrich herself, was only what was best for the peasants she had fought for. That's why even today she is so important. We know history has and is judging the revolution. If all the rest of us have failed in some ways, many ways, she never did. 'Power corrupts and absolute power corrupts absolutely.' Is that an axiom of history? Well, in Cuba Fidel made sure Celia had absolute power from 1959 till she died in 1980. And the Celia we buried in January of 1980 was the least corrupted person in history. It was her revolution. We are the caretakers. If we corrupt it, or if we ever cave in to the Miami Mafia, we will have shamed her. And if we do, history should crucify us for having besmirched that which she fought for."

Fidel Castro's idolatry of Celia Sánchez is well known. But other still-living and prime revolutionary figures — such as Raúl Castro, Marta Rojas, Juan Almeída, and General Teté Puebla — all share that adoration. In the US, disparagement of Fidel Castro and of the revolution is easy; but disparagement of Celia Sánchez has never been attempted.

Except when it comes to military matters, Raúl Castro is a man of few words, at least in public before a US media that he doesn't trust. But in 2002, he used many words to explain that Celia Sánchez remains the heart and the soul of the Cuban Revolution, and not just in the eyes of his big brother Fidel. Georgie Anne Geyer wrote: "Even those who despise Fidel love Celia." Her banner has, for all these decades, sustained revolutionary Cuba.

Even today, university students in Havana will tell a visitor: "If the US attacked Cuba today I would fight...for her. She cried when they murdered her Cuban children; the US laughed. She's someone to die for, even today."

Her true power in the Sierra and later in Havana evolved from the respect she commanded from the next four most important revolutionary figures, namely the Castro brothers, Che, and Camilo. That respect was warranted and unconditional, and it superseded or, in effect, smoothed over any divisions in the revolutionary hierarchy.

After the Battle of Jigüe, for example, by August of 1958 in the Sierra the four key men, in varying degrees, were receptive to the two peace overtures from Batista, especially the notion of giving the rebels the eastern third of the island. For a couple of weeks the three typed copies of that offer floated around the rebel base camps, provoking considerable discussion. All the while Celia ignored the peace overtures, which she thought she had ended at Clearing #9 when she told Fidel, "I didn't promise little María Ochoa a negotiated peace settlement. I promised her a do-or-die fight." In the ensuing days she got back to preparing for the next battle. She became irked, really irked, to discover that her four prime commanders were distracted by the peace offer.

Celia called a council at a little round table in Clearing #4. She sat the four men down and told them to wait until Ada arrived. Ada showed up, with two of the three copies of the offer. She was sent back to round up the third. They waited.

In about twenty minutes she was back. Then Celia tore the three pages to shreds and tossed them aside.

"Now, gentlemen," she said, "let's get back to the revolution. I want no distractions. The next battle, at Yara, is going to be a tough one. You are not here to talk peace. Che, give me your opinion on the best way to attack Yara!" He did, and so did the others.

On occasion, Celia could be "pushy." This was one of those occasions.

***

On September 18, 1958, after two days of fierce fighting, the Battle of Yara ended with a resounding victory over the best Batista army in the Sierras.

On September 28, 1958, the rebels defeated another Batista army in a three-day battle at Cerro Pelado in Oriente province. At Cerro Pelado, the sheer tenacity of the Maríana Grajales Platoon in holding the left flank on the third day of hostilities proved decisive to the outcome of the battle. The Maríana Grajales Platoon was comprised entirely of young women led by Major Teté Puebla.

On October 9, 1958, Celia formed a new rebel army and assigned it to defend the captured territory in Oriente province. That new army was led by Major Teté Puebla and Lt. Delio Gómez Ochoa, María Ochoa's uncle.

On October 10, 1958, Celia used Radio Rebelde to announce a new "Rebel Proclamation." It stated that the peasants in Oriente province could now own the land that they had been working as sharecroppers.

On October 27, 1958, the rebels captured a Batista garrison at Güinía de Miranda. The supplies captured at Güinía de Miranda included seven jeeps.

On October 31, 1958, US Secretary of State John Foster Dulles hosted a gala reception at the Cuban Embassy in Washington to celebrate a victory in the Spanish-American War in 1898 by then future president Teddy Roosevelt's "Rough Riders." Roosevelt's victory had kept a rebel army from taking Santiago. Sixty years later — on October 31, 1958, while Dulles celebrated Teddy Roosevelt's 1898 victory — Celia Sánchez was planning her own rebel attack on Santiago, Cuba's second largest city and the key bastion in the Sierra.

On her way to Santiago, Celia's rebels captured another Batista garrison on November 2, 1958, at Alto Songo in Oriente province. She had developed a fetish for US jeeps. At Alto Songo, the rebels presented her with nine more.

On December 9, 1958, the rebels captured two more towns in Oriente province — Baire and San Luis.

After a bruising three-day battle, a rebel army commanded by the fearless Che Guevara defeated a newly refurbished Batista army at Fomento on December 18, 1958.

On December 19, 1958, rebel armies were victorious in the Las Villas areas of Jiguaní, Caimanera, and Mayajigua.

Between December 22 and December 25, 1958, rebel armies captured the towns of Sancti Spíritus, Sagua de Tánamo, Puerto Padre, Guayos, Cabaiguán, Manicaragua, Placetas, Cumanayagua, Lajas, Cruces, Lajas, and Camarones!

On Christmas day, 1958, the rebels captured the towns of Caibarién, Remedios, and Palma Soriano.

Between the Sierra and Havana, the rebels now held every town and city except the final two still circled in red on Celia's map — Santiago, on the southeastern coast of the Sierras, and Santa Clara. Santa Clara is in west-central Cuba and it was where Batista had stationed his last major army to block the rebel advance toward Havana itself.

Holding Santiago, the city on the island's southeastern tip, and capturing Santa Clara far to the west in central Cuba were now the final two challenges for the rebels. Then the march on Havana itself could commence.

After Che's big victory at Fomento on December 18, 1958, Celia ordered Camilo Cienfuegos' column to hook up with Che and head toward Santa Clara.

Celia and Fidel would stay back in the Sierras to make sure the vital city of Santiago was captured and secured. They maintained radio contact with Che and Camilo as the critical advance on Santa Clara commenced.

On the evening of December 27, 1958, Che and Camilo could see the lights of Santa Clara. Celia and Fidel were camped on the western edge of Santiago, which they considered secured. At 3:00 A.M. Fidel and Che had a blistering conversation on a radio hook-up with Fidel verily gloating to Che about the capture of the old Moncada garrison on the edge of Santiago. Then Fidel handed the speaker to Celia.

She calmly said, "Che, we are fine here. The fighting was easy, except for securing the prisoners. The last Batista army between here and Havana is in Santa Clara, and it's a strong one. They know it's the last protection for Havana and they will defend it furiously. But when you and Camilo take Santa Clara, march straight to Havana. Fidel and I will be a full week behind you. So, when you and Camilo enter Havana I want you to do something special for me. Over."

"I hear you. You're soft and clear, like on Radio Rebelde. No static. What can I do special for you? Over."

"Che, if you can, capture three men and hold them for me in Havana till I get there. Those three men are Batista, Lansky, and Rafael Díaz-Balart. Over."

"Celia, I know all about Batista and Lansky, and I'll do the best I can. But who is Rafael Díaz-Balart? Over!"

"He happens to be the brother of Fidel's ex-wife Mirta. And he was a classmate of Fidel's in law school. But he's one of Batista's key cronies. After we captured most of the towns in the Sierras, I got a communication from Havana that told me Rafael, if we win, plans to set up a sanctuary in Miami and then, with the US military's help, come back after us. So, if they haven't fled by the time you and Camilo get to Havana, the three I want most of all are Batista, Lansky, and Rafael Díaz-Balart. If you get them alive, hold them so they will answer directly to me. Over."

"I'll do my best, Celia. First, Santa Clara. Then Havana. Tell Fidel to get on his knees and pray for me. Santa Clara is fortified like hell. We'll attack tomorrow. I love you. I'll see you in Havana in about a week. Over."

"I'll tell Fidel. It's 3:30. You have your hands full. I'll sign off now. But, Che, I love you too. Tell Camilo I love him. Oh, gosh! You know that. I'm wasting time. I'll pray for you till morning. Over and out."

A tape recording of this December 28, 1958 discussion with Che remains in the Cuban archives.

The supremely inspired rebel army led by Che Guevara and Camilo Cienfuegos attacked the city of Santa Clara on December 28, 1958. Fierce fighting raged throughout the day. The rebel armies had always had guerrilla fighters much more motivated than Batista's soldiers and the rebels had the most brilliant and the bravest commanders. However, till these closing months of 1958, they had been sorely out-numbered and out-gunned.

At Santa Clara, the last big battle of the war, they were still out-gunned because the US had helped Batista fortify the last major outpost designed to protect Havana. But Che and Camilo were not out-numbered at Santa Clara, just out-gunned. No problem. Che, Camilo, and their rebels fought with a "do-or-die" posture; the Batista army initially battled back furiously but, faced with the continued tenacity of the advancing rebels, they soon adopted a "do-and-live" posture. Many soldiers guarding Santa Clara simply threw down their rifles and ran, leaving behind powerful US-artillery batteries, as a rebel unit on the left flank led by black-bearded Camilo moved toward them.

The rebel unit attacking Santa Clara on the right flank — led by the young Argentine doctor Che Guevara — was even more scarier to Batista's defenders. In the early fighting Che had been wounded in the right shoulder and the left buttocks, turning his green rebel uniform a bright red. The new coloration merely urged him onward at the head of his equally determined rebels, scaring Batista's batteries of officers and soldiers.

Che captured 1300 of them and later said, "I wasn't concerned with those who ran like rabbits away from us. They wouldn't be a future problem."

The fighting in Santa Clara on December 29, 1958, decided the outcome of the battle, but mop-up operations led by Che and Camilo continued throughout the next day. On December 29 and 30 Che had talked with Celia three times — twice via telephone and once on a radio hook-up, which Celia taped.

"We've got it, Celia!" Che said. "Santa Clara is ours."

"Che, do you have enough men to leave Santa Clara secure and still race to Havana, or shall you wait for us? Over."

"No! No waiting, except to pen up these bastards. Then it's Havana. When you get there I want to have a dining table waiting for you, and a little wine. If I'm lucky, I'll introduce you to Fulgencio, Meyer, and Rafael. Over."

"The decision when to advance on Havana is yours, Che. God knows, I love you. I hope you know how much. Santiago and the rest are very secure on this end. Oh, be careful, but always be Che! I've come to believe your fearlessness keeps you alive. You have my coordinates. Don't forget the wine. Over and out."

The Battle of Santa Clara solidified the legends of guerrilla leaders Che Guevara and Camilo Cienfuegos, and left them #3 and #4 in the hierarchy of the revolutionary leaders, right behind Celia and Fidel and right ahead of Raúl.

Che and Camilo secured Santa Clara and then raced toward Havana.

On January 1, 1959, Havana was not a military problem for the rebel band led by Che and Camilo, except for the chaos they encountered. Batista had received telephone updates from his losing commanders in Santa Clara. He prepared himself in the fashion typical of leaders who are in it for personal gain rather than the general good. He and the other top leaders fled, choosing not to confront the guerrilla fighters.

Celia had hoped fervently that her adversaries would stay in Havana and fight. If they won, they would still have control of the island; if they lost, they would answer to her.

Batista, with the first telephoned bad news from Santa Clara, had his US-supplied getaway airplane on stand-by at Camp Colombia on the edge of Havana. His family was aboard the plane, which was also famously stuffed with the last many millions of dollars from the Cuban treasury (Newsweek Magazine estimated Batista's Cuban loot totaled $600,000,000). Batista left Camp Colombia just prior to 3:00 A.M. on January 1, 1959. The first stop was the nearby Dominican Republic, which was ruled by Rafael Trujillo. Batista would spend the rest of his life in extravagant luxury in his mansions, fully protected by the US and Spanish governments. He died of natural causes in 1975, after sending huge amounts of his vast fortune to the Batistianos in southern Florida.

Meyer Lansky, the Mafia kingpin who was Batista's best friend for thirty years and also Batista's co-ruler of Cuba, used his own getaway airplane to fly to southern Florida. Lansky already had a mansion there, as did many of the other Mafiosi who had robbed Cuba for years. With an estimated worth of $500,000,000, Meyer Lansky died of old age in Miami on May 15, 1983.

Che was unable to capture Fulgencio Batista and Meyer Lansky for Celia. The US government, which had partnered with Batista and Lansky in the cruel dictatorship, was very active in making sure they escaped.

And what about Rafael Díaz-Balart, the third member of the Batista dictatorship that Celia specifically asked Che to try to capture for her? Rafael — the brother of Fidel's ex-wife Mirta and also Fidel's law school classmate at the University of Havana — also fled to southern Florida. With the support of the US government, Rafael quickly ensconced himself in regal splendor with havens in

Madrid as well as in southern Florida, where he ruled the Batistianos from 1959 till he died at age seventy-nine in May of 2005.

Three particular US politicians have been crucial supporters of the Batistianos. Those three are: (1) former CIA director, Vice President, and President George H.W. Bush; (2) Florida governor Jeb Bush; and (3) the US President George W. Bush. As leader of the CIA, as Vice President, and as President, George H. W. Bush danced to every tune the Batistianos ever sang, including the order to pardon Batistianos like Orlando Bosch. G.H.W.'s sons Jeb and George dance in similar fashions

Naturally, Batista's supporters and those who made their fortunes under his rule want Jeb Bush to continue as Florida's governor. And naturally, the Batistianos also want George W. Bush to go on as president of the United States. George W. Bush is at the mercy of the Batistianos, and affords them exclusive control of America's Cuban policy.

In his first administration, George W. Bush put two anti-Castro zealots, Otto Reich and Roger Noriega, in full control of Cuba policy. Cuban-born anti-Castro Mel Martinez, a former member of the Bush administration, was elected to the US Senate in 2004. Two sons of Rafael Díaz-Balart, Lincoln and Mario, are also members of the US Congress from what amounts to the banana republic of south Florida.

And so, as Celia Sánchez feared in 1958, Rafael Díaz-Balart, from 1959 till his death in 2005, ran America's virulent Cuban policy, with the supreme advantage of having both the governor of Florida and the president of the US in his pocket.

For the past forty-six years, the Díaz-Balart dictatorship in southern Florida along with other off-shoots of the Batista dictatorship in Cuba, such as the Cuban American National Foundation and Brothers to the Rescue, have used US military bases and US tax dollars to stage continuous attacks against Cuba. This is documented in Chapter 14.

***

Celia and Fidel, having to stay far to the east to secure the vital city of Santiago, were a week behind the January 1, 1959, capture of Havana by Che and Camilo. "I could only share their euphoria over the telephone and radio hook-ups," Celia later told Nora Peters. "During these halcyon days, I felt so strange and a bit lost. What had we wrought? I missed fighting the battles, because that is what I promised little María I would do. But Damn! Now we've won. So, now what do we do? I was a guerrilla fighter, but no battle action to look forward to."

History records that, after securing Santiago, Celia and Fidel actually took their time on the western trek to Havana — even after they knew the capital city and the entire island was theirs. They seemed reluctant to claim it.

On January 1, 1959, the first day of the new Cuba, Celia and Fidel spent the night in a sugar mill on the edge of Palma Soriano. "It was a strange and mellow night, Nora," Celia later confided. "And, yes, we made love."

A couple days later they had only reached Cienfuegos, where they had a fish dinner at the La Covadonga Restaurant.

Then they stopped off in Matanzas and visited a convent-run orphanage. They bought the nuns a television set and left them some money, according to Georgie Anne Geyer.

Next, they visited the rural home of José Echeverría's parents; José, Fidel's young supporter at the University of Havana, had been machine-gunned Mafia-style by Batista two years earlier. Celia would later tell Nora Peters: "The first time ever I saw tears in Fidel's eyes was when he hugged José's mother... for the longest time."

They toyed around for twelve hours one day, waiting for Fidel to be interviewed by Ed Sullivan.

Even after they saw the lights of Havana, they made camp on the outskirts. Fidel's now nine-year-old son Fidelito, whose mother was Mirta Díaz-Balart, joined up with them. Like all others close to Fidel, Fidelito loved Celia passionately the rest of her life, and he cuddled with her all that night on the edge of Havana.

"I don't know, Nora," Celia reminisced years later. "I guess I slowed Fidel's triumphant trek to Havana as Che and Camilo waited for us. He was anxious but tolerant of me. My revolutionary heart missed the camaraderie we had all shared fighting in the Sierras. They would be the happiest days of my life. I never dreamed of being a guerrilla fighter, but fate made me one and I came to relish it. I knew our cause was just. But then I didn't relish arriving in Havana and helping to rule Cuba. I only wanted the majority, the peasants, to rule Cuba in a democratic way with our colossal neighbor, America, our best friend."

Celia also explained to Nora her reluctance to race from Santiago to Havana even after the bloody revolutionary war had miraculously ousted the malicious leadership: "I knew the Batista and Mafia leaders had settled in southern Florida and, with the US government still backing them, they would always be attacking us. Maybe that's why the historians like Herbert Matthews wondered why Fidel took so long on the trek from Santiago to Havana after we had won. His procrastination was for me. He knew I was worried. He knew I was worried about whether the US would let us have a democracy that would care for the peasants the way little girls like María should have been cared for. Fidel believed now that the US would let us do that, although we would not let rich Americans just feast on Cuba. But, Nora, I told Fidel the first night in January, when we stopped over at the sugar mill, that I disagreed with him. I told him we would now always be fighting the Batista coterie in Miami because America would always want them back in charge of Cuba. I knew their hatred of us would only increase now that we had chased them from Cuba."

On January 7, 1959, Celia and Fidel finally arrived in Havana. They were greeted by over a million wildly cheering Cubans. Celia still had that strange feeling of being lost. She had come to relish the purposeful guerrilla warfare in the Sierra, but suddenly it was over. Now what?

CHAPTER 9. THE WHITE DOVE

The dilatory trek Celia and Fidel made from the eastern city of Santiago to the western city of Havana, even after the euphoric capture of the capital city of Havana by the rebel unit led by Che Guevara and Camilo Cienfuegos, puzzled observers.

When they stopped off at the sugar mill on the edge of Palma Soriano; when they took time to visit the mother of the martyred student José Echeverría; when they stopped off to buy a television set and leave it along with some money with the nuns at an orphanage in Matanzas; when they stopped in Cienfuegos to have a leisurely fish dinner at La Covadonga Restaurant; etc., the media that trailed the now freshly famous pair were shocked. They knew Castro's pent-up impatience; why wasn't he eager to get to Havana and claim Cuba? Young revolutionaries could only bask in this special moment once in their lifetimes, but this particular revolutionary was observed spending leisure moments at an outdoor ocean-side dining table, chatting softly with a petite, moody woman.

The media and the everyday Cubans were witnessing the one exception in Fidel's life where he displayed unexpected patience, and that was when it came to Celia. After all the adrenaline wore off, with the battles won, the let-down was overwhelming. She felt no inspiration drawing her to Havana. He understood, even if the media and the public did not. To him, now, she was more important than anything else, including Havana. And this would always be so.

But then Celia, the media, and the elated Cuban people would witness the first of Fidel's soon-to-be-legendary hours-long, extemporaneous, raucously emphatic speeches. With over a million wildly cheering supporters before him and dozens of guerrilla heroes and heroines pressed shoulder to shoulder around him on a rickety platform, Celia would always remember Fidel's initial speech as the leader of Cuba.

> At the height of the euphoria on that stage, Nora, with Fidel fully animated and shouting above the roar of a million peasants, a white dove flew down and landed on his left shoulder. Fidel glanced at it and then continued his tirade and the very animated shouting. That white dove, Nora, stayed perched on his shoulder for the longest time. I covered my face with my hands and closed my eyes. I believed, I still believe, that white dove was the spirit of little María Ochoa. It had come down from heaven just to represent María on this historic occasion. When I opened my eyes again, that white dove was still perched there, amid all that amazing pandemonium and Fidel's own exaggerated movements of his arms and upper body. Then the white dove flew back into the nighttime sky.

And the improbable dove is actually documented on videotape. In the Arts & Entertainment cable TV network's biography of Castro, entitled El Comandante, the dove is shown landing on Fidel's shoulder and remaining there during his speech marking his arrival as the new leader of Cuba. If this uplifting vignette was "incredible" to historians, it was all the more so for Celia.

In the Sierras, Celia Sánchez had carved out a niche as the greatest female revolutionary of all time. Her defeated enemies — the Batista dictatorship, the Mafia, and the United States — were proof of that. But now, with the full blessing of the idolatrous Fidel Castro, she would essentially have absolute power in Cuba.

"Power corrupts and absolute power corrupts absolutely." Celia was more afraid of fulfilling that axiom than she had ever been in the bloody front-line battles in the Sierras.

Celia wrote years later (1973), "I relished the challenge from Batista, the Mafia, and the US in the Sierra. But not the challenge from that damned axiom, which Raúl reminded me of the first week I was back in Havana. Ready or not, I had so much work to do and I never liked distractions. And all I had to do now was reshape Cuba with María's white dove watching me!"

***

Professor Robin Blackburn wrote: "The remarkable triumph of the Cuban Revolution thrust the island onto the world stage. And just as remarkable, it has remained there all these decades because it has not been overthrown. Considering that its two prime virulent enemies have always been the United States (the strongest nation in the world) and the Mafia (the strongest criminal organization in the world), what we pundits/historians/professors call Revolutionary Cuba is indeed a remarkable and historic phenomenon."

On January 2, 1959, in far-off Moscow, the leader of the Soviet Union, Nikita Khrushchev, pored over the front-page article in Pravda about the victory of little Cuba's peasant revolution over the US-backed Batista dictatorship. According to his son Sergei, who later became a US citizen and a professor at Brown University, he turned to Deputy Premier Anastas Mikoyan and asked where Cuba was located. They got a map, and were shocked to see that it lay just ninety miles off the coast of Florida. At the height of the cold war between Communist Russia and the United States, the world's only two nuclear superpowers, this represented an unimaginable opportunity.

That week in 1959 put Cuba on the map, and many of the world's renowned historians have written profusely about its political, theoretical, and historical impact from an international standpoint. In the US, many historians have focused on trying to figure out how the Cuban Revolution triumphed. The highly respected Terrence Cannon, for example, rationalized it with these famous words: "The US did not fear the revolution till it was too late. It was inconceivable to the US policy makers that a revolution in Cuba could turn out badly for them. After all, US companies owned the lush little island and longed to keep it."

Cannon's analysis is both typical and accurate. But it needs to be considered within the context of two pertinent quotations left behind by Celia Sánchez. As she told historian Carlos Franqui, "They loved gluttony. I loved Cuba. I guess I loved Cuba more than they loved gluttony." And, as she told Nora Peters in a 1970s letter, "Our leaders fought from the frontlines in a do-or-die posture. Their leaders sent others to do their fighting in a do-and-live posture."

In the messy world of guerrilla warfare, Celia adapted quickly and thrived; but the turmoil of revolutionary politics always tested her patience.

The fact that the Cuban Revolution pitted a tiny woman against some of the greatest powers in the world — and the tiny woman won — sets it apart from all other historic phenomena.

A little synergy played a key role, meshing two 1953 Cuban events that would one day link Celia Sánchez and Fidel Castro for eternity.

When Fidel Castro led an over-matched little band of would-be rebels in an attack on Batista's heavily fortified Moncada Army Barracks in July of 1953, like others across the island, Celia was touched — but not stirred. When her beloved María was killed the following month, she declared war.

Castro joined her in the final week of December, 1956, at the farm of Epifanio Díaz in the Sierra foothills. His synergy with Celia altered history. Cuban historian Pedro Alvarez Tabío stated that Castro was stunned by her "organizational skills that had created the viable revolution from scratch....The responsibility rested with Celia," Tabío said, "and Fidel would never see fit to change that fact. It was her movement, her revolution."

Celia's revolution dispossessed many wealthy investors and business owners, who had enjoyed a free hand in exploiting a helpless island population under the US-protected Batista regime. Many of them retreated to their palm-fringed estates in Florida, and even now they foment trouble for Cuba in their efforts to regain "paradise lost."

Celia Sánchez always believed she won in the Sierra because she was the most motivated, and she believed the revolution continued to succeed in Cuba for the same reason. "The Batistianos and the Miami Mafia," she told Nora Peters, "...want Cuba back real bad. Robbing a little island and killing dissidents seems so easy.... But they don't have the guts we have. They hide behind the US government's skirts. We have a motivational edge, although their motivation for money is limitless.... The motivation I derived ... offsets all their advantages.... The US, the Mafia, and the Batistianos could still be robbing Cuba blind if they [had] remembered not to devour little peasant girls."

Fidel, Teté, Raúl, Marta, and Juan are still there, leading Cuba, but they are all in their seventies or eighties now. What will happen after they pass on? How would Celia view present-day Cuba? "For some reason," Marta Rojas said in an e-mail from Havana on January 9, 2005, "that question is always filtering through my mind because I still think of Celia each day. We all do. She would want the peasants to have more material things. She would be very sad over the fact the US never became Cuba's best friend and key trading partner. But she would be pleased that the revolution exists. None of us doubt what that would mean to her."

***

In the first months of 1959 in revolutionary Cuba, Celia was buoyed by the fresh opportunity to reshape Cuba on behalf of the long-maligned people; but also heartbroken by the terrorist attacks that came almost immediately from Florida. In the new Cuba, she handled the new war with the skill, determination, and precision that had made her a legend in the Sierra Maestra Mountains. And, as Roberto Salas stated in his 1998 book, "Celia made all the decisions for Cuba, the big ones and the small ones."

The three prime members of the Batista dictatorship that Celia wanted "to answer" to her — Fulgencio Batista, Meyer Lansky, and Rafael Díaz-Balart — all escaped to lucrative safe havens. But several thousand others deemed key villains were rounded up by rebel units led by Che Guevara and Camilo Cienfuegos, and they were put on trial. Celia named the lawyer Fidel Castro, the public face of Cuba's new leadership, to be the Chief Prosecutor.

She closely monitored the trials, as did many others, and she determined that Castro was "too soft" on the miscreants. She fired Fidel as Chief Prosecutor and replaced him with Che Guevara, whom she considered "more of a hard-liner like me," as she later told Nora Peters. Several hundred firing-squad executions followed. "Some of the child-killers paid for their crimes, Nora," Celia wrote in December of 1971, "but too many of them escaped to Florida where they thrive under the protection of the US government, a veritable sponsor of terrorism, at least when it comes to Cuba." Many pundits in the US media, who never mention the wholesale slaughter of children and women in Batista's Cuba, still harp about the executions of the Batista criminals.

One of Celia's first decisions in January of 1959 was to send 300,000 volunteers across the island to begin teaching the peasants, who were mostly illiterate. Then she mandated that all Cuban peasants would be granted free education, through college, once she reopened the University of Havana (which Batista had closed) and once she had refurbished the other twenty major educational institutions in Cuba.

Free education for all the rural poor remains a hallmark of revolutionary Cuba, a fact that Americans are not supposed to factor into the Cuban equation.

In February 1959, two Batistiano airplanes strafed a tobacco farm near Playas del Este just east of Havana. A couple of young workers and their two children, trying to take cover in a shed, were killed. A teary-eyed Celia attended their funeral.

In fighting Batista and then in reshaping Cuba, Celia was forever fueled by her love of the Cuban people; and the Cuban peasants love her to this day. They now celebrate "Mother's Day" on May 9, Celia's birthday.

"The US chants how much it wants to return 'freedom and democracy to Cuba.' That's easy to chant after you've been kicked off the island for preventing it! 'Return freedom and democracy to Cuba?' Do US citizens believe that joke,

Nora? The US had every chance in the world to create a free and democratic Cuba. But the US teamed with the Mafia and Batista to create a dictatorship that robbed the island blind and killed peasants like they were flies. Return! Return! Damn that word! Damn it!"

In January of 1959, as soon as she had the authority to do so, Celia began moving poor families into the luxurious mansions left behind by the Batista team. She put exactly ten peasant families in the mansion once owned by Rafael Díaz-Balart, the dictator of southern Florida's Banana Republic and of America's Cuban policy from 1959 to May 2005 (when he died at age seventy-nine).

For herself, Celia's primary abode was her little apartment on 11th Street in Havana. That meant it was also Castro's primary residence. In fact, using radio and telephone hook-ups, Celia and Castro began the Bay of Pigs defense of Cuba from that apartment in April, 1961. Fancy cars, yachts, airplanes, and furniture had no appeal for Celia, who was known as a "tight-wad." She famously set out to spend Cuba's wealth on the peasants and the island's infrastructure, and she pointedly did not allow government officials to squander it.

Celia was famous for driving a cheap Italian-made Mehari jeep convertible that is now stored in a public museum in Havana. Contrary to depictions of Revolutionary Cuba in the US, Celia's imprint pertaining to government honesty still prevails.

For example, Felipe Peréz Roque, Cuba's young Foreign Minister, may be the second most powerful person in Cuba in 2005, right between the Castro brothers. He has been Fidel's key aide for twenty years and Castro envisions the now 39-year-old Felipe as Cuba's leader in post-Castro Cuba. Yet, he has none of the imperial trappings that tend to go with such a lofty position.

The best profile of Peréz Roque in America was an article written by Linda Robinson in US News & World Report. Ms. Robinson noted that Peréz Roque is paid the equivalent of $25 a month, lives with his wife's parents (she's a doctor), and drives a very old automobile.

In Celia's eyes, and thus in Castro's, the top government officials are public servants, not aspiring millionaires. Peréz Roque has a very positive image in Cuba.

In the first week of April, 1959, a large speedboat sailed along Cuba's northern coast and sprayed two hotels at Varadero with blistering machine-gun fire. One Cuban worker was killed as were two tourists, one Spanish and one Canadian. Six other Cubans were wounded, one losing an eye. As the speedboat circled to its left and headed back in the direction of Florida, a US Coast Guard boat was observed in its wake, with a white uniformed coast guardsman standing on the bow looking through binoculars, which were mounted on a tripod, to assess the damage on shore. From 1959 to the present day, the US government has condoned and also funded, trained, and protected Florida-based terrorism against Cuba. Aware of this, the Cuban-exile anti-Cuban terrorists brag about their deeds in the southern Florida media when they return to US soil.

Just three months into the revolutionary rule of Cuba, Celia had already mandated free education and free health care as well as greatly subsidized shelter and food for all the peasants. But the deadly airplane bombing of the tobacco farm at Playas del Este, the strafing of the two hotels at Varadero, and other such terrorist acts also commanded much of Celia's attention and much of the island's resources.

Celia negotiated a deal with England to buy fighter planes and speedboats to patrol Cuba's coastline, but the United States persuaded England to cancel the purchases. Celia adamantly refused to curtail the expensive social services for the peasants. "We must defend the island but we also must care for the peasants," she told Herbert L. Matthews. "We'll find the resources...somehow. But it's painful to contemplate the purchase of weapons with money that could be spent building shelter, schools, and hospitals."

Still in April of 1959, just four months after the revolutionary victory, Celia arranged for Fidel Castro to visit America to get approval for what she had fought so long and so hard for — a democratic Cuba that her beloved peasants, who easily constituted the majority on the island, would rule with their votes. Castro had been invited to the US by the Society of Newspaper Editors. Celia decided to take them up on the offer, after the US State Department promised that Castro could meet with President Eisenhower at the White House to make the proposal for a democratic Cuba. After the revolutionary triumph, she believed the United States might allow such a development.

Pragmatism was a vital part of Celia Sánchez's character. She realized that if her dream of a thriving democratic Cuba — one that was safe for little girls — was to come to fruition, the island needed peaceful relations with the US.

Celia not only craved peace with America but she also wanted America to be Cuba's best ally and key trading partner. "We are and forever will be, because of geography, next-door neighbors, Nora," Celia said in a 1973 letter. "The big and powerful neighbor should not devour its little neighbor just because it believes it has the power to do so. They should be friends, partners."

With all that hope and pragmatism, Celia was ebullient about the promised Castro—Eisenhower meeting. Further, Celia had in mind that Fidel would ask Eisenhower to send a battery of monitors to Cuba to make sure the democratic elections were fair.

The US State Department gave assurances that the meeting between Castro and Eisenhower would take place. However, Vice President Richard M. Nixon hustled Ike off to Georgia on a golfing trip, and Castro met with Nixon. The Vice President revealed the subtle manipulator that Americans would recognize in him much later.

The ambitious Nixon, reminiscent of the 1950s power-crazed "Joseph McCarthy era," flagrantly tried to make political hay by accusing Castro of being "a closet Communist." He was no such thing, and neither was Celia Sánchez. The Communist Party of Cuba had supported Batista, the Mafia, and the US during the bitter fighting. But both Celia and Castro got the message from the US government, delivered by Nixon to Castro in April of 1959: the US planned to reclaim Cuba — and planned do it in short order.

To Celia, this meant the US sought the quick return of a Batista-like dictatorship to Cuba, one that would help US capitalists to shamelessly exploit the resources and the people. The last thing the US wanted, Celia now realized, was a democracy in Cuba that would spend a good portion of the local resources on the Cuban people and on the island's sorely neglected infrastructure.

The US Secretary of State, John Foster Dulles, and his brother Allen Dulles, the head of the CIA, were major stockholders in the United Fruit Company, the front company that was most involved in ripping off the Cuban economy (and many other countries in the Caribbean and South America). And it was the Dulles brothers who had to sign off on the terrorist and military strikes against Cuba.

Celia was devastated and unmerciful in her critique of the US "democracy" and of the US citizenry from then on. And, she blasted the media for ignoring the obvious corruption.

Back home, Celia discussed the Nixon debacle with Fidel in her apartment on 11th Street in Havana. Marta Rojas witnessed that discussion. In an e-mail to me, Marta said, "Celia got up from the kitchen table where she and Castro had discussed Nixon. She then went to her bedroom and lay down, leaving the door cracked open a little bit. She cried for two hours, one of only two times I have ever seen her cry. Her tears were for the democracy in Cuba that she now knew the US would not let her have. When an angel cries, those around her suffer, too. I suffered that day. When she rejoined Fidel and me in the kitchen, the first thing she said was, 'We tried. That's all we could do. We now have to deal with Nixon and the other crooks in the US, and still do the best we can for Cuba.'"

Celia retained a copy of Newsweek Magazine that depicted Castro's visit to the US in April of 1959 — with Castro pictured on the cover above the glowing headline identifying him as a "hero." In every aspect except the double-cross orchestrated by Nixon, Castro's visit was a rousing success. He was wildly cheered by huge crowds, as were other "heroes of the peasant revolution" such as Camilo Cienfuegos.

But efforts to better the lives of the Cuban peasants would face opposition at every turn from the US. In an April 1969 letter to Nora, Celia said:

> In five years of bloody fighting, Nora, I never lost a battle and I didn't lose the war. But ... they wanted Cuba back, a Batista-style Cuba and surely not a democracy.... But now, Nora, my time and much of Cuba's resources could not be devoted to [providing health care, education, and other services]; I knew America would attack us. I didn't plan to lose, and yes, the US attacked rather quickly at the Bay of Pigs. But before and after that it has been just one cowardly terrorist act after another against us. I longed for one big battle with the damn Batistianos, like the big ten-day Battle of Jigüe against Batista! But the Batistianos don't fight face-to-face. Their style is terrorist acts that kill children. So, that's what I mean by saying this is a different kind of war for both me and for Fidel. And all the while, Nora, I try so hard to protect and care for the peasants each day. I believe the white dove, María's white dove, is watching me.

Perhaps the closest the US-Batistiano-Mafia assassins ever came to killing Celia was on May 17, 1959. She was in the passenger seat and "Dani" Ortiz was driving. Three Cubans and one American working for the CIA — two each in two big black cars — blocked the little jeep convertible fore and aft. The scene played out on a narrow street directly in front of the sign "Havana Café" near the entrance to the Melía Cohiba Hotel in the Vedado section of the old capital city. The four assassins jumped out of their cars, firing pistols. Celia, sliding out the right side of the jeep, barked, "I've got the two in back, Dani! You take the two in front!" With their own pistols, Celia and Dani each killed one assassin and wounded one. The quick battle instantly drew a crowd from the café and the street, and the throng circled the bullet-scarred vehicles. Recognizing Celia, the angry crowd instantly realized what had happened. The two surviving suit-and-tie-attired assassins were pounded into the pavement and were about to be stomped to death when Celia and Dani fired into the air so they could cut through the mob. The two prisoners, along with the two bodies, were shipped back to Miami the next day, after the US State Department was notified of the failed assassination attempt.

Castro was furious. Normally, on his orders, Celia was accompanied by five bodyguards — Dani in her jeep, and two others in each of two jeeps that preceded and followed her — whenever she was on short trips without him. Celia realized her mistake this day. She had been at her office in the Palace of the Revolution when a telephone call informed Ada Martinez that the jeweler had fixed María Ochoa's broken chain. Celia told Ada to send Dani to fetch it; but, then she decided to go with Dani, dropping the usual discipline of taking a full entourage of bodyguards.

Later that day, Celia put María's repaired chain and medallion of Christ around her neck, keeping the promise she had made to the murdered little girl that she would fix it and then wear it "forever."

This was only one of the continuing attempts by the CIA to kill her. Three weeks later, all three tubes of toothpaste in the 11th Street apartment were poisoned — by a trusted maid. Always alert, Celia barely discovered that first one, and then all three, tubes had been tampered with; later they were determined to have been poisoned. The maid confessed that she had been paid $7500 by a CIA agent. She was fired but not punished; she returned $7100 in cash to Celia, who gave the money to three peasant families.

The CIA during this period also tried conventional methods such as gunmen and bombs to kill the new Cuban leaders. But it is the inept unconventional methods that most intrigue historians and writers. For example, a long article written by Marc Frank in Financial Times magazine on February 5, 2005, told about a smoking ban decreed in Cuba by Castro, the famous cigar smoker who quit smoking entirely in 1986. In that article Frank noted that the CIA had even tried "an exploding Cohiba cigar" rigged to detonate when he lit it. The CIA, according to the BBC, tried to "kill Castro up to 600 times."

Many historians are also aware that when Castro was imprisoned by Batista, the US government repeatedly told Batista to kill him, warning Batista that "Castro will be a problem for all of us if he ever gets out."

In Guerrilla Prince (page 182), Georgia Anne Geyer notes that Arthur Gardner, the US ambassador to Cuba, personally told Batista to kill the imprisoned Castro. Only the close watch kept by local and foreign journalists, and others, stayed his hand. When Castro was released in 1955 in a sham "amnesty" by Batista, the plan was for death squads to kill Castro somewhere far from the prying eyes of the peasants and media. Castro evaded the death squads, traveled to New York and Mexico and then joined Celia's revolution in the Sierras.

One of her domestic political problems concerned the four Sierra point commanders that she wanted to be top leaders in Revolutionary Cuba — Fidel, Che, Camilo, and Raúl. None of the four, to her surprise, wanted to be "tied down" running a nascent government that was going to be turned into a democracy, anyway. They were still fired up with the revolutionary fervor that had served them so well in the Sierras. Many times, as Roberto Salas notes in his 1998 book, only Celia "saved" Cuba from "hair-brained" schemes.

Castro, for instance, wanted to take a Cuban army and "eliminate" Rafael Trujillo, the notorious dictator of the nearby Dominican Republic who was, like Batista, staunchly supported by the US. Celia refused.

Next, Che wanted to go off and start revolutions against American-supported dictators all across Latin America. Celia spent two hours begging him to stay with her in Cuba. He relented, at least for seven years.

And then Camilo (who had been a tailor prior to the revolution) told Celia he wanted to open "a big clothing store in Havana." Raúl wanted "to be a farmer, like my Papa."

Celia called both Camilo and Raúl to her office and heatedly told them, "After the new Cuban government is safe and established, both of you can be any damn thing you want to be! Till then, I need you and Cuba needs you!" Then she mellowed. A little calmer and a lot sweeter, she smiled and said, "I needed both of you in the Sierra and I need both of you now. One day, Camilo, I'll buy a dress in your store. And one day, Raúl, I'll visit your farm to get some fresh air and look for some walking trails. By then, I hope I can be concentrating on my own dream job, which is to administer a hospital."

"When need be," Marta Rojas told me in an e-mail, "Celia could be stern as hell and no one ever intimidated her. But just as quickly she could temper all that and be as mellow and as sweet as an angel. If honey didn't work, she tried vinegar. If vinegar didn't work, she tried honey.... I don't believe I ever noticed anyone resisting her very strongly."

That combination kept the revolutionary adventurers Fidel and Che and the entrepreneurial hopefuls Camilo and Raúl in her government.

Batista in 1956 had closed the University of Havana and he never did concern himself with educating the peasants. In 1959, Celia reopened the University of Havana and decreed free educations for all the peasants; this free education persists to this day and the results have been outstanding. Since the island did not have nearly enough teachers, Celia sent an astonishing 300,000 volunteers across the island to begin teaching the peasants. Then she drew up plans for all of the Cuban universities to train teachers and doctors as a top priority. The newest and largest teacher training complex, located in Holguin province, is named for her.

In Batista's Cuba, only the rich had adequate access to decent health facilities. In 1959, Celia decreed free and excellent medical attention for all the peasants. Nowadays, Cuba sends highly trained physicians to assist Venezuela and other neighbors.

The health of the Cubans quickly and drastically improved under Celia's watch. Soon, Cuba had for its population as a whole the highest ratio of doctors and teachers in the world.

In the 1980s, the island's infant mortality rate became lower than that in the United States; and in the 1990s, President Bill Clinton's Surgeon General, Joycelyn Elders, toured Cuba and, upon her return to the US, stated that, "Cuba's health system cares for its people better than America's system cares for its people."

Instead of reacting positively to that statement, Americans tended to ignore or ridicule it.

On January 12, 2005, the lead editorial in the New York Times was entitled "HEALTH CARE? ASK CUBA." In the editorial, Nicholas D. Kristof documented that, in the year 2005, Cuba's infant mortality rate is lower than that in the United States despite the nation's resources. Celia would not have been surprised.

Among the many historical records held by the Cuban Revolution is its longevity — almost five decades and counting. What other nation, big or small, has survived that long under daily assaults from the strongest and richest nation in the world? Even minus the terrorist and military attacks, a 44-year American embargo would have brought most nations to their knees.

In 2004, a US foreign subsidiary was found "guilty" of selling "two infant vaccines" to Cuba. The generous-spirited Bush Administration told the public that: "Those two infant vaccines helped Castro and put money in his pocket, and the policy of this Bush administration is to starve the Cuban people so they will be encouraged to get rid of Castro so we can return freedom and democracy to Cuba."

Celia Sánchez blamed the American public for Batista's brutal reign in Cuba and for the massive brutality of the Florida-based Batistianos against the Cuban people.

The US taxpayers paid the federal lawyers who won the lawsuit against the US company whose subsidiary sold those infant vaccines to Cuba. Even so, Cuba's infant mortality rate is lower than America's. The US taxpayers paid for the CIA-Batistiano suitcase bomb that blew a Cuban airplane out of the sky on October 6, 1976. The US government maintains to this day that those murders hurt Castro. Is that correct, or did the attacks help keep him in power? Celia Sánchez decided that the American people had neither the intelligence nor the guts to ask such questions.

One other decree handed down by Celia in 1959 is still reverberating in the New York Times. She lamented the fact that peasant children under the US-backed Batista were treated like dogs. Therefore, in addition to providing shelter, health, and education, Celia did a myriad of other remarkable things.

She asked Fidel Castro himself to knock on the door of a Cuban woman named Alicia Alonso. In America and elsewhere in the 1940s and 1950s, Alonso had earned a reputation as one of the world's greatest ballerinas. Celia had Fidel tell her that the new Cuban government would give her an initial sum of $200,000 if she would start a national ballet in Cuba.

Celia mandated that the ballet would give full scholarships to promising children from across the island, and that the Cuban government would continue to fund such a program. History registers the fact that Alicia Alonso accepted that offer. She scoured the island in search of candidates for her new Havana academy. In the decades to come, Alicia awarded thousands of scholarships and devoted fifteen-hour days to training her pupils. Her touring troupe has won far in excess of 300 first-place awards at major international competitions, and played to standing-room-only audiences around the world, including the US. Top ballet companies around the world, especially the US, now feature Alicia-trained superstars.

Alicia Alonso is now eighty-three-years old, and blind. But she is provided talented aides, such as her likely successor Loipa Araújo. And to this day she still trains Cuban peasant children and turns them into world-class ballet stars. In January of 2005, the Cuban government — always depicted in the US as destitute — somehow found enough money to sharply increase its funding to Alicia Alonso's National Ballet, just as it still finds enough money to fund free education and health care for all Cubans.

On February 6, 2005, the longest article in the New York Times and on its website was about the "aged matriarch of Cuban ballet," Alicia Alonso. Erika Kinetz took note of Ms. Alonso's age, eighty-three, and her blindness, but also noted, "Ms. Alonso has aged with a grandeur so willful it can be frightening." The article also mentioned that "her dancers have been leaving at an alarming rate" and that "Alicia-trained dancers now grace American Ballet Theater, the Boston Ballet, the San Francisco Ballet, the Washington Ballet, the Cincinnati Ballet, and the Royal Ballet, among others....Despite the weight of its accumulated years, her body still holds the clarity, passion and light that distinguish the Cuban school of movement. Ms. Alonso rose from behind her desk and began to dance. Her face was rapt with remembered glory. She lifted her unseeing eyes toward a far balcony, gripped the desk with one hand and sent the other wafting gaily in the air. With perfect, flirtatious grace, she pranced like a muse in Balanchine's Apollo. Then her press secretary walked swiftly over and helped her back into her chair."

The pro-Batista émigrés in southern Florida control the US media and the US government when it comes to perceptions and projections of Revolutionary Cuba. But when Celia Sánchez told Nora Peters "the best Cubans stayed on the island and didn't run to Florida seeking fame and fortune, mostly fortune," she was speaking of Cubans like Alicia Alonso, a world treasure.

Celia also endeavored tirelessly to afford the average Cuban child with access to team sports. She created and funded sports academies across the island, sports academies that are still thriving to this day. The Olympic gold medals in baseball, boxing, and other sports that little Cuba won in 2004 are testaments to Celia Sánchez, as is the island's now long-standing reputation for its disproportionate success in international sports competitions. She attended training sessions at Alicia's ballet academy as well as at the youth athletic facilities that her resolve had created.

Celia Sánchez, the greatest female revolutionary of all time, is as topical today as she was in the 1950s in the Sierras. That's because so many of the revolutionary improvements she mandated solely to help the Cuban peasants are still helping them today.

***

The year 1959 led to the decade of the 1960s, an important time for Cuba and for Celia.

She took a keen interest in the 1960 presidential election in the US, hoping and praying that the Democrats would win, preventing Vice President Richard Nixon from ascending to the presidency; and ousting John Foster Dulles, the Secretary of State, and his brother Allen Dulles, the head of the CIA, from their positions of power. It was a reasonable bet that a new US government, led by Democrats, might treat Cuba fairly and allow the island to promote the welfare of its people without terrorist and military attacks from Florida.

Celia got her wish. The Democrat, John Kennedy, nipped the Republican, Richard Nixon, in 1960's US presidential election.

Chapter 10 . Over the Rainbow

Antagonists often create unlikely protagonists in a set of circumstances that permeate history. Dwight Eisenhower, for example, had languished for almost two decades with the same modest military rank till the circumstances of World War II elevated him into a legendary five-star general and a two-term US president.

The circumstances of the Batista dictatorship in Cuba elevated Celia Sánchez from a shy, modest, and petite doctor's daughter into "the greatest maker of Cuban history" (according to Pablo Alvarez Tabío) and into the realm of history's greatest revolutionaries.

Clearly, Celia did not welcome or relish those circumstances. Her daunting revolutionary fervor created an adorable leader but she would have very much preferred the comfortable, inconsequential life she had enjoyed prior to the revolution. Celia's staid demeanor contrasted with Castro's electrifying personality, but together they comprised an imposing team. Guided by the unobtrusive Celia, Castro absorbed or deflected any attacks on the revolution while shielding the prime decision-maker, Celia. "He did so with aplomb," Marta Rojas told me in a January 2005 e-mail. "To him, protecting Celia was defending the revolution. And to him that has always constituted the main focus in his life."

In little Media Luna, with a loving father who was an anti-Batista Cuban patriot and former head of the Cuban Medical Association, she grew up with privileges and social stature but she reveled almost exclusively in the beauty of her island and its rural people, the peasants who surrounded her and with whom she sympathized.

American movies and music influenced Celia, and perhaps everyone of her generation, especially the 1939 classic "Wizard of Oz" and its immortal song "Over the Rainbow." Prior to the revolution, the gentle Celia had dreamed of the fanciful world portrayed in the movie; later, when her life had become far more harsh and hard, she found comfort in the haunting lyrics — "Somewhere over the rainbow, bluebirds fly... Somewhere over the rainbow — why, oh why, can't I?"

The frequent rainbows that adorned the skies over Cuba enthralled Celia, whether in Media Luna, in the Sierras, in Havana, or at her lovely little getaway cabin in Viñales Valley. To this day, many Cubans think of Celia Sánchez when they see a rainbow overhead and many believe it is a sign that she is still looking down wondrously and protectively on her "beautiful little Cuba."

The June, 1999, edition of National Geographic Magazine featured a twenty-page photo-essay of Cuba with text by John J. Putman. Putman and his photography crew walked the trail leading to La Plata, the old mountain camp in the Sierras for the guerrilla fighters. Rubén Araujo Torres, an old guerrilla fighter himself, served as the guide. Torres led Putman to a "house of thatch and wood, set on a steep slope above a spring-fed stream in a sea of green." This was the house in the Sierra Maestra where Fidel and Celia "planned the final battles that broke the spirit of Batista's army." As Putman pointed out, "The house had two rooms. The little kitchen held a kerosene fridge with a bullet hole in it." Araujo Torres told Putman about other things still in the house. "Fidel built the bookcase, those chairs. He built this chair for himself, that one for Celia."

Outside, he was constantly reminded of Celia — when a rainbow appeared overhead, when they stopped at a flower garden. "Celia planted these," Araujo Torres told Putman, as he pointed down at what he called, "hibiscus, mar pacífico." Putman wrote, "I had noticed the bright red petals on the trail coming in. They seemed to me now souvenirs of a time when everyone here was young and all the world was green."

Soon realizing that the return to La Plata had most reminded the old guerrilla of Celia, Putman asked him what he remembered of her. "She was very nice," Rubén said. "She was the mother of the troop. She was constantly by Castro's side — taking notes, keeping watch, running things." Many Cubans believe she is still "by his side, running things."

Castro's trip to the US in April of 1959 had exposed the duplicitous attitude of Washington, which had to be factored in as well as the Dulles brothers' interest in the United Fruit Company, when assessing possible threats to Cuba and its new leaders. Throughout 1959, the first year of revolutionary rule in Cuba, the US government's alliance with the Mafia and with the pro-Batista faction in Florida resulted in constant assassination attempts and terrorist attacks against Cuba. Celia mandated that Cuba would not retaliate in kind, even with strikes at what she termed "the cesspool in Miami." She did not want to give the US a ready excuse for an all-out military attack on her little island.

Instead, Celia focused sharply on the 1960 presidential election that pitted President Eisenhower's Vice President Nixon against the young US senator from Massachusetts, John F. Kennedy.In Havana, Celia was euphoric when the results were announced — Kennedy had won. Her visionary plans — grooming Cuba for democracy while continuing to massively upgrade the educational, health, and shelter available to the peasants — could now proceed without the distractions of terrorist and military attacks emanating from southern Florida. Or so she fervently hoped.

"Oh, God, Nora," Celia reflected years later, "I was Kennedy's biggest fan, if briefly. I didn't associate Democrats with the United Fruit Company or the Mafia." The image the Kennedys projected was as alluring as that "land that I heard of, once in a lullaby."

Very quickly, Celia learned that the election was a gigantic fraud, an historical fact that the American voters minimized but one that she could not afford to overlook. Kennedy's narrow victory over Nixon was predicated upon the support he was given in Mafia-dominated states such as Illinois and West Virginia, support purchased by Joseph P. Kennedy on behalf of his son (Joe's first millions were garnered via his Mafia-connected bootlegging of illegal whiskey from Canada during the era of prohibition in the US). And, in exchange for its crucial help in putting John Kennedy in the White House, the Mafia insisted on payback — Cuba!

"Despite all I knew about the US government's maniacal support of fiendish dictators like Batista in Cuba, Nora, I drastically over-estimated the honesty and decency of the American democracy when I put such hope in Kennedy beating Nixon in the 1960 presidential election" (Celia's letter to Nora Peters dated 08-19-74).

OPERATION MONGOOSE

President Kennedy appointed his younger brother Robert Attorney General, Robert McNamara Secretary of Defense, and John McCone the new Director of the CIA. Instead of acting in the best interests of the American public, the new leaders began by rewarding the Mafia. Robert Kennedy was the prime architect of a secretive US government scheme code-named Operation Mongoose. It was a lushly funded top priority item that called for CIA, Mafia, and Batistiano operatives to assassinate the leaders of Revolutionary Cuba. Time and again they tried; time and again they failed. The Mafia and the CIA were two of the world's best killing machines and Cuba was right next door; they had insider knowledge via the Batistianos in southern Florida and should have been able to capitalize on all the best entry points and hiding places on the island. Their failure intensely frustrated the Kennedy White House.

The assassination project evolved into plans for a military attack.

Terrorist attacks from Florida were escalated for the purpose of provoking Cuba into a response that could be used as a pretext to justify the attack. A blistering series of airplane and speedboat strafings assaulted coastal areas, and saboteurs bombed bridges as well as intercity landmarks such as the Pepsi-Cola plant in Havana. Cuba responded by filing protest after protest with both the United Nations and the US State Department. The Kennedy brothers and Secretary of Defense McNamara seriously considered a unanimous (7-0) suggestion from the Joint Chiefs of Staff, headed by General Lyman Lemnitzer, that entailed having the CIA blow up boats and airplanes, killing Americans, so they "could blame it on Castro." (This Joint Chiefs of Staff proposal was not revealed until 1998 when US documents were declassified under the Freedom of Information Act at the behest of historian James Bamford). Meanwhile, Cuba studiously avoided giving the US any excuse for military action.

Unable to document or fabricate a suitable excuse for attacking Cuba, the Kennedy White House proceeded anyhow. Only, now the US government's role would be kept secret.

Military bases in Florida would be used to train Cuban exiles, the Batistianos, to attack Cuba under the clandestine direction of the CIA and US military officers. The US would also call on Trujillo, in the Dominican Republic, and Somoza in Nicaragua. The government would deny any participation. It would be a land, sea, and air attack launched from Florida and Nicaragua. US warplanes disguised as Cuban airplanes would initiate the attack by wiping out Cuba's three military airbases and destroying Cuba's fledgling air force. The date for the attack was changed several times, and then was slated for mid-April of 1961, give or take a few days depending on the weather forecast in the Caribbean.

***

On April 3, 1961, Celia Sánchez and Fidel Castro were spending the night in their office on the fourth floor of the five-story Hotel Cohiba, formerly a favorite haunt of Mafia kingpins as well as celebrities such as the author Ernest Hemingway. A man reputed to be "an officer" at Florida's Homestead Air Force Base had been trying for a week to talk "personally" with Celia over the telephone about what he termed "an urgent matter." Such calls were not unusual and were always closely screened. Celia's aides gradually convinced her this one might be important and not just a nuisance or a hoax.

Thus, if the man called back, Celia left instructions for him to call her at a specific number after midnight on April 3, 1961. The number was in her office at the Hotel Cohiba, where she also had a studio apartment as well as her best equipment for recording incoming phone calls — something about which she was particularly concerned since her guerrilla days.

The call came in at 4:12 A.M., April 3, 1961.

"Hello."

"I need to talk to Celia Sánchez."

"This is Celia Sánchez."

"Thank you for arranging this. Listen carefully. I am a flight officer at Homestead Air Force Base in Florida. I am also a patriotic American. But ... I believe what you have done and hope to do for your people is far better than what the Batista crowd did ... [W]ithin two weeks the US ... will attack Cuba ... I believe the first attack will be on your three main airfields and I believe the ground attack will start on your southern coast near Trinidad..."

Celia and Fidel listened to the tape recording of the phone call several times. They believed in its authenticity and they began planning accordingly, beginning with a phone call to Raúl. As Fidel talked with Raúl on the telephone, Celia sat at her desk underlining this note to herself: "Move fighter planes from the three main air bases!"

The next morning at the Palace of the Revolution Celia and the Castro brothers had a three-hour meeting. They listened several more times to the telephone tape recording. To Fidel, the most interesting part was the projected date of the attack — April 15, 1961; two weeks away. They had already anticipated that the series of terrorist attacks would be followed by a military attack. Raúl pored over maps marking and circling coastal areas as he guessed where the major land assault would commence. The officer had said "on your southern coast near Trinidad." Trinidad was an ornate and quaint old Spanish colonial town located on the island's south-central coast. Just to the northwest was another important seaport, Cienfuegos. With Nicaragua being used as a base to launch the attack, targeting the heart of Cuba's southern coastline was a logical plan; the invading force would have a direct line from the eastern Nicaraguan coast, right between the Cayman Islands and Jamaica, to Cuba's soft underbelly between the cities of Cienfuegos and Trinidad. Attacking the south-central area of Cuba from a base in Nicaragua would also serve the US goal of trying to mask its involvement in the attack; otherwise, the military bases in Florida would be used to attack the nearby northern coast of Cuba between Havana and Cardenas.

One thing was quite apparent to Celia and the Castro brothers: Cuba was very vulnerable to such an attack. It was the largest island in the West Indies and the sixteenth largest in the world. A third of the island, from Cardenas westward, was just 100 miles south of the Florida Keys and the other two-thirds of the island, from Cardenas to Baracoa, meandered southeasterly from Florida. Just off the coasts of the main island there were thousands of smaller islands, with the Archipelago de Sabana and the Archipelago de Camaguey the biggest.

The Archipelago de las Canarreos, due south of Havana, included the large island of Isla de la Juventud where, in the city of Nueva Gerona, the young Fidel Castro had been imprisoned. The vast coastline of the main island, bordered by thousands of smaller islands, and the close proximity to Florida as well as US-backed dictatorships like Somoza's in Nicaragua, made defense almost impossible. Celia and the Castro brothers all agreed on that; but they had done the "impossible" in the revolutionary war and they would try once again.

Celia later described that session with these simple words: "Yes, Nora, we believed we would die because we didn't believe the US leaders, the Kennedy brothers, would be so stupid as to attack a small island and lose. We believed we would die because we never gave a thought to do anything but to stand and fight. Giving up and running never crossed our minds. That entire session was devoted to devising the best way to fight, with our very limited resources, to the end."

It was Celia who stood and summarized that session as the Castro brothers sat at the table in front of the map. Using a pointer, she traced back and forth along the southern coast from Surgidero de Batabano, due south of Havana, to Trinidad on the south-central coast. "So, we agree now that the ground attack and the supply ships from Nicaragua will target this area. Raúl, just before you got here Fidel said he believed the invasion will start halfway between Surgidero and Trinidad...right here at the Bay of Pigs inlet just east of Cienaga de Zapata. He will explain his reasoning to us later. But we agree, prior to the ground attack, the US fighter planes will blow to bits the Ciudad Libertad Airport, San Antonio de los Baños Airport near Havana, and Santiago de Cuba Airport on the southeast coast. I saw the reports on what we have at those three airports — mostly old commercial DC-3s and some good fighter planes that lack spare parts, which may now be too late to refurbish... [since] the US blocked that [spare parts] deal with England."

Raúl gave an update on their air power. he reported that they had fifteen of the best young pilots in the world, but only had eight top-notch fighter planes ready to go.

Celia turned, pondering, and stepped away from the table. Then she looked at Fidel and said, "You and I will drive down to Trinidad today and spend the night. Tomorrow we'll drive west along the southern coast. You can explain your prediction that the main ground attack will occur at the Bay of Pigs."

Then she looked back at Raúl. In order to leave the impression that the attack came as a surprise, she proposed leaving the DC-3s and older fighter planes out in the open. "But we must have those eight planes with those fifteen pilots ready for a counterattack."

Raúl nodded, and slowly pushed up from his chair. He shook Fidel's hand before hugging Celia and kissing her cheek. Then he left the room.

Celia's left hand went to her chest, grasping María's medallion of Christ. She squeezed it tightly and stared out the window. Words from her favorite song were now whispering softly in her mind. "Somewhere, over the rainbow..."

Chapter 11. Camelot

On April 12, 1961, President John Kennedy was asked at a major news conference what the US government was doing to help the Cuban exiles in Florida reclaim Cuba. His exact words were: "First, I want to say that there will not be, under any circumstances, an intervention in Cuba by the United States Armed Forces. This government will do everything it possibly can; I think it can meet its responsibilities, to make sure that there are no Americans involved in any actions inside Cuba. The basic issue in Cuba is not one between the United States and Cuba. It is between the Cubans themselves."

As is so often the case, public pronouncements are used to mask, rather than to reveal, the truth. As Geyer wrote, in Guerrilla Prince, "All the historic indications support the theory that Kennedy had been briefed by CIA chief Allen Dulles that a Cuban exile invasion force had been set in motion by the Eisenhower administration. Yet, when he faced Nixon [in the 1960 campaign debate], Kennedy vigorously denied it and indeed even attacked the Eisenhower and Nixon administration on its targeting of Cuba." Yet, early in his presidency, Kennedy's two Cuban projects were: (1) Operation Mongoose, the covert operation by the CIA and the Mafia to murder Cuba's leaders; and (2) extensive training operations for a military attack on Cuba being conducted on military bases in Florida and at an expensive new base on the eastern coast of Nicaragua. The CIA was paying each trainee $400 a month plus $175 for their wives and $100 for each of their children. Of the first 500 Cuban exiles recruited by the CIA, there were 200 who had been charged with gross crimes, including murder, in Cuba.

The young officer at Homestead Air Force Base in Florida who had warned Celia Sánchez of the impending attack was not the only decent American who was appalled by the imminent attack. On March 29, 1961, Senator William Fulbright personally handed President Kennedy a scathing memo that stated: "To give this activity even covert support is of a piece with the hypocrisy and cynicism for which the United States is constantly denouncing the Soviet Union in the United Nations and elsewhere. This point will not be lost on the rest of the world — nor on our own consciences." No one in the US Senate was more powerful than Fulbright, and yet President Kennedy was beholden to the Mafia. His allegiance to them was apparently stronger than his allegiance to "democracy" or to decency.

Under Secretary of State Chester A. Bowles on March 31, 1961, handed Secretary of State Dean Rusk a three-page note signed by ten more well-known politicians who were trying to avert the attack on Cuba. Bowles literally got down on his knees and begged Rusk, "For God's sake and for America's sake please don't let him do it! Please let him know that this country cannot stoop to this level of madness! Oh, God, no! The Cuban people, the American people, do not deserve this!"

The operation continued unabated.

Meanwhile, Celia and the Castro brothers prepared for the impending attack as best they could. Raúl had hidden Cuba's eight serviceable fighter planes — one B-26, three T-33s, and four British-made Sea Fury light attack bombers.

The DC-3s and unusable fighter planes would be left exposed at the three military airbases — two outside Havana and one on the edge of Santiago to be sacrificed in the initial stages of the attack.

Fidel and Celia had walked the coast at the Bay of Pigs, where Fidel had told her he believed the ground attack would take place. There were, of course, thousands of other possible target areas, but luck — and a few good guesses, and a few good tips — was on their side.

On April 12, 1961, Celia and Fidel spent the night at 11th Street in Havana. They received several phone calls, one telling them that "a large US warship" was just off the northern coast of Cuba. Historians recount that Fidel immediately recognized that as a diversion. "I'm not worried about any action in that area ... [Kennedy will attack] as far from Florida as he can, in the southern area west of Trinidad."

Fidel and Celia got five hours of "peaceful" sleep that night, as Celia later told Herbert L. Matthews of the New York Times. On Friday, April 14, 1961, Celia and Fidel spent the day at Punto Uno (Point One), the main military head-quarters in the heart of Havana. They were attired in their green guerrilla uni-forms. Their plan was to not contest but to survive the expected bombing attack, and then make the US fight them on the ground.

Cuba could not match the US Air Force, but if it survived the initial bombing, they thought they could very severely punish the ground invaders. Cuba had 25,000 regular soldiers and they were backed by 200,000 militiamen. The CIA had informed Kennedy that "large elements of Cuba's regular army and most of its militia will turn against Castro once it realizes America is launching an all-out bombing attack." Celia and Fidel calculated otherwise.

At 9:00 P.M. on April 14, they drove to her 11th Street apartment to spend the night. They went to bed at 1:15 A.M., earlier than usual for the two well known "night-owls." At 5:15 A.M. they were awakened — not by a phone call or by their aides, but by the ominous roar of American B-26 bombers flying over Havana.

"We got up," Celia later told Matthews, "and did morning things. The first thing I did was to fix a pot of coffee."

As they did those "morning things," the cacophonous blasts of bombs assaulting their two military air bases on the edge of Havana echoed through the apartment. A phone call from Raúl informed them that the airfield at Santiago de Cuba on the island's eastern tip was also under attack. Celia, in a second com-munication from the officer at Homestead Air Force Base in Florida, had been informed that one of the attacking B-26s would be assigned to bomb "any building or location that the CIA determines you and Fidel may be at." The CIA was apparently late in targeting the 11th Street apartment.

Otherwise, the bombers did their job. The three military air fields were blown to bits, as were the commercial DC-3s and fighter planes that had been left exposed. And the strategy worked. The US B-26 pilots informed their bosses that "the Cuban air force now ceases to exist."

After breakfast, Celia reluctantly separated from Fidel. She drove to the military headquarters at Punto Uno to control the overall radio communications; he headed south of Havana in the direction of the Bay of Pigs, where he now expected the major ground assault to occur. Their instincts and their knowledge of military history had served them well, to this point. They had remembered the events of 1956, when Nasser, in Egypt, had let his entire air force be destroyed on the ground.

They also knew that, after the initial bombing of Guatemala on May 17, 1954, the US ground attack had followed exactly twenty-four hours later. That one was successful and the US installed a "friendly" dictatorship in Guatemala.

They believed the US would replicate these attacks when they targeted Cuba. They guessed correctly.

On April 14, 1961, just prior to the air attack on Cuba, six US warships sailed from the port of Puerto Cabezas in Nicaragua bound for Cuba. The Nicaraguan leader, Luis Somoza, famously stood on the dock and bade them bon voyage with these historic words: "Bring me back some hairs from Castro's beard!"

The six US warships headed for the Bay of Pigs, just as Fidel had amazingly predicted. Just after dark on Sunday, April 16, 1961, US frogmen went ashore and established landing lights to guide the ships to the right spot. Just after midnight, the attackers hit the beach and divided into six battalions with CIA operative Manuel Artime the overall commander. The CIA had told Artime that the landing area around Playa Girón and Playa Largo was lined with harmless seaweed. In fact, razor-sharp coral reefs sliced into the landing crafts and many of Artime's men, making a mockery of a tightly orchestrated military landing.

The commander of the Cuban militia, José Ramón Suco, monitored both the frogmen and the landing; he kept Castro informed via walkie-talkies. Castro was inside a tank and he kept Celia informed via a radio hook-up.

The unexpected coral reef acted like razor-wire, cutting off the US troops from the supplies and armaments that were still on supply ships just off shore. At that moment, as the soldiers began to exchange fire, Fidel and Celia launched their little air force — eight fighter planes that they were not supposed to have!

Captain Enrique Carreras Rojas swooped down and sank the US command ship Maropa and the prime supply ship Houston. The CIA-orchestrated attack began to unravel because of the poor information that had let the coral injure Artime's attacking Brigade 2506 even before Fidel ordered a barrage of rifle, machine gun, and tank fire.

As he directed the fighting from the frontline, Castro looked more like a scholar or professor than a commander. Black and white photographs from the frontline reveal he wore glasses and a beret, not a helmet. At one point, Geyer reports, firing his rifle from his tank as bullets whizzed all around him, Fidel radioed another of the young pilots these exact words: "Chico, I need you to take out that other supply ship." Chico did.

A bit later, Raúl was in radio contact with him when Fidel fired off a few rounds — "Hear that, brother? You're missing all the fun!" That radio hook-up is said to have been recorded by Celia and it was released to the world media decades later.

US warplanes joined the action in a last-ditch effort, but the first four were shot down and all four US pilots were killed; five other US warplanes fled. The four US pilots who were shot down and killed, despite assurances that "no person connected to the US military or to the US government is or will be involved in any military action against Cuba," were Thomas "Pete" Ray, Riley Shamburger, Leo Francis Baker and Wade Gray.

Amazingly, at the same time — on April 17, 1961 — US Secretary of State Dean Rusk was giving a news conference in Washington, in which he emphatically stated, "The American people are entitled to know whether we are intervening in Cuba or intend to do so in the future. The answer to that question is no. What happens in Cuba is for the Cuban people to decide."

From that day to this day, top US government officials including Secretary of State Condoleezza Rice in 2005 during her confirmation hearings before the US Senate, have dissembled in regards to the continuous US effort to regain control of Cuba. And from that day to this day, Washington's Cuba policy has been directed by the rich, powerful, and self-serving Batistianos in southern Florida.

In the White House, President John Kennedy, shaken by the unexpected turn of events, was receiving telephone updates on the disaster he had created at the Bay of Pigs. Aides later confirmed that both Kennedy brothers cried as they received the reports.

The information regarding the four downed airplanes and Cuba's overwhelming land defense prompted President Kennedy to call off the attack. This left the attackers on the beach defenseless, unable to even retreat back to the ships that had brought them. That decision earned John F. Kennedy some deadly enemies — the Batistianos, the Mafia, and even anti-Castro zealots within the ranks of the CIA.

On Kennedy's desk at the time was a furious telegram from Nikita Khrushchev, Premier of the Soviet Union, the only true rival and the one nation that should have been Kennedy's main focus. That Khrushchev cable has since been declassified and is well known: "It is still not too late to avoid the irreparable. The USA now still has the possibility of not allowing the flame of war ignited by interventions in Cuba to grow into an incomparable conflagration. As far as the Soviet Union is concerned, there should be no mistake about our position: We will render the Cuban people and their government all necessary help to repel an armed attack on Cuba."

The above words represented a credible threat, since Moscow had nuclear weapons easily capable of annihilating America. Kennedy had played into Khrushchev's hands. To attack was one thing; but to attack and lose was quite another. Khrushchev was startled that the only other superpower in the world could produce such infantile leaders.

The Bay of Pigs fiasco branded the Kennedy presidency reckless and criminal in its disregard for human life. Even in the lead-up, Herbert L. Matthews (Revolution in Cuba) wrote that: "Beginning in January of 1960, CIA planes from Florida, some with American pilots, raided Cuban fields with napalm-type bombs to burn sugar cane fields." The US, of course, denied that any CIA planes or any Americans took part.Some of those "napalm-type bombs," as documented earlier, killed innocent women and children, including one entire family of four. The CIA, always slow to realize that such actions create enemies, convinced Kennedy prior to the Bay of Pigs that the Cuban peasants would "turn against Castro" once the US started its attack. Kennedy fired Allen Dulles, but the CIA is the CIA. Howard Hunt wasn't fired. He remained in place, and masterminded the Watergate debacle a few years later.

Contrary to the CIA predictions, the Cuban troops were prepared to fight to the death and not a single one defected to the US side. Someone in the CIA had also predicted that Fidel would "turn tail and run once the attack commences." Any study of Castro would have refuted that.

It is also odd that the CIA was unable to instruct its B-26 bomber as to Celia's and Fidel's whereabouts. The New York Times knew where they were; how is it that the military could not find its quarry?

Fidel's forces easily killed or captured those attackers who made it to shore. The final tally of prisoners totaled 1,189. Because the attack on Cuba was unprovoked and broke all international laws, including those in which the US was a signatory (including Article 2, paragraph 4, and Article 51 of the Charter of the United Nations; Articles 18 and 25 of the Charter of the Organization of American States; Article 1 of the Rio Treaty; and The Act of Bogota), Cuba probably had the right to put all the prisoners on trial and then shoot them —

particularly considering that the attackers did not wear any nation's uniforms; they could be termed terrorists and not soldiers.

The attacking US airplanes were disguised as Cuban airplanes, complete with the Cuban Air Force insignia. But Cuba did not shoot the 1,189 prisoners. It sold them back to the US for $53 million. By all rights, the Kennedys should have paid that bill out of their own deep pockets, just as they had paid the Mafia to get elected. But, it was the US taxpayers — not the Kennedys or the Batistianos — who would pay for all the aftermath, monetarily and otherwise. After the Bay of Pigs attack, the young and arguably incompetent US president, John Kennedy, marveled as the taxpayers even covered the massive public relations campaign designed to embellish his role in the debacle. Kennedy's famous comment — "The worse I do the more popular I become" — mocked those voters for their ignorance and naiveté.

The US representative at the UN at the time was Adlai Stevenson, the two-time Democratic presidential candidate and one of America's most honest and most respected politicians. At the UN Stevenson staunchly maintained the US position that it was not involved "in any manner" with the attack on Cuba. Duped, Stevenson was caught in the lies when photographs revealed that the attacking US airplanes and pilots were American, in disguise. The revelation humiliated Adlai Stevenson for the rest of his life. President Kennedy laughed as he said, "Adlai is my official liar." The US taxpayers laughed with him, so they thought.

The stage was set for many more decades of underhanded bullying of Cuba on behalf of the remnants of the Batista dictatorship who had so easily taken over both southern Florida and the US government's Cuban policy. Celia Sánchez, in a 1976 letter, revealed what the Bay of Pigs taught her:

> The worst elements of a deposed US-supported dictatorship settled on US soil and immediately created a dictatorship there, using that soil to launch military and terror attacks against a small neighbor. The US people who paid for such things but did not benefit from them were too stupid to object. The two-party system of the US democracy caved in when both parties were controlled by the Mafia. In the 1960 election I learned that the Mafia wing Sam Giancana represented controlled the Democrat Kennedy and the Mafia wing run by Carlos Marcello controlled the Republican Nixon. Looking back, Nora, I realize Cuba didn't have any hope in that election because there was no alternative, no honest option, when both parties were bought and paid for by the Mafia, the capitalists, and the Batistianos — the three elements that most wanted Cuba back. The greatest and strongest country in the world, and history's greatest democracy, was usurped. In time, I realized, this degradation would destroy your democracy from within, like a cancer that is inopera-

ble or untreatable. In a two-party system, it is imperative that at least one is not bought-and-paid for. Cuba and 1960 tested the US, and the US lost.

"Bahia de Cochiños" is Spanish for "Bay of Pigs."

The American people remained fully and very conveniently disengaged (except via their checkbooks). This would enable Kennedy, and the nine presidents that succeeded him, to continue to do the bidding of the Batistianos and the Mafia when it came to Cuba. Kennedy's vast army of public relations hacks and biographers would gloss over all of his puerile, murderous, cowardly, and foolish mistakes. These public relations wizards included three brilliant speechwriters ("Ask not what your country can do for you...") and sycophants — Ted Sorenson, Arthur Schlesinger, Jr., and Raymond Price. With the cooperation of the mainstream media, especially such powers as the Washington Post, they would promote misleading stories and craft incredible excuses to smooth over Kennedy's Cuban and sexual misdeeds, establishing precedents that undermined the values we think of as American democracy. A sharp political mind like that of Joe Kennedy knows that even Mickey Mouse can be elected president — especially if his only opponent is Donald Duck.

Like Celia, latter-day US political strategists have studied how Joseph Kennedy purchased the 1960 presidency for his son. He paid John's Ivy League writer-friends to ghost-write Profiles in Courage, the book and the movie that made JFK a World War II PT-109 hero. It later became assigned reading in many schools. Joe bought a seat in the US Senate for his hero as a steppingstone to the prime goal, the White House. But JFK was losing the 1960 presidential election to President Eisenhower's Vice President Richard Nixon, until his father asked his Mafia buddies to secure the pivotal states of Illinois and West Virginia. Thus, the Kennedys owed the Mafia, and the return of Cuba was the price they demanded.

In the White House itself, Kennedy carried on innumerable sexual escapades including an affair with Judith Exner, the girlfriend of Mafia kingpin Sam Giancana. But neither the Bay of Pigs disaster nor the sexual binging presented problems for President Kennedy. His public relations team and the docile media still lionized the good-looking and youthful president, equating it to the legendary Camelot of King Arthur.

"I had to learn the hard way," Celia wrote to Nora Peters in 1973, "the true meaning of Camelot as related to the Kennedy White House. While "Over the Rainbow" as related to the movie was beautiful and harmless, I discovered that Camelot as related to the Kennedy White House was ugly and hurtful."

Little Cuba's incredible victory at the Bay of Pigs would astound the world, thrusting the island more than ever onto the world stage. That didn't impress Celia, except she was now aware that the Soviet Union had taken notice. Even Arthur Schlesinger, Jr., a prime associate and apologist for Kennedy, wrote after the Bay of Pigs:

> The reality was that Fidel Castro turned out to be a far more formidable foe and in command of a far better organized regime than anyone had supposed. His patrols spotted the invasion at almost the first possible moment. His planes reacted with speed and vigor. His police eliminated any chance of sabotage or rebellion behind the lines. His soldiers stayed loyal and fought hard. He himself never panicked; and, if faults were chargeable to him, they were his overestimate of the strength of the invasion and undue caution in pressing the ground attack against the beachhead. His performance was impressive.

Celia too had "overestimated" the invasion force, telling Nora, "Fidel and I believed we would die because we would stand and fight and because we did not believe the US, the strongest nation in the world, would be so stupid as to attack a small island and lose."

In a letter dated September 3, 1974, Celia explained to Nora Peters what Cuba's victory at the Bay of Pigs meant to her:

> After the Bay of Pigs I hoped the pressure from the US people and the US media would blunt further military attacks and terrorist attacks on Cuba. America should be our friend and top trading partner, and it should be embarrassed for its support of Batista, the Batistianos, and the Mafia, especially now that most of the world is enlightened. But after the Bay of Pigs, I didn't know what to expect. But I knew this, Nora: As long as I lived or as long as Fidel lived, neither the Batistianos, the Mafia, nor the US capitalists would ever regain control of Cuba. And I was tired of terrorist acts from Florida killing the peasants and the tourists; and I was tired of anticipating gutless attacks like the Bay of Pigs. I preferred a big and definitive war, once and for all. After the Bay of Pigs, as America's targeting of Cuba resumed, I began looking far away to Russia. They had a bigger army than the US, and they had nuclear weapons. I wanted the terrorist attacks and Bay of Pigs attacks to end, even if it took a Big War to end it. I had nothing in common with Russia but the Bay of Pigs pricked my interest in Russia, an option I would cultivate if I had to.

John and Robert Kennedy, never held to account by either the US electorate nor the US media — were still in charge of the US government and the US military. Their hubris would only grow. The "Camelot" lie was now more obsessed than ever.

Georgia Anne Geyer, the nationally syndicated columnist, hates Fidel Castro to this day and she was no fan of his when she authored the Castro biography entitled *Guerrilla Prince*. And Geyer loved Camelot, then and now. Geyer described Kennedy (p. 181) "in the immediate aftermath of the Bay of Pigs" as being "humbled but still determined." Then Geyer wrote these painful but accurate words:

> John F. Kennedy, leader of the powerful United States, and Fidel Castro, leader of the small and "powerless" island nation of Cuba, were now competitors for what was, in effect, the soul of the developing world. Kennedy's pledge was...to defeat his nemesis, Fidel Castro. President Kennedy was inconsolable about the failure of the invasion, whose prospects in retrospect looked so clearly and criminally absurd that he could not believe he could have made such a mistake. While his brother [the president] agonized in the Oval Office, Bobby Kennedy grew more and more enraged over the failure and more determined than ever to get rid of Castro, this time in his own way. After all, the Kennedy brothers were supreme competitors, and this was their first — and perfect — failure. It was Bobby's "push-push-push" that would lead the Kennedy administration and the CIA to intensify "Operation Mongoose," a series of bizarre attempts to poison Castro, to assassinate him, even to make his beard fall off — and to do it with the help of the Mafia. The obsession with Castro would drive American policymakers to extremes they would never dream of entertaining in their relations with "real" countries. (p. 182.)

Real or not, the Cuba that Celia dreamed of, the land that she'd heard of once in a lullaby, would still stand and fight "Camelot."

Chapter 12. Spanish Eyes

In the pantheon of revolutionary icons, Celia Sánchez holds a few records, such as: the "greatest maker of Cuban history" (per Pablo Alvarez Tabío); the "greatest female revolutionary of all-time," (per Rich Haney); and "the greatest chronicler of the Cuban Revolution," (per fellow revolutionary heroine Marta Rojas, the internationally acclaimed author).

Cuban writers such as Marta Rojas and Carlos Franqui as well as noted American writers were all aware that Celia was a notorious note-taker and note-receiver, and that she preserved those records for posterity. Marta Rojas provided the author with copies of many notes and records that no other American writer has ever had access to.

Pedro Alvarez Tabío notes in the Cuban archives that "Celia Sánchez preserved even simple records such as the purchase of 'cough medicine' even as she also conducted the major aspects of the Sierra revolution, such as the guerrilla fighting. Her records are fetishistically meticulous." Celia told Nora Peters, "I did not want any lies about the revolution to take hold. If we needed to validate the revolution with lies, I would have been ashamed of it. All revolutions begin, I guess, with noble purposes. But many dissolve into greed and lust for power. Not my revolution, Nora."

The most famous note ever written by Fidel Castro was the one he penned to Celia Sánchez dated June 5, 1958, while they were fighting in the Sierras and while the outcome of the struggle against Batista was undecided. All such notes were kept by Celia Sánchez because she was very determined to maintain a true history of the Cuban Revolution. US historians and other anti-Castro writers use it to make the point that, from the very beginning, Fidel was determined to wage war against the US.

> Sierra Maestra June 5 '58
>
> Celia:
>
> After seeing the rockets they shot at Mario's house, I've sworn that the Americans are going to pay dearly for what they are doing. When this war is over, a much wider and bigger war will begin for me, the war I am going to wage against them. I realize that that is going to be my true destiny.
>
> Fidel

That note has been used over and over again to disparage Fidel Castro and the Cuban Revolution. But seldom if ever is the genesis of that note explained, although it is well known. Admitting to the event that inspired that note would give the other side of the story, and in the US that is not permitted when it comes to Cuba.

On June 5, 1958, Fidel had just seen the burned and mangled bodies of a peasant family in the foothills of the Sierras — a farmer, his wife, and their four children — after their home was targeted by a US jet flying in support of a Batista army. The farmer's name was Mario Sariol. Fidel knew Mario and his family well, and he knew they had nothing whatsoever to do with the war. Fidel and Celia had helped Mario's family with food and money. Like other peasant families in the area, they were wiped out merely to spite the rebels, the "peasant-lovers."

The aftermath of the April, 1961, Bay of Pigs attack has had unfortunate results for both the US and Cuba. Historian J.A. Sierra wrote: "Aside from being at once a major victory for the Cuban Revolution and a major embarrassment for Kennedy and the CIA, the attack at the Bay of Pigs set the stage for the major confrontation between the US and the Soviet Union: the missile crisis that brought the world to the brink of nuclear war. In the meantime, perhaps as a result of the Bay of Pigs embarrassment, Kennedy's obsession with eliminating Castro grew."

Celia Sánchez astutely labeled the Kennedy brothers "Three-year-olds, but three-year-olds with nuclear weapons to play with and a thirst for killing."

After the Bay of Pigs debacle, John McCone became CIA director. The Deputy Director of the CIA, Richard Bissell, was actually the man in charge of the Bay of Pigs; Bissell later blamed the CIA and ordered a full investigation, which was written by the CIA inspector general, Lyman Kirkpatrick. There were twenty copies of that report and McCone quickly destroyed nineteen of them. The twentieth copy was classified until 1998.

By that time the blind-folded US citizens had moved on. Cuba was no longer on their minds. Bamford unveiled material that included intriguing details such as a discussion between President Kennedy, the Joint Chiefs of Staff, and Secretary of Defense Robert McNamara regarding plans to blow up ships and airplanes in order to kill Americans and "blame it on Castro." And every year, the US pushes its embargo on Cuba. But, of the 196 nations that vote in the UN, the US can only purchase or intimidate just two votes — Israel's and the Marshall Island's — to support its Cuban embargo.

Richard Bissell, the Deputy Director of the CIA who was in charge of the Bay of Pigs attack, later wrote in *Reflections of a Cold Warrior: From Yalta to the Bay of Pigs,*

> To understand the Kennedy administration's obsession with Cuba, it is important to understand the Kennedys, especially Robert. From their perspective, Castro won the first round at the Bay of Pigs. He had defeated the Kennedy team; they were bitter and they could not tolerate his getting away with it. The president and his brother were ready to avenge their personal embarrassment by overthrowing their enemy at any cost. I don't believe there was significant policy debate in the executive branch on the desirability of getting rid of Castro. Robert Kennedy's involvement in organizing and directing Mongoose became so intense that he might as well have been deputy director for plans for the operation.

In Cuba, civilians were routinely targeted as signals to the leadership.

Assassination attempts against Cuba's leaders as well as attacks targeting Cuban hotels, factories, homes, and farms not only continued but accelerated. The assassins murdered Cuban civilians out of pure frustration or simple vengeance. The need to defend the island diverted a significant portion of resources to defense and away from the social programs that had already been instituted.

Celia's sole solace during this period was to break away from her work to attend daytime activities involving children. She loved watching the ballerina Alicia Alonso teaching the children at the Cuban National Ballet. She opened sports facilities for peasant children. Under tight security, she stood at home plate and spoke at the opening of a new baseball field on the edge of the city of Camagüey. She sat on the first row behind home plate and watched the first game played on that field, and then went onto the playing surface to personally hug every player on both teams.

By the time she got back to Havana, she was heartbroken to learn that a bomb had gone off in front of the press box in the third inning of the second game at Camagüey, killing four people.

This policy of violence resulted in part from Washington's partnership with notorious criminals. The ruthless dictator Fulgencio Batista had support from the Mafia, especially kingpins such as Meyer Lansky and Santo Traficante, Jr. These are names that pop up in many books exploring the underside of the Kennedy dynasty.

Next to Meyer Lansky, Traficante was the second most significant Mafia man in this business. Both had plush mansions in southern Florida. Traficante had two mansions in Tampa — at 2505 Bristol Avenue and at 3010 N. Boulevard Avenue; his mansion in Havana was located at Calle 12, No. 20 Vedado. Traficante also owned property in Miami, St. Petersburg, and Clearwater, Florida, as well as in New York.

Traficante was born in Tampa on November 15, 1914. On Batista's watch, the Mafia had the freedom to inundate Cuba with prostitution, gambling, and drugs. Traficante ran those illicit and lucrative activities in Havana. Batista provided Traficante two prime hotels in Havana — the Sans Souci and the Casino International. Traficante also directed operations at the Riviera, the Tropicana, the Sevilla Biltmore, the Capri, and the Havana Hilton hotel/casinos in Havana. He also owned such businesses as the Colombia Restaurant, the Nebraska Bar, the Tangerine Bar, and the Sands Bar in Tampa. When he was in Tampa, Traficante's Havana operations were watched over by James Longo. The main Mafia headquarters in Havana at this time was National Casino, which was owned by Meyer Lansky and run by his brother Jack. The Lanskys moved most of their key casino personnel from Las Vegas to Havana.

The Lanskys and Traficante organized a pipeline of Peruvian cocaine from Cuba to the US, with an associate named George Zarate. Other notorious US crime figures such as Norman Rothman joined Traficante in the Havana gambling, prostitution, and drug businesses.

All these names, locations, and activities were well known to the US government but as long as they appeared to enrich US entities, no action was taken to stop the crimes. American businesses or families owned most of the island's farms and many of the financial institutions and railroads.

Given their failure to bring Cuba back into the fold, Traficante and the other Mafia and Batistiano men developed a furious hatred for the Kennedy brothers. Traficante especially resented their failure to win back the Mafia's cash cow in Cuba. Now, the Kennedys had the Mafia as an enemy rather than a partner.

John was assassinated in 1963 and Robert in 1968. Giancana was killed by the Mafia for talking too much to reporters about the assassinations; but Traficante also famously talked — on a secret FBI wire tape. Traficante lamented one thing about the Kennedy assassinations. In hindsight, he said, "We should have killed Robert before we killed John."

In her seventeen letters to Nora Peters from 1959 to 1979, Celia Sánchez talked of specific historical events as "water over the dam." Yet, one of the most startling revelations in the letters concerned the assassinations. In a letter dated February 19, 1978, she said:

> When President John Kennedy was assassinated in 1963, I immediately knew Cuba would be blamed, Nora.... the triggerman Lee Harvey Oswald was quickly depicted in the US as being "pro-Cuban." I had to use all my sources, and I had many, in the US to prove to the US that Cuba had nothing at all to do with JFK's assassination. As usual, many sources inside the US government, including the military and even the CIA, were sympathetic to Cuba and volunteered vital data to me.... After that Cuba was not seriously blamed.... My policy, Cuba's policy, for all these years has been not to give the United States an excuse for an all-out attack on this island.

Celia was most concerned with avoiding and staving off assaults designed to "provoke" Cuba into actions that would give the US military a pretext to attack Cuba on behalf of the cabal in Florida.

A CIA agent named Grayson A. Lynch is credited with firing the first shot on behalf of the US in the Bay of Pigs attack on Cuba in April of 1961; Fidel Castro is credited with firing the last shot, a signal to his soldiers as they rounded up the last of the prisoners. Fidel later decided to send the prisoners back to the US in exchange for $53 million, and Celia Sánchez reluctantly agreed. Lynch proved that it was a risky choice. Once he was back in the US, he resumed working for the CIA in the continuing terrorist attacks on Cuba, and in July of 1998 Lynch admitted that he had directed 2,126 "clandestine CIA assaults on Cuba" from 1961 to 1967. He said he "personally participated in 113" of those assaults. In his book *Decision for Disaster: Betrayal at the Bay of Pigs*, Lynch blamed Kennedy "for canceling the air attacks in fear of widening US involvement." Lynch and other CIA operatives, as well as Carlos Marcello, never forgave Kennedy for that decision. Marcello would later tap into that CIA dissension when he devised his plans to assassinate both Kennedy brothers. The FBI heard Carlos Marcello discussing such plans when they taped telephone conversations from his small office located in a New Orleans motel.

On May 1, 1961, two weeks after the Bay of Pigs attack, Fidel Castro led a May Day celebration in Havana. Much of the world listened as he said:

Humble, honest blood was shed in the struggle against the mercenaries of impe-rialism. But what blood, what men did imperialism send here to establish that beachhead, to bleed our revolution dry, to destroy our achievements, to burn our cane? We can tell the people right here that at the same instant that three of our air-ports were being bombed, the Yankee agencies were telling the world that our air-ports had been attacked by planes from our own air force. They cold-bloodedly bombed our nation and told the world that the bombing was done by Cuban pilots with Cuban planes. This was done with planes on which they painted our insignia. The world's strongest nation attacked our island, David vs. Goliath, and they lost.

The dismay that overwhelms America's naïve admirers around the world when they see beneath the surface is touchingly reflected in a note from Celia in her later years.

Growing up as a girl in Media Luna, Nora, my father had the best library in the province. I loved reading about the American Revolution that broke away from England. I also learned that Thomas Jefferson, who wrote your Declaration of Inde-pendence, later wrote in two letters to well-known friends that his greatest fear for the new US democracy was the threat from what he termed "unchecked capital-ism." As I observed what the US-installed Batista dictatorship was doing in Cuba, as I fought in the Sierras against Batista, as I have struggled all these years since 1959 against the murderous terrorism from southern Florida, I have recognized all along the way exactly what Thomas Jefferson warned about so long ago. The capi-talism that fueled America's unrivaled economic growth began to take over your democracy when it could buy up your prime politicians and thus eliminate the checks and balances that Jefferson envisioned and hoped would rein it in. Then, in Cuba and elsewhere, the unchecked capitalists began to devour little nations, using a secretive and powerful governmental organ, the CIA, to do its bidding whenever and wherever it chose. That's how the US could stamp out any hints of democracy in these little countries because the capitalists wanted puppet dictators, not democracies... in democracies that wealth would be spent on its own people and on its own infrastructures. In that manner, the democratic leader the Cuban people wanted, Antonio Guiteras, was murdered so Fulgencio Batista could be Cuba's US-beloved dictator.... But the point I make, Nora, is this: If the US capitalists ... do not care about [Cubans], will they care about the working class or the middle class, while they rob America blind, which they surely will do? The capitalists who robbed Cuba and so many other helpless nations blind by blocking democracy and installing their own thieving dictators will surely destroy democracy in America by simply buying it up."

José Basulto epitomizes the type of individuals utilized by the US gov-ernment, especially the CIA, to terrorize Cuba. Basulto is a Cuban exile who was dropped off in Cuba by the CIA as a saboteur to blow up bridges and railroad tracks prior to the Bay of Pigs attack. He was carrying out his assignment when he heard and then saw the US warplanes begin their bombing. José bragged that he ran to safety and jumped the fence at the US-controlled Guantanamo Naval Base on Cuba's southeastern tip. Afterwards, Basulto simply melded back into the Batistiano stronghold.

The US government has supported and protected all of Basulto's activities. In their book *The Fish Is Red*, Warren Hinckle and William Turner write that the cannon attack on the Cuban hotel in 1962, in which Basulto led the exile attack group DRE (Directorio Revolucionario Estudiantil), "was a raid carefully planned and approved by the CIA." Basulto's CIA training occurred in Guatemala.

As Basulto told the *Wall Street Journal* in 1987, he was closely tied to the Oliver North-directed Iran-Contra scandal; notorious CIA agent Felix Rodriguez told the Kerry Congressional Committee that he and other Contra leaders, Enrique Bermudez and Adolfo Calero, met at Basulto's Miami home. In his book *Shadow Warrior*, Rodriguez states that he and Basulto "have been like brothers" since their Guatemalan training days prior to the Bay of Pigs. Miguel Recarey reportedly had a budget of $30 million a month as part of the Contra scandal that otherwise was funded by the CIA, Oliver North's illicit operation, and by drug trafficking. Rodriguez ran the Contra operation at Ilopango Air Force Base in El Salvador that was primarily involved with "smuggling cocaine and marijuana," according to an article dated January 20, 1987, in the *New York Times*. Celerino Castillo, the DEA agent who compiled the data for the Kerry Commission, wrote that "Hundreds of flights each week through Ilopango delivered cocaine to the buyers and returned with money headed for Panama. From Panama, the money was wired to a Costa Rican bank account held by the Contras." In his 1994 book *Powderburns: Cocaine, Contras, and the Drug War*, Celerino Castillo further detailed those operations. The CIA directed illicit drug-running to support the infamous Contra deeds in Nicaragua and the assaults on Cuba. Felix Rodriguez, who escaped Cuba when Batista was ousted in 1959, trained with the CIA-funded Brigade 2506 that attacked Cuba at the Bay of Pigs in 1961. Rodriguez entitled his biography *Shadow Warrior: The CIA Hero*.

Rodriguez was the main CIA agent assigned to capture Cuba's famed revolutionary hero Che Guevara in Bolivia in 1967, and it was Rodriguez who interrogated Che. Before Che was executed on orders of the CIA, Rodriguez stole his Rolex watch. In his book, Rodriguez says that he wears Che's watch as a souvenir "to this day."

And to this day, CIA operatives such as Felix Rodriguez and José Basulto target Cuba with the intention of overthrowing the revolution. In 1991, Basulto founded *Brothers to the Rescue*. He defines it as a benevolent, charitable organization based in Miami to rescue Cubans in the waters between Cuba and Florida. Cuba has always defined *Brothers* as one of many anti-Cuban terrorist groups. For decades, groups such as Brothers to the Rescue, the Cuban-American National Foundation, and even the US Interests Section in Havana concoct schemes designed to provoke Cuba into some action that can be used to justify the US treatment of Cuba. For example, in 1996 the Clinton Administration was ready to ease the US embargo of Cuba, with the blessing of the US Congress. Basulto himself flew a Brothers to the Rescue airplane directly over Havana, dropping leaflets and scaring the Cuban people. Most nations, including the US, would have shot down such an intruder. Cuba instead chose to file protests with the US State Department and the UN. The over-flights continued, as did the Cuban protests. Finally, Cuba proclaimed that if the over-flights did not stop, it would be forced to take action.

In the Miami media, Cuba was ridiculed by spokesmen for Brothers to the Rescue for being "unable to do anything" to stop the incursions. The US State Department did nothing. Basulto was the lead pilot in a three-plane convoy that headed back to Cuba on February 24, 1996. This time two Cuban MIG fighters, piloted by the young Perez-Perez brothers, went out to meet them. Basulto's plane turned back to Miami but the other two planes were shot down and the four occupants were killed. As usual, only one side of that story is told in the US media; there is no context provided, no mention of the unlawful over-flights, of Cuba's pleas to the US and the UN, of the bragging and the pledges to continue the abuse in the Miami media. Instead, almost without fail, the downing of the two "Brothers" planes is depicted as a mercy mission that was heartlessly destroyed. And, as usual, Cuba paid a price. Not only were the plans to ease the Cuban embargo scuttled, a much harsher anti-Cuban embargo, via the Helms-Burton Act, was rammed through Congress. Lawyers for "victims" of the downed planes quickly sued and easily won a $189 million judgment. The major *Associated Press* article in the *Miami Herald* on January 21, 2005, reported from Fort Lauderdale that José Basulto himself had just been awarded $1.7 million as a judgment against Cuba relating to his 1996 provocation against Cuba.

Should Cuba, for balance, be able to hold trials in Havana without US representation and sue Batistianos such as José Basulto, Orlando Bosch, and Luis Posada Carriles for acts they have publicly bragged about?

The January 21 article in the *Miami Herald* began with these words:

> Cuba was ordered by a US judge Friday to pay $1.75 million to a Miami pilot who was "scared to death" in 1996 when Cuban MIGs attacked his flight of three private planes over the Florida Straits, downing the two other planes. Although the pilot, José Basulto, evaded the jets and was able to fly home, he deserves the money because he was traumatized by the knowledge that his four companions in the

other two light planes of Brothers to the Rescue had been killed, said US District Judge Kenneth A. Marra.

That article never mentions the provocations, Cuba's efforts to stop them, Cuba's rights under international law to protect itself, and the fact that Cuba was not represented in the courtroom.

In the early 1960s, Celia Sánchez had set in motion programs to drastically upgrade the living standards and, in stark contrast to the Batista regime, she made it a very salient point that Cuba's resources not be pocketed by governmental officials.

To her, government work was a "public service," not a means to enrich someone personally.

In 2003, according to a major article in the *Miami Herald*, the Batistianos, namely the Cuban-American National Foundation, publicly offered Felipe Peréz Roque a chance to be "in the post-Castro government" if he would defect to their side. They seem to believe that cynicism, American-style, must have infiltrated the island by now, even if an appreciation for bare-knuckle free market capitalism has not.

Felipe Peréz Roque is a public servant and may perhaps become the next leader of Cuba, if an informal poll of the citizenry is any guide. (I base my opinion on feedback from Cuban peasants; I utilized a car and driver to traverse the island in 2004, and the peasants with whom I spoke invariably mentioned their love for Peréz Roque and equated him to Celia Sánchez. They accept the fact that when Fidel dies his also elderly brother Raúl would likely be Cuba's leader, albeit briefly. After that transition, they believe the Castro brothers will not (posthumously or otherwise) block their path to democracy. However, they believe the Batistiano-dominated US government will block them — but only after the US showers Cuba with "billions of dollars to ease the Miami Mafia back to power," to quote Alfredo Carvajal Fuentes, a farmer in Oriente province. Most Cubans I encountered refer to the exiles in Florida as "the Miami Mafia.")

In the early 1960s, Celia Sánchez lived in her 11th Street apartment in Havana as she tried desperately to preserve Cuba's resources for the people.

Celia clung quixotically to the hope that the attacks would cease, that the US military and the US treasury would stop supporting the continuing quest to regain Cuba. She was wrong, and that miscalculation pained her deeply and everlastingly. The protective cocoon that she tried so hard to create for Cuban children was still penetrated by a range of terrorist acts emanating from the Cuban exiles in Florida.

Both Cuban and US history document CIA-funded airplane bombings of sugar mills in Pinar del Río and Camagüey provinces in the 1960s as well as attacks on tobacco farms in Matanzas province and elsewhere. In Las Villas province, an airplane strafed a train full of civilian passengers. Within a five-day span saboteurs bombed three Havana stores, two Santa Clara stores, and one store in Santiago. Between the towns of Colón and Sagua la Grande southeast of Havana, an airplane flew low over a sugar cane field. A fifteen-year-old girl named Alina Peréz Torres scooped up her three-year-old sister Vivian from the edge of the field and ducked into a holding shed. The airplane circled back and bombed the shed. Celia Sánchez attended the funeral of the Torres sisters in Colón, and peered down into the single casket in which Alina was still holding her little sister. Someone snapped a black-and-white picture of Celia as she leaned down and kissed Alina's forehead.

Just before and just after that funeral in Colón, the Soviet Union sent high-level trade missions to Havana. The most important such mission was headed by Russia's Deputy Premier Anastas Mikoyan, second in power only to Khrushchev.

Mikoyan arrived on a day when Celia was to host the arrival of twelve rural girls honored with free scholarships to Alicia Alonso's ballet academy. She skipped the official reception that greeted Mikoyan at the airport, leaving the task to be performed by Fidel and Che. After preliminary agreements preceding Mikoyan's trip, Russia's second-in-command was to sign the final trade papers. That meeting was scheduled for 11:00 A.M. in the conference room at the Palace of the Revolution. Celia was due back from the ballet academy for that session, where she would meet Mikoyan for the first time. However, she was so beguiled by the girls that she was late leaving the academy.

Celia didn't arrive at the meeting until 11:55 A.M. She wore a baseball cap with her ponytail sticking out the back, and she didn't have time to shower and change. Fidel was embarrassed and Mikoyan was miffed — Fidel would not start the session without her. All eleven men stood in silence. There was a palpable tension in the room.

Later, back in Moscow, Mikoyan would tell his associates that "That session was held up for an hour while we twiddled our thumbs and waited for what turned out to be the little ashtray girl wearing a baseball hat. Cubans, I thought to myself! Of course, I quickly learned she was more than that. The big meeting *just couldn't begin* without her. In the next two days, she made the final decisions for Cuba, some of which Castro and myself didn't fully agree with but we signed them anyway" (Herbert L. Matthews "Missile Crisis Revisited," *The New York Times*, April 17, 1965).

Mikoyan had a three-day stay in Havana. He was smitten with the "ashtray girl," especially after he figured out why they had waited for her. Mikoyan would learn that Celia, with the full backing of Fidel and Che, not only "made the final decisions for Cuba" but that she was the legendary fighter of the Sierras.

At the gala dinner marking Mikoyan's last night in Havana, the brash Russian refused to be separated from her and flirted shamelessly. Celia, always pragmatic, sweetly accepted the adoration. He gave her a nickname, *"Spanish Eyes."*

In the coming days, Celia and Mikoyan exchanged cables and telephone conversations, severely taxing their translators at times. "I didn't want to use Mikoyan," Celia told Nora Peters, "but I cultivated him in case I did need him." Meanwhile, the relentless attacks from Florida continued unabated; a mother and daughter were killed by a bomb at a cigar factory in the city of Manzanillo, where Celia's reputation as a fearless recruiter of rebel fighters and supplies had first surfaced.

After attending the funeral, Celia spent the night with Fidel on the fourth floor of the Cohiba Hotel. Celia composed a cable for Moscow. Here, word-for-word, is that cable:

> Deputy Premier Mikoyan:
>
> I am tired, my friend, of the continuous terror attacks from Florida that almost daily now kill Cuban peasants, including children, as if they are just pawns to be stomped on to smite the Cuban leaders. The US has nuclear missiles aimed at Russia from Turkish soil. I propose that Russia install nuclear missiles on Cuban soil aimed directly at the US. Such missiles at least in stages can be transported on the big Russian ships that now enter our harbors. I will not permit Cuba to use terror attacks against Florida in retaliation for the terror attacks against us because of the innocent civilians that would be hurt. But I would love to fight the terrorists and their US soldier-backers. They have nuclear missiles. So do you. I want to counter their missiles with missiles of our own. Then, if they want to fight face-to-face instead of just as cowards targeting innocent children, I and a few million other Cubans would love to fight them as tenaciously as we fought in the Sierras and at the Bay of Pigs. Let me know your feelings as soon as you study this cable.
>
> With much love,
>
> Spanish Eyes

CHAPTER 13. THE WORLD TREMBLES

The "Spanish Eyes" cable from Celia Sánchez to Russia's Deputy Premier Anastas Mikoyan set in motion the "Cuban Missile Crisis" of 1962, the closest the world has ever come to a nuclear holocaust. Shy, modest, genteel, and always ready to give the appearance of being deferential to Fidel and Che, Celia not only accepted this image but orchestrated it. If Fidel and Che were projected as the dominant forces, it was because Celia had decided that was the way it would be. But she reserved for herself the final decisions on all major issues pertaining to the revolution and to the new Cuba. No one in the Sierras or in Havana challenged her, least of all Fidel and Che.

Celia told Nora Peters that her "Spanish Eyes" cable to Mikoyan was written and sent before Fidel was aware of it. She was confident that Fidel would and did support her 100%, even when he disagreed with her. The "Spanish Eyes" cable is usually ignored by historians, even though it can now be found in the Cuban archives translated from Spanish to English, Russian, and French; and since 1993, shortly after the collapse of the Soviet Union, it can be found in the Russian archives. Only in the mid-1980s, after Celia's death, did it find its way to the Cuban archives because, till then, it was kept among Celia's secret papers in Havana's Office of Historic Affairs, which was solely created by the historic-minded Celia herself, the Celia who always wanted the true history of the Cuban Revolution to be meticulously documented.

The Office of Historic Affairs in Havana housed a blue, shoebox-sized little container that held twenty-eight different Celia-related documents, including the "Spanish Eyes" cable. A white note in black ink on that box said: "Till my death only/then Cuban archives."

In all this author's research, Nora Peters stands out as nearly the only American who could distinguish Celia Sánchez from Peter Pan. That is under-standable. Like a novelist creating antagonists and protagonists, the Batistianos in partnership with the US government easily constructed Fidel Castro and Che Guevara as the prime villains in the US-Cuban imbroglio. In doing so, the strategy has always been to avoid, if possible, the mention of two names — Ful-gencio Batista and Celia Sánchez. Batista was not only a dictator but also a thief and a murderer, so the less he is mentioned, the better. Unbound by any inconve-nient association to him, the misinformed US citizens can be continually hit with the mantra: "Our only goal is to RETURN freedom and democracy to Cuba!" By the same token, any mention of Celia Sánchez accentuates the brave and selfless aspects of the Cuban Revolution. Any critique of Celia would reveal her extraordinary devotion to the Cuban populace, especially the children.

***

On October 22, 1962, President John Kennedy told the national television audiences that Russian nuclear missiles aimed at the US had been installed on the nearby island of Cuba. Everyone trembled that night, and the trembling didn't begin to subside till the end of that week — on Sunday, the 28th of October — when Kennedy announced that the Russians had finally agreed to withdraw those missiles.

One misconception in America about the missile crisis is that Cuba was just a pawn caught between the two superpowers. That is not so. According to the record left by Celia, little Cuba had the audacity to request the missiles. This claim is buttressed by the acute remembrances of Sergei Khrushchev, a highly regarded historian and professor at Brown University. At the time of the missile crisis, Sergie was a key advisor at his father Nikita's side. He wrote a long article about the missile crisis that was published in the October 2002 edition of *American Heritage Magazine.* He portrays Kennedy and Nikita Khrushchev as fearing the nuclear confrontation this stand off could lead to. Indeed, Nikita Khrushchev cabled orders to Havana that US spy planes flying over Cuba were not — ABSOLUTELY NOT — to be fired at or in any way harmed. But a Cuban missile did shoot down a US plane over Cuba and the pilot was killed. Kennedy, just as frightened as Khrushchev, did nothing.

Sergei Khrushchev wrote, in *American Heritage*: "But at almost the same time Father sent orders not to shoot down American planes, Fidel Castro issued a command to open fire on them. Yankee aircraft were making themselves at home in Cuban skies just as in Batista's day and he (Fidel) had no doubt that his northern neighbor would recognize only force. He was the president of Cuba, and the planes were flying over his not Soviet territory. Told about the downing of the U-2 spy plane, Kennedy rejected a proposal for an immediate and all-out attack on the Soviet anti-aircraft batteries in Cuba. The president wanted to know if it was a chance attack or if Moscow had hardened its position. One possibility he did not admit was that Castro, who everyone in Washington thought was nothing more than a puppet of the Kremlin, might act independently. Thus, Castro was the focus, not Father and not Kennedy."

Sergei Khrushchev then wrote that the next day six American F-8U spy planes flew over Cuba, "hugging the ground and hiding behind every hill." When those planes returned to America, Sergei said they were riddled "with holes from 30-millimeter shells. This was reported to Kennedy. Everything indicated that the U-2 had been shot down deliberately. Still the president decided not to act."

According to these reports, Havana was not a pawn between Washington and Moscow during the crisis. In fact, Havana is depicted as responsible for the risky confrontation. That image may flatter Cuba as much as it appears to absolve the superpowers for reckless conduct.

Celia Sánchez had an acute mind and an acute memory. Even so, it is a matter of some wonder that years after the Cuban Missile Crisis, she correctly remembered the name of the US pilot of that downed spy plane, Rudy Anderson; and she correctly remembered those tough Russian names — General Issa Pliyev and Colonel Georgy Voronkov.

In October of 2002, the 76-year-old Fidel Castro hosted a series of meetings in Havana marking the 40th anniversary of the Cuban Missile Crisis. At his side were key Cuban leaders such as Felipe Pérez Roque, Ricardo Alarcón, José Ramón Fernández, and Ramon Valdés. The Russian delegation included Anatoly Gribkov, the Soviet general who directed Operation Anadyr, the code name for the installation of the missiles in Cuba; Dmitry Yazov, the former Russian defense minister who led an elite army unit that protected the Cuban missiles; and even Sergo Mikoyan, the son of Russia's 1962 Deputy Premier Anastas Mikoyan, the man who called Celia "Spanish Eyes."

Americans who were deeply involved in the missile crisis also attended, including the then Secretary of Defense Robert McNamara and key White

House aides such as Arthur Schlesinger, Jr., Richard Goodwin, and Ted Sorensen. Ethel Kennedy, widow of then Attorney General Robert Kennedy, was also there. All the Americans in Havana for that 2002 anniversary were warmly greeted by Fidel Castro, who was pictured shaking hands with McNamara, the US secretary of defense who was not only deeply involved in the Bay of Pigs attack and the Cuban Missile Crisis but was also a key man in devising Operation Mongoose, America's code name for the all-out attempts to murder Fidel Castro.

The event was widely covered by the media. Don Bohning of the *Miami Herald* noted that "a number of intriguing and previously unknown disclosures were made." The first such example was: "The important role played in the decision to install the missiles by Operation Mongoose, the US covert action program against Cuba." Thus, at the 2002 conference in Havana, the US delegation finally admitted Operation Mongoose's role in the Missile Crisis. History as well as US documents plainly register the fact that Kennedy tried to destroy Cuba. Also at the 2002 Havana conference, Arthur Schlesinger and Robert McNamara admitted to having roles in Operation Mongoose and confirmed that it was a precursor to the missile crisis. Bohning went on to say, "If there was a single theme underlying the two days of discussions, it was the role of Operation Mongoose as a catalyst for the crisis. Both the Russian and Cuban delegations left little doubt that they saw Operation Mongoose as the precursor to an invasion." And of course the key American Arthur Schlesinger Jr. concurred with that.

***

During the 2002 40-year anniversary of the Cuban Missile Crisis, all the American TV networks craved interviews with Fidel Castro. Castro granted ABC's Barbara Walters an exclusive interview, which was aired on ABC's 20/20 program. Fidel remembered back a quarter of a century when Barbara Walters had interviewed him in Cuba and had treated him fairly.

In the 20/20 interview, the 76-year-old Castro was both insightful and charming, always enthusiastically calling his renowned host, "Barbara!" He told Ms. Walters that back in 1962 he had told Nikita Khrushchev not to lie to President Kennedy about the nuclear missiles in Cuba. "Kennedy believed what Khrushchev told him," Fidel told Walters. "Therefore Kennedy was misled. That was a very big mistake on the part of Khrushchev, one that we opposed vehemently."

In one of history's startling paradoxes, on November 22, 1963, Celia Sánchez was heartbroken when she got word in Havana that John Kennedy had been assassinated in Dallas. One of Kennedy's very last communications with a foreign leader was his exchange of notes with Celia, designed to belatedly "normalize" relations between the two neighbors. As will be shown in the following chapter, this exchange included the first ever conciliatory cable from the US to Cuba, and Celia's sweet letter back to JFK, an exchange that, sadly, helped seal the fate of the young US president. JFK had many enemies, even including associates of Vice President Lyndon Johnson — who resented the fact that he was blocking the path to the White House — and included elements of the Batistianos in Florida, the CIA, and the Mafia. The startling change in Kennedy's attitude toward Cuba was the preamble to his assassination, an event that devastated Celia Sánchez because she feared that it also marked the death knell of any possible future overtures on America's part in defiance of the Batistianos and the Mafia who are determined to thwart normalized relations with Cuba.

CHAPTER 14. THE BATISTIANOS

It was the Eisenhower-Nixon White House in April of 1959 that informed Havana that America would not allow a democratic Cuba controlled by the popular vote, but instead wanted another Batista-type regime that would give US businesses and the Mafia control of the economy. But it was the presidency of John F. Kennedy that raised the stakes, with an unimaginable succession of assassination, terrorism, and military attacks emanating from Florida.

Decent members of the US media who have dared to challenge or denounce the Batistianos have discovered that their efforts are futile, leading them to otherwise unthinkable "suicidal tendencies," as the pro-Batista Mafia terms it. ABC-TV anchorwoman Lisa Howard in New York in 1965, News Director Emilio Milán of WQBA Radio in Miami in 1976, and noted author/newspaperman Gary Webb in 2004 in California are prime examples of "suicides" resulting from notable reporting critical of Batistiano or CIA actions against Cuba.

Decent members of the US government who question America's Batistiano-directed Cuban policy are just as unfortunate. Ana Belén Montes is perhaps the best example of this. In 2002, Belén Montes was sentenced to twenty-five years in prison for "being the most senior spy for Cuba ever to penetrate the top ranks of US intelligence." For seventeen years she had an impeccable record as the top Cuban expert and a senior analyst for the Defense Intelligence Agency. She was a highly respected State Department expert on Cuba who was not recruited by Cuba and was not paid by Cuba, but who informed Cuba of covert action upcoming from the US. She simply did this to save lives in Cuba and she was never accused of harming any American. But her case was heard in an anti-Cuban courtroom presided over by an anti-Cuban judge named Ricardo M. Urbina.

Because Ana was the State Department's top expert on Cuba and knew many things, she could have plea-bargained and offered an apology or a sign "of repentance." She refused, choosing instead to read a statement in court: "Your Honor, I engaged in the activity that brought me before you because I obeyed my conscience rather than the law. I believe our government's policy towards Cuba is cruel and unfair, profoundly unneighborly, and I felt morally obligated to help the island defend itself from our efforts to impose our values and political system on it. We have displayed intolerance and contempt towards Cuba for most of the last four decades. My greatest desire is to see amicable relations emerge between the United States and Cuba. I hope my case in some way will encourage our government to abandon its hostility towards Cuba and to work with Havana in a spirit of tolerance, mutual respect, and understanding. Today we see more clearly than ever that hatred and intolerance — by individuals and governments — spread only pain and suffering."

Meanwhile many terrorists — such as the well-known figures who have boasted of killing seventy-three people via a suitcase bomb that downed a Cuban airplane in 1976 — still roam free and are cheered as heroes by the four members of the US Congress from Florida — Lincoln Diaz-Balart, Mario Diaz-Balart, Ileana Ros-Lehtinen, and Mel Martinez. Meanwhile, the compassionate Ana Belén Montes, considered by many to be a political prisoner, is in a federal prison. In a way, she too has essentially "committed suicide" by trying to bring conscience to America's Cuban policy.

Her statement in court concluded: "I hope for a US policy that recognizes that Cuba, like any nation, wants to be treated with dignity and not with contempt. Such a policy would bring our government back in harmony with the compassion and generosity of the American people. It would allow both Cubans and Americans to learn from and share with each other. It would enable Cuba to drop its defensive measures and permit the two neighbors to work together to promote tolerance and cooperation."

Ana Belén Montes sacrificed her successful and fulfilling life trying to save Cuban lives.

The *Miami Herald* generally shows a strong bias against Cuba and its reporter Tim Johnson called Ana "a turncoat for Cuba." Yet, his October 17, 2002 article included a lengthy report on her trial and included her statement to the court; he coyly claims it is "Still a mystery is what motivated Montes."

In many instances the anti-Castro Cuban exile-zealots use the courtrooms that they control to punish Cuba and via the US treasury they reap financial rewards, exploiting frozen Cuban bank accounts in America and loopholes such as the 17% of AT&T revenues for Cuban telephone calls that by contract is supposed to go to Cuba. Instead, it goes to the US government, which then funnels it to the Cuban exiles. Brothers to the Rescue, which Cuba and others consider a terrorist group, received $93 million in 2001 when George Bush ruled the White House.

A young man named Juan Pablo Roque was arrested in southern Florida and charged with being "a Cuban spy perpetrating a scheme intended to infiltrate Miami's exile community." Then his ex-wife, Ana Margarita Martínez, sued Roque. In the Miami-Dade Circuit Court system, Martínez was awarded $27.18 million by Judge Alan Postman. Her lawyer, Fernando Zulueta, was quoted in the November 19, 2002, *Miami Herald* as saying, "Cuba should pay their debts like anyone else." On April 29, 2005, an update by the Reuters News Agency in Miami revealed how such money is collected: "President Bush on Friday ordered that $198,000 in frozen Cuban funds be sent to a Miami woman who sued Cuba for rape because her husband turned out to be a spy for Fidel Castro's government. Ana Margarita Martinez married Juan Pablo Roque in 1995 but months later he left her to go back to Cuba. A Miami judge ruled that the couple's sexual relations constituted rape because of the deception."

Roque (and Cuba), of course, were not represented in that courtroom, and neither were the US taxpayers. The Bush administration routinely lavishes US treasury checks on the Batistianos, tax money that otherwise could go to causes that serve the average American.

A column written by Marie Cocco of *Newsday* on May 26, 2002, indicates that the Bush administration gives them money even when the Batistianos have said they do not need it.

> With many eager hands outstretched, it is hard to imagine the US government would try to give cash to people who do not want it. Yet that is what Washington insists on for Cuba's dissidents. Cuba policy is an image in a funhouse mirror. The American trade and tourism embargo, an anachronism of the Cold War, against Fidel Castro's government continues while the rest of the world soaks up the sun and investment opportunities. The Bush administration has peopled the foreign-policy apparatus with Cuban exiles and their sympathizers. So far in the geopolitical struggle between the farm states and South Florida, Miami is winning. It holds the keys to the White House and the Florida governor's mansion, after all.

This is a dreadful embarrassment. But not more so than the US determination to finance Castro's political resistance, despite pleas from the resisters themselves that we close our wallets. Then there is the International Republican Institute, a Washington-based organization with close ties to the Bush administration. The institute was a supporter of opposition groups that staged an unsuccessful coup against the democratically elected president of Venezuela, a coup the White House seemed to welcome. Institute officials also served as back-channel contacts between the Venezuelan plotters and the Bush administration. Now they are to 'build solidarity with Cuba's human rights activists.' This list could go on but even in this funhouse, the picture is clear enough. When it comes to Cuba, we do not strive for success. Only for domestic political gain and international shame.

"Funhouse?" Cocco has used an apt description of the Bush administration, and "international shame" is an apt term for the administration's Cuban policy. President Bush has put Otto Reich and Roger Noriega, two men whom Cuba consider terrorists, in charge of "Cuban and Latin American affairs." The coup that attempted to overthrow Venezuela's elected president, Hugo Chávez (because of his close ties to Cuba), was just one in a continuing string of anti-Cuban offshoots of the Reich/Noriega-orchestrated Cuban policy that is harmful and costly to Americans.

USA Today founder and columnist Al Neuharth repeatedly has used the word "shameful" to describe America's Cuban policy. The *New York Times* in a famous editorial called it "indecent." Penelope Purdy, an editorial writer for the *Denver Post*, writes that America's Cuban policy for all these decades "has been conducted with the IQ of a salamander."

Meanwhile, lawyers in Miami get rich by finding someone like Ana Margarita Martínez.. In the October 19, 2002, Miami Herald, staff writers Jennifer Babson and Luisa Yáñez wrote of the $93 million given to the Brothers' families: "That success emboldened others, such as Ada Martínez, who have claims against Cuba, to take the Cuban government to court." To court in Florida, that is, where Cuba is not represented.

And, how about another of those partners in crime who were dipping so deeply into Cuba's economy — Sam Giancana? As John Morgan explained in *Prince of Crime*, "Sam Giancana, always active in Cuba, seems to have been persuaded by rogue elements in the CIA that he could play a heroic role (in the retaking of Cuba)." Joseph Geringer, in his book *Sam Giancana: Live and Die By the Sword*, wrote, "When Fidel Castro took over Cuba, ousting Batista, the Mafia winced. With his regime came the end of their gambling and whoring in that country, and something had to be done about that. The CIA agreed. As it had done many times before and would do many times in the future the CIA married the Mafia for convenience."

Both Giancana biographers recount that he received $150,000 of CIA money for his personal attempt to kill Fidel Castro after several CIA attempts had failed. Geringer states, "President Kennedy knew of the conspiracy and sanctioned it; so did the FBI chief J. Edgar Hoover. Mafia bosses like Santo Traficante played their various roles, inciting Batista loyalists to move against Castro while delivering arms to anti-Castro Cubans off the Florida coast. One of the gun runners was a man named Jack Ruby, a close associate of New Orleans Mafia boss Carlos Marcello."

Many of these names have been implicated with the darkest episodes of recent US history, including the JFK assassination. It was Jack Ruby, of course, who pulled off another job for Carlos Marcello: silencing Lee Harvey Oswald, whom history has declared was one of the Kennedy assassins.

To call Batistiano-controlled southern Florida a Banana Republic is not fair to other weak and struggling republics, some of which are only partially corrupt. All of southern Florida's major entities intended to serve its citizens are goldmines for a handful of fortunate leaders. Take, for example, the Miami-Dade County School System or the Miami-Dade County International Airport.

Carl Hiaasen is the top columnist for the *Miami Herald* and also a noted author. His column on December 22, 2002, notes: "Once again we learn that airport riches are flowing copiously to friends and political cronies of Miami-Dade Mayor Alex Penelas. Once again, he claims to know nothing about it.

> This time the disgrace involves an outfit called World Wide Concessions, made up of so-called minority partners who were supposed to run eight restaurants at Miami International in association with Host Marriott Services....Gosh, you don't suppose that World Wide was set up as a front for Host, which needed minority participation to land the 10-year concession contract? The fellow who arranged this lucrative little charade is Chris Korge, a local lobbyist who for years has had Penelas on a leash. Korge is a big fundraiser, for the mayor in particular. His sticky fingerprints can be found on virtually every major MIA contract approved since Penelas joined the county commission in 1990. In the voluminous annals of airport sleaze, the Host Marriott deal will go down as a classic. It's very common knowledge that nobody does business at MIA without piercing out the mayor's pals, so Host went right to the top. Not only did the company hire Korge as a lobbyist, it agreed to pay him 10 percent of its final take on the deal. An additional 10 percent was routed to Paula Gomez, another Penelas fund-raiser. No one seems exactly sure what Gomez does at the airport to earn all that money. Don't worry. It gets worse. The "minority partners" at WWC quietly send 10 percent of their net profits to Rodney Barreto, another influential lobbyist. A second 10 percent goes directly to Korge.

The state of Florida and the US government look the other way. Yet, even as the taxpayers are bilked for the benefit of the Cuban "ex-pats" and projects such as Miami International Airport and the Miami-Dade County School System languish, the lust to regain control of Cuba has never subsided.

The only way to "cure" the evils of Florida's banana republic is to rein in the leaders and make them accountable. That won't happen; those leaders spend large portions of their revenues courting favor with governors like Jeb Bush and presidents like George W. Bush, who know what to do if they want to keep the campaign contributions coming in.

On May 2, 2000, *Denver Post*'s Penelope Purdy discussed what she called the "folly in US-Latin American policy." She was livid about the US treatment of Cuba under the pretence of "getting rid of Castro," and pointed out that the "regime that preceded him hardly qualified for sainthood."

Celia Sánchez wrote a letter to Nora Peters in 1978, shortly after she had been diagnosed with cancer: "You .... worried about ... how tired and sad I am these days. Perhaps my phone call encouraged that, although it was not my intention. I weigh 93 pounds and today I promised Fidel that I will be at 100 pounds by the time you get here. Actually, Nora, I am not sad. I am at peace with my influence on the Cuban landscape as I gaze at it each day. I believe I have done all I could do."

Penelope Purdy wrote in the article mentioned above, "Yet even as we raged against Castro we supported Haiti's Papa Doc and Baby Doc Duvalier, among the most ruthless despots ever in the Western Hemisphere. And as we chided Castro about open elections, we ignored the dearth of democracy elsewhere. In Guatemala, we supported a corrupt, latter-day feudal system, mostly because it enabled US businesses to keep laborers in dismal working conditions. Over much of Central America your US tax dollars figuratively fertilized the killing fields. In Nicaragua, we were the chief champions of the greedy, brutal Somoza regime. In both Guatemala and Nicaragua, US-backed forces, who often learned their brutal "interrogation" techniques at the US Army's School of the Americas — tortured and murdered women, children, civilian men, and members of the clergy. America spread the war by illegally building secret bases in Costa Rica, a peaceful democracy with no armed forces. Remember Manuel Noriega? He was our guy in Panama — until we got tired of his drug-running, an illegal enterprise we had tolerated for years. And our diplomatic lunacy isn't relegated to history. In Colombia, we're now sending millions of dollars in aid to a military infamous for violating human rights. Instead of weakening drug lords, we make them richer. Our track record doesn't improve further south. For generations, Chile was a democracy but in 1973 our CIA — that cheerleader for despots everywhere — choreographed a military coup that ushered in two decades of government-sponsored terror. We helped keep General Augusto Pinochet, a man accused of hideous crimes against humanity, in power. We committed similar sins in Argentina, supporting fascist thugs in fancy uniforms. The Dirty War that Argentina's military carried out against its own country's civilians killed an estimated 30,000 people. Blessed with millions of US tax dollars and US military support, the Argentine generals killed more citizens in torture chambers and back-room execution chambers than died in all its honorable wars. The US-supported Argentine generals proved far more efficient at slaughtering defenseless college students than at fighting foreigners, including the British in the Falkland Islands War. Uncle Sam was the Argentine military's biggest fan."

Of course "Uncle Sam" was also the "biggest fan" of Fulgencio Batista in Cuba.

In an article dated September 13, 2002, Lucy Morgan, the *St. Petersburg Times*'s bureau chief in Tallahassee, told *USA Today*,: "There have been proposals in the state legislature to cut it [the banana republic] off and set it adrift." The headline was: "South Florida Like A Whole Other State."

Also in *USA Today*, that August, James Bamford wrote: "The Joint Chiefs of Staff saw a grand opportunity for the military to launch an all-out war against Cuba. But they needed a pretext. The Joint Chiefs would secretly launch a war of terror on the US public — and blame it on Castro. Operation Northwoods called for innocent people to be shot on US streets..."

During the most bitter fighting in the Sierra, Celia Sánchez easily earned the reputation as the most fearless guerrilla fighter, with Haydée Santamaría coming in second. Cuban women and the children they loved were the most brutalized in Batista's Cuba. We know what motivated Celia to fight; what about Haydée? Her extraordinary role alongside Fidel and Raúl Castro in the ill-fated attack on the Moncada army garrison on July 26, 1953, left her imprisoned and targeted for a torture-death. But first, Batista's men wanted to make her divulge information about the nascent underground opposition. Beating her and burning her with cigarettes got nothing from her.

Then Haydée was tied to a chair and forced to watch as they tortured her 25-year-old brother, Abel Santamaría Cuadrado. They cut out both of Abel's eyes and placed them in Haydée's lap. She still refused to give them the information they knew she possessed, information that she knew would only cause many others to be arrested and tortured to death. Then they forced Haydée to watch as they gruesomely murdered her brother. Still, Haydée did not divulge one iota of information. Two days later, Haydée's fiancé Reynaldo Boris Luis Santa Coloma was brought to her cell. She was tied to a chair and forced to watch as he was beaten to death. Then Reynaldo's testicles were cut off and rubbed over Haydée's face and chest. And through it all, she refused to provide the killers any information about the anti-Batista underground.

But history registers the fact that Haydée did get out of prison; that she went to the Sierra and joined Celia's revolution; and that she never lost another battle against the Batista men.

After the victory of the revolution, Haydée Santamaría founded a museum in Havana (with a branch in Paris, France) that championed Latin American literary figures. Haydée lovingly nurtured her museum, Casa de las Américas, till the day she died in 1980. The book *Haydée Santamaría: Woman Guerrilla Leader in Cuba Whose Passion for Art and Revolution Inspired Latin America's Cultural Renaissance* was published in 2003. The book lists Celia, Haydée, Melba Hernández, and Vilma Espin as the Big Four in the pantheon of Cuba's revolutionary heroines. It should probably list a Big Five, with Teté Puebla.

The camaraderie of the guerrilla fighters in the Sierra, almost without fail, has been everlasting. The female leaders, from the 1950s to the present day, have always been the heart and soul of the revolution, and their resolve is what created it and what has held it together for all these years. Fidel Castro and Che Guevara agreed with that assessment, as reflected in Betsy Mcclean's Haydée Santamaría biography. At the dedication of the Haydée Santamaría Printing Complex in Santiago de Cuba, Fidel began his long tribute thusly: "Haydée has a really beautiful revolutionary history." He then told how in the revolution's nascent days she "had to carry guns and bullets in suitcases, under cover." With tears in his eyes, Fidel concluded, "Yeyé's [Haydée's nickname] name is essentially linked to the Cuban Revolution."

The Betsy Mcclean biography of Haydée includes an excerpt from a letter Che Guevara wrote to her in the 1960s:

> Dear Yeyé:
>
> .... I see that you have become a literati with the power of creation, but I will confess that how I most like you is on the that day in the New Year, with all of your fuses blown and firing cannons on all sides. That image, and that of the Sierra —

even our fights in those days are pleasant memories — are what I will carry of you for my own use.

Love, your colleague,

Ernesto "Che" Guevara

That letter is one of several documents in which Che Guevara stated that his most "pleasant memories" were the battles in the Sierra — a common theme, it seems, of all the guerrilla leaders.

In October of 2004, after a nasty fall that resulted in nine broken bones, the seventy-eight-year-old Fidel told his Marta Rojas, "My greatest fear is that I will die in bed. If the fates are kind to me, Marta, I will die fighting on the front lines, like in the Sierra with Celia."

According to Betsy Mcclean, Haydée likewise never recovered from the end of her "glory days" as a guerrilla fighter in the Sierra. To her, the Sierra fighting was "a moment when all things were beautiful, heroic — that moment when life defies death and defeat. At such a moment, one risks everything to preserve what really counts. Life and death can be beautiful, and noble, when you fight for your life, but also when you give it up without any compromise. All I have wanted to show our young Cubans is that life is more beautiful when you live that way. It is the only way to live."

And that's the way Santamaría died, as well as lived. She herself chose the time to end it, in 1980, as she mourned the death of her compañera, Celia Sánchez. The one thing Haydée could not accept was Celia's death from cancer on January 11, 1980. She had considered suicide right after the death of her friend Che Guevara, as she wrote this tribute to him (cited by Betsy Mcclean):

"Fourteen years ago I witnessed the death of human beings so immensely loved that today I feel tired of living; I think I have lived too much already. I do not see the sun as so beautiful, I do not feel pleasure in seeing the palm trees. Sometimes, like now, despite enjoying life so much and realizing that it is still worthwhile to open one's eyes every morning if only for those two things, I feel like keeping them closed, like yours." The reference is, of course, to the torture-murders of her brother and her fiancé by Batista goons.

Celia Sánchez and Haydée Santamaría were together as unmatched guerrilla fighters in the Sierra. They essentially died together in 1980.

On my visit to Cuba in March of 2004 I talked with some 250 Cuban workers about Celia Sánchez. I was surprised how many times the name of Felipe Peréz Roque, Cuba's young Foreign Minister, came up in relation to her.

The Cuban peasants, who revere Celia, believe Felipe is cast in her mold as a true Cuban patriot and fierce lover of the island and its people. That happens to coincide with Fidel Castro's view. Felipe is a Celia Sánchez disciple, one who has worked tirelessly the past two decades at peasant wages (as documented by Linda Robinson in *US News & World Report*) for the Cuban people.

Felipe monitors Cuba's world-renowned production of pharmaceuticals and vaccines for children, and he is proud that Cuban scientists in 2003 developed the world's best and cheapest vaccine for treating childhood meningitis, and Cuba provides that vaccine free of charge to poor African and Latin American nations. (On April 26, 2005, the Associated Press reported that Malaysia's Deputy Prime Minister Najib Razak sought and received Cuba's help "in the pharmaceutical sector." In early 2005 Cuba's economic situation showed sharp improvement thanks to major new trade agreements with Venezuela, China, and Canada; immediately Peréz Roque made sure that Celia's favorite projects for children received infusions of new funds.

During a ceremony at the huge Celia Sánchez Hospital Complex in Holguín province, Felipe was asked what Celia Sánchez means to him. He said: "Everything. She will always be the angel in my heart, the angel that wakes me each morning and the angel that tucks me in each night."

***

One American scholar who comprehends Celia Sánchez's dominant role in the Cuban Revolution as well as her huge significance to present day Cuba and Cuban-American relations is Tiffany A. Thomas-Woodard. Her article, "Toward the Gates of Eternity: Celia Sánchez Manduley and the Creation of Cuba's New Woman" was published in 2003 by the University of Pittsburgh Press in its *Cuban Studies, Volume 34* series. Tiffany Thomas-Woodard writes, "The death on 11 January 1980 of Celia Sánchez is a special historical event that has earned its place in the biography of Cuba. For a nation coming to terms with a turbulent and often violent history, Celia has become the symbol of a revolutionary ideal. Little is known of Celia's early childhood, but it is generally accepted that she was born and raised in the small town of Media Luna. She enjoyed a relatively affluent lifestyle. While Celia's father is frequently identified as having been her primary intellectual influence, there is a gaping hole in our knowledge of why Celia became committed to the revolutionary cause."

The "gaping hole," I believe, is filled in by the information conveyed in Celia's own letters to Nora Peters, letters that time and again reference "the legal torture-murder of ten-year-old María Ochoa" in 1953 as the inspiration for Celia's declaration of war against Batista, the Mafia, and the United States.

Thomas-Woodard expertly traces Celia's epic life as a revolutionary, and states, "Perhaps no aspect of Celia's life has received more attention from the international academic community than her relationship with Fidel Castro. What is less clear is whether or not Celia's relationship with Fidel was purely professional — and neither Fidel nor Celia ever publicly addressed this issue. The Cuban exile community in the United States has proven to be a major source of countermemories of Celia."

Celia was a very private person and she did not leave a personal diary behind. However, she left seventeen letters to Nora Peters, and Nora gave them to the author for the purpose of this book. In those private letters, Celia did "address" her relationship with Fidel — although many mysteries still remain.

Thomas-Woodard writes, "Several of the histories of the Cuban revolution in the US derisively refer to Celia as the 'proverbial lion at Fidel's door' who also happened to be 'sharing his double bed,' or as 'Fidel's long-term companion.'" That quote, of course, relates to what Thomas-Woodard calls "the countermemories of Celia" fostered by "the Cuban exile community in the US." In other words, the Cuban exiles (Batistianos) have reserved the right to be the sole chroniclers of the Cuban Revolution.

Thomas-Woodard writes, "Despite the popular discretion with which Celia's personal life is treated, it is clear that within Cuba's national mythology Celia Sánchez is widely recognized as an important revolutionary figure. Beyond the basic biography sketched above, however, it is difficult to find any specific information about who Celia was as an individual." Even the "Celia Sánchez Library" references primarily "male revolutionary leaders." (Some say this is because the shy and modest Celia herself set those parameters.)

In 1976, Celia was unable to save 73 innocent souls, including her entire Cuban Youth Fencing Team, in the terrorist bombing of the Cuban airliner. Thomas-Woodard states that she "conducted multiple interviews with Cubans who had known Celia personally or who had fought with her in the Sierra Maestra." Thomas-Woodard discovered "that Celia herself may well have been one of the primary architects of the official silence surrounding the particularities of her lived experience. Celia is said to have believed firmly in the notion that all people are equal. She chose to be buried among her compatriots in a modest grave, marked only with the number '43' in the mausoleum in the Colón Cemetery in Havana. In short, many believe that Celia's silence was self-imposed. Thus, perhaps, Celia's belief that her deeds were no more laudable than those of her compatriots provides an additional explanation for why so few details of her life are known. Yet, she is no less real to those Cubans who guard her memory."

Thomas-Woodard quotes Armando Hart Dávalos (Haydée Santamaría's husband and a key revolutionary figure) as saying, "Celia was the heroine not only of the war, but also of work. In her, legend acquired real form and content." Celia, in a 1974 letter, wrote: "God knows, Nora, I strive daily to diminish any legend that is attached to me. Haydée, Teté...so many others...are my heroes. In the Sierra and here in Havana, a non-legend can get much more accomplished. I keep telling Fidel how uncomfortable I feel taking bows or being applauded. Such things distract me."

Despite her lifelong efforts to diminish her legend, Celia failed, at least posthumously. Within a week after her death, the magazine *Bohemia* devoted an entire issue to her. "Of the thirty-five photographs of Celia in that issue," Thomas-Woodard writes, "nineteen show her standing directly at Fidel's side." As with other legends, including Che Guevara's, Celia's "will grow more profoundly each year following her passing," as Armando Hart predicted.

CHAPTER 15. SEVEN SPANISH ANGELS TAKE HER HOME

There were seven Spanish angels at the altar of the sun. They were prayin' for the lovers in the valley of the guns. When the battle stopped and the smoke cleared, There was thunder from the throne; And seven Spanish angels took another angel home.
—Troy Seals/Edward Setser

Celia made all the decisions for Cuba, the big ones and the small ones. We all knew no one could ever replace her.
—Roberto Salas

Like the soft warm echoes of a gentle wind after a stormy tropical day long ago, the simmering pathos and joys, the trials and tribulations of Celia Sánchez's life still linger over the island of Cuba as if the imprinted memories somehow will always survive the shifting sands of time.

Marta Rojas — the greatest living authority on the revolution, Celia, and Fidel — wrote in an e-mail dated December 19, 2004: "Fidel by his nature has always been defiant and authoritarian, except when it came to Celia. He was always a puppet in her tiny hands. He still is — defiant, authoritarian, and her puppet. He rules Cuba day-by-day only as he perceives Celia would want him to rule it."

Entering the 1960s, the leadership in Cuba resided in a Big Four — Celia, Fidel Castro, Che Guevara, and Raúl Castro. It had been a Big Five till the lovable but fearless guerrilla commander, Camilo Cienfuegos, died in the crash of a small Cesna-310 airplane during a coastal storm on October 28, 1959, a mere ten months after the triumph of the revolution. Celia and Fidel were devastated by

Camilo's untimely death, which the anti-Castro forces in the US, of course, blamed on Fidel, claiming he eliminated Camilo because of his popularity among the peasants. In a speech at Camaguey on October 28, just before his return flight bound for Havana, Camilo as always had spoken lavishly about Fidel and the revolution. Georgie Anne Geyer notes that Castro, at his majors speeches, would often turn and ask his guerrilla pal Camilo, "How am I doing, amigo?" The reply from Camilo would always be, "You're doing great, commander! You're doing great!"

Camilo was extremely close to Celia, Fidel, and Che but, as Geyer pointed out, Camilo and Raúl did not like each other, and this personality conflict pitted the staid Raúl against the flamboyance of Camilo. Meanwhile, it is typical of any regime's enemies to accuse their rivals of murdering or causing the murder of any prominent figure who dies. This ploy has been used in an attempt to turn the Cuban peasants against the revolutionary leaders. It has generally succeeded in the US but if it had gained traction on the island the revolution would have ended long ago. As far back as 1959, if the peasants had believed Fidel was responsible for Camilo's plane crash, Fidel would have been doomed. Anti-revolutionary propaganda in the US is one thing; on the island it is something else altogether.

In the early days of the revolution the young teacher Frank País was the second most important rebel recruiter/organizer after Celia. Batista put bounties on their heads. Frank was captured and tortured to death on a public street in Santiago by Batista goons, after which the peasants created a three-day disruption in the city. Even with the public execution of Frank País, Fidel was blamed for the murder and for the same reason — to eliminate a popular rebel. Geyer tries to perpetuate the lie by insinuating that rebel heroine Vilma Espín betrayed País's hideout. That does not mesh with the fact that Vilma was Frank's chauffeur and she loved him.

Later Vilma would marry Raúl Castro and become the President of the Federation of Cuban Women in revolutionary Cuba. Geyer, in her research for *Guerrilla Prince*, mostly interviewed Castro's enemies such as Huber Matos, who told her, "There is no question that they killed Camilo." Another typical source for Geyer was Rafael Díaz-Balart, a top official in the Batista dictatorship who set America's Cuban policy from January 1959 to May 2005.

The propinquity, or nearness, of the revolutionary leaders began in the Sierra and has continued to this day — accounting for the fact that the Castro brothers, almost five decades later, remain Cuba's leaders. Revolutionary warriors such as Vilma, Marta, Teté, and Juan Almeída remain on the island as loyalists. It they had not, the revolution would have been finished years ago.

Celia Sánchez, in her letters to Nora Peters, discussed the deaths of rebel leaders as well as the deaths of her parents and Fidel's parents. Fidel's mother Lina was sickly, entering her eighties, and this became a distraction for Celia in the early 1960s. Lina frequently asked for Celia, once just to hear her dispel rumors that Fidel "caused Camilo's death." Celia told Nora, "I just took her hand and told her: 'Mama Castro, Fidel and I loved Camilo. Please understand that the CIA and the exiles in Florida will blame us for every revolutionary death, to justify their own actions and to cause dissent within the revolution. You have always trusted me. Trust your son. You were a lowly maid who married Fidel's rich father. I think you framed his love for the peasants. Respect that. He loves the peasants as I do. And you well know he would not do anything against my wishes. We loved and needed Camilo."

Fidel was close to his mother and his sisters Emma, Lidia, Angelita, and Juanita (although he later became estranged from Angelita and Juanita, after he felt they became jealous of Celia and he heard that they derisively called the revolutionary heroine a "dictator"). Fidel's younger brother Raúl has always been loyal and, apart from nepotism, Raúl earned his revolutionary and governmental stripes alongside his big brother. Ramón, Fidel's older brother, was never as close with his younger brothers.

Fidel's most famous son is Fidelito, whose mother was Fidel's first wife, Mirta Díaz-Balart. A doctor, Fidelito has always been close to his father. Fidel has a total of eight loyal sons on the island; they all live quietly and modestly, never flouting their relationships to Fidel. Fidel's only known daughter, Alina Fernández, the offspring of his affair with Havana socialite Naty Revuelta, is the only one of his children that turned against him. Alina moved to America and makes a living criticizing her father.

Fidel, like Celia, has always burnished his image as one who sympathized with the downtrodden. One way his enemies in the US seek to put a burr under his saddle is to make mention of his "accumulated wealth." For example, the March 2005 *Forbes Magazine* "estimated" Fidel's personal wealth to be "$550 million." Castro issued a scathing rejoinder via the Cuban embassy in Mexico City. Forbes then admitted it was a "wild guess." Indeed, the trappings of immense wealth are not evident to observers in Cuba, for Fidel or any of the other revolutionary leaders.

Fidel was never close to his father, Angel Castro. Angel had a contract with the United Fruit Company, the US-owned enterprise. He owned 36,000 acres and was a multi-millionaire when he died, in his eighties, on October 21, 1956, soon after Fidel had been released from prison and was refining his approach to the Batista and United Fruit Company cabal. Ramón, Fidel's older brother, managed to send a cable that said: "Tell Alejandro that Papa died this morning. Ramón." Alejandro was Fidel's code name in the rebel underground. He made no effort to attend the funeral, which was conducted out of Ramón's home in Birán. Batista, hoping to trap Fidel, had "the entire town surrounded by soldiers" according to Georgie Anne Geyer. Geyer also stated that several rebel friends of Fidel sneaked into Birán and laid roses on Angel's bier before "fading away again into the steamy, hot tropical night." Those rebels with the roses were sent by Celia from her guerrilla camp in the Sierra.

By 1967, the leadership in revolutionary Cuba was reduced to three, consisting of Celia and the Castro brothers, Fidel and Raúl. Che Guevara, the dynamic young Argentine doctor who had emerged in the Sierra as a talented point commander, had told Celia in the summer of 1959, that he was "besieged with wanderlust" but that he would stay and help her and Fidel in the new transitional government as long as he was needed. She asked him what he meant. He replied, "A Cuban-type revolution is needed all over Latin America, country by country, where the US has thieving dictators and the United Fruit Company is poised to rob those poor countries of what little they have, just like they were robbing Cuba. Apart from this new Cuban government, I want to start the type of revolution you started in the Sierra, country by country, till the US kills me."

She replied, "I need you with me, Che." And he stayed, for the next seven years, and did what Celia and Cuba asked. Like the other revolutionary leaders, Che came from an elite background but gave almost every peso he ever had to the poor. He also gave them all the value of his wits and devotion.

After the revolution, he would work shirtless all day side-by-side with the campesinos (peasants) in the sugar cane and tobacco fields.

But Che also flew around the world and made daunting political speeches on behalf of the new Cuba. On such excursions, he liked to stop off in African countries and toil in the fields with those peasants.

Che's favorite writers included Keats and Sara de Ibáñez. He could speak coherently about Marx, Aristotle, Kant, Gide, and Faulkner. In a letter to Señora María Rosario Guevara, Che wrote perhaps his most famous line: "If you are capable of trembling with indignation each time that an injustice is committed in the world, we are true comrades...."

Still reviled in the capitalist world, and revered worldwide by the multitudes of poor people, he was fearless in waging guerrilla war on behalf of peasants and he well knew that he was destined to die in that struggle.

The legendary Che finally left Cuba. In 1967, after bidding a sorrowful farewell to Celia and Fidel, Che disguised himself and headed for Bolivia. There, in the jungles, Che tried to form a guerrilla army like the one Celia had so successfully created in the Sierra Maestra Mountains and its swampy foothills. Celia had begged Che not to try, reminding him of the unique circumstances that had played in favor of the Cuban Revolution.

Bolivia, including its army, was tightly controlled and led by the CIA. Within days of his arrival, the CIA managed to get a photograph of Che. This became a famous photograph when it was later released. A large Bolivian army went after Che, who at the time had recruited just twelve Bolivian guerrilla fighters. Che was wounded and captured on October 7, 1967, by a Bolivian army led by Captain Gary Prado Salmón, who was trained, directed, and paid by the CIA. Che was held in an old schoolhouse till the Bolivian soldiers received instructions from Washington. When additional CIA agents had arrived on the scene, Che was executed by a Bolivian soldier name Mario Tenán, who shot Che nine times. Tenán lived out a long life in Bolivia with that one claim to fame.

Che's hands were cut off, because the CIA believed that would help prevent his body from being identified by the Latin American peasants who were sure to worship their martyred hero. The body was not found and identified by DNA tests until 1993. Che's beloved widow had remained in Cuba working as a biologist for the Cuban government. Instead of returning his remains to his native Argentina, she wanted them brought back to Cuba and buried forever in the city of Santa Clara, where Che's brilliant, fearless leadership had won the last great battle of Cuba's revolutionary war.

In a 1977 letter to Nora Peters, Celia wrote: "I still miss him. I knew from the fighting in the Sierra that he one day would die fighting for the poor and the oppressed because that's the way he wanted to die. In the decade since he died, he has gained more fame each passing year. The poor and the oppressed need him. I...need him."

One seldom-mentioned note in Che's biography concerns the fact that the KGB once sent a female East German spy to Cuba to monitor Che because he had been outspoken against Russia's Communism during its Cold War with the

US. Her name was Tamara Bunke Bider and she used many aliases — Laura Gutiérrez Bauer, María Aguilera. Her KGB code name was "T." But her historic name is Tania. She was strikingly beautiful. Inconveniently, she fell in love with Che and, yes, they became torrid lovers even as Tania sent reports on him back to the KGB in Moscow. Tania was destined to die with Che in the jungles of Bolivia. Geyer and many historians have been mesmerized about Tania. In the 1970s, Marta Rojas wrote a book entitled *Tania: The Unforgettable Guerrilla.*

The CIA made sure Che's death was blamed on Castro. Geyer and others, subscribing dutifully to the CIA's disinformation campaign, claim that Fidel had two reasons to kill Che: (1) Che's popularity among Cuban and Latin American peasants; and (2) Che's opposing Fidel regarding Cuba's tightening alignment with Russia as a counterbalance to the US in the Cold War.

The CIA's fears about Che's martyrdom were justified. Each year since the CIA conducted his execution in Bolivia in 1967, his fame has grown. T-shirts bearing his image are big sellers worldwide. Tourists visiting Havana are greeted by a famed five-story image of Che that fronts the building that looks across the parking lot at the Palace of the Revolution, reminding visitors what the doctor meant to Cuba and to the revolution. "As long as the poor and the weak are exploited by the rich and the strong, Nora," Celia wrote, "Che will stand tall as a revolutionary icon."

***

The 1960s were sad times for Celia Sánchez, prompting her to write: "My Treasure Island doesn't seem much like an island anymore." She had lost two of her greatest point commanders and devoted government officials with the deaths of Camilo and Che; she had lost Fidel's mother, Lina; and she had buried too many Cuban children.

She had buried three-year-old twin sisters killed by a terrorist attack from a speed boat on a coastal cabin. She had buried a 13-year-old catcher killed by a bomb at a new baseball field that she had just dedicated. She had buried a twenty-year-old Cuban mother of two little boys killed by a bomb at Havana's Pepsi-Cola factory, one of four Havana buildings bombed that week.

The continuing CIA and Mafia assassination attempts against Fidel and her didn't faze Celia; to the chagrin of their security details, they continued to spend most nights in her small apartment on 11th Street. How do you fight terrorists who target children and then race back to Florida and brag about it? Terrorism stymied Celia, and mystified her.

The last thing she ever wanted was for Cuba to always be at war with mighty America. Twice during the Lyndon B. Johnson presidency — as declassified US documents posted on US government Websites confirm — Cuba presented America with detailed offers to reimburse US companies for property nationalized after the revolutionary victory. The efforts merely spawned more and more US government-sanctioned terrorist attacks from the Batistianos, the Mafia, and the CIA.

"For Cuba's sake," Celia told Nora Peters, "I prayed for any little sign that America would treat us fairly, and I was willing in an instant to forgive and to forget all that we had suffered from those shores."

History documents that Celia did get a "little sign," one glimmer of hope from America. Moreover, history records the fact that her quick reaction to that overture was precisely as she always said it would be, "for Cuba's sake."

In the early 1960s Celia began to get calls from an American named Lisa Howard, who had become the first female national news anchor in the US, hosting "The News Hour with Lisa Howard" on ABC-TV. She got the first US interview with Nikita Khrushchev. She had two interviews with Fidel Castro, arranged via a friendship she had cultivated with Celia. Lisa became obsessed with what Celia was accomplishing for the Cuban people. Ms. Howard was upset by "the cowardly and dishonorable" Bay of Pigs attack and at one point she angered the ABC-TV brass when she inserted into an interview a personal observation that "America's Cuban policy can be construed as hypocrisy without principles for always pounding Cuba while supporting some of the worst dictatorships on this planet."

Lisa Howard made efforts to encourage a normalization of relations between the US and Cuba. Her fame, beauty, and forum afforded her exceptional influence.

On her visits to Cuba, Lisa walked sandy beaches at nighttime with Celia. One moonlit night the two women sat on the cement banking along the Malecón, Havana's famed oceanfront highway. Lisa said that Senator Eugene McCarthy was working with her secretly to normalize relations and wanted face-to-face assurances from Celia, Fidel, and Che that Cuba was sincere and would honor that commitment. She said that President Kennedy wanted to break from the Mafia and make amends to the Cuban people; and that Senator McCarthy wanted one of them to attend a meeting at her apartment.

Celia agreed.

***

By the summer of 1963, with Lisa Howard the catalyst, it seems that President John Kennedy had indeed decided to normalize relations with Cuba, believing his Camelot presidency was now popular enough to shed the shackles of the Mafia as well as the remnants of the Batista dictatorship that ruled southern Florida. Just days before he left for Dallas in November of 1963, Kennedy had told his staff to make "normalizing relations with Cuba our top priority." Key members of Kennedy's staff, including Press Secretary Pierre Salinger, confirmed the sharp policy change regarding Cuba. The CIA quickly spread the news to the Batistiano and Mafia strongholds in Florida. Mafia kingpins Carlos Marcello in New Orleans, Traficante in Tampa, and Sam Giancana in Chicago went on the warpath. This was a complete betrayal.

Even between the 1963 assassination of John Kennedy and the 1968 murder of Robert Kennedy, Celia and Lisa doggedly tried to normalize relations between the US and Cuba. Historian Peter Kornbluh writes, in his 1999 book *JFK & Castro: The Secret Quest For Accommodation*, that: "Recently declassified US government documents reveal that, at the height of the Cold War, John F. Kennedy and Fidel Castro were exploring ways to normalize US-Cuba relations."

In August of 1961, just four months after the Bay of Pigs, Che Guevara met with Kennedy's key aide, Richard Goodwin, in Punta del Este, Uruguay. Che expressed to Goodwin Cuba's desire that the US "become our best friend and key trading partner." Kornbluh also documents that Che told Goodwin that Cuba would "pay for expropriated US properties" on the island, along with a myriad of other generous concessions.

But that and other such overtures fell victim to a JFK administration dictated to by the Batistianos and the Mafia.

Even after JFK was killed, Celia is said to have instructed Fidel to send a letter to LBJ, pleading for normalized relations. That letter, now declassified and available on such websites as the George Washington University archives, stressed conciliatory offers from Cuba, yet asks, "Please don't consider this a sign of weakness on Cuba's part." But the President was not about to challenge the Batistianos and the Mafia. Still, the Cubans did not give up.

In 1960, actress Lisa Howard had become a reporter and was soon covering the UN, where she secured the famed interview with Nikita Khrushchev. By 1963, she was covering world events such as the dramatic Kennedy-Khrushchev summit in Vienna, where, as she would later tell Celia, JFK "noticed that I was a woman." Back in the US, partly due to her unique access to the world's two most powerful leaders, Ms. Howard was hired by ABC-TV in 1963 as the anchor on

"The News Hour With Lisa Howard." She also had unique access to Fidel Castro, who would soon become one of the three most famous leaders in the world. On at least two occasions, according to Nora Peters, Castro made love to Ms. Howard — once at the Cohiba Hotel and once at Celia's apartment. After that revelation to Nora, Celia wrote: "The bimbos around Fidel, I controlled. But never was I jealous of either Naty or Lisa. I told you of my respect for them. Some of his one-nighters I accepted in the best interests of Cuba. Cuba! Anything for my beautiful little Cuba!" (There is no evidence that Lisa ever had sex with JFK.)

Lisa not only went to Cuba to conduct two interviews with Fidel, but she frequently flew to Cuba clandestinely for brief strategy or friendship sessions with Celia, whom she knew dictated Fidel's leadership of Cuba. A May 1, 1963 White House document that is now declassified states: "Interview of US Newswoman with Fidel Castro Indicating Possible Interest in Rapprochement with the United States." The document included Kennedy's "P saw" scrawl, confirming that the president had "seen" it.

Celia, in her letters to Nora Peters, and Peter Kornbluh, in his respected book, indicate that Lisa Howard's beauty helped her gain the vital attention of JFK, Castro, and Cuba's UN representative Carlos Lechuga. Her skill as a journalist and her love of Cuba also brought those three key men together in a quest to normalize relations between Cuba and the US. But Ms. Howard also won over such US politicians as UN advisor William Attwood, UN Ambassador Adlai Stevenson, Under Secretary of State Averill Harriman, and JFK's confidant and State Department advisor McGeorge Bundy — all of whom spoke positively at her Park Avenue apartment with her and Cuba's UN Ambassador Carlos Lechuga. After each session, Lisa phoned Celia in Havana. Surprisingly, Ms. Howard was even able to convince the influential Senator Eugene McCarthy to meet with Che Guevara at the Park Avenue apartment. That historic meeting took place on December 16, 1964.

But, while some factions seemed to be entertaining the thought of normalization, CIA Director John McCone and the Deputy CIA Director Richard Helms were constantly having Howard interrogated and hounded.

By the summer of 1963, John Kennedy and Fidel Castro seemed to have agreed and affirmed that normalizing relations was in the best interests of both countries. After an exchange of cables between Kennedy and Celia, Kennedy informed his staff that "normalizing relations with Cuba is my top priority." That historic pronouncement, however, was made on November 15, 1963 — one week prior to his ill-fated trip to Dallas, Texas. At least as early as July of that year, the Batistianos in Florida, elements within the CIA, and the Mafia were discussing rumors of JFK's drastically altered plans regarding Cuba. This "double cross" is considered to have been a major factor motivating the conspiracy to kill Kennedy.

And shortly thereafter, Celia Sánchez linked President Johnson's White House and the CIA to something else — the murder of Lisa Howard!

The LBJ White House immediately began targeting Lisa Howard. They pressured ABC-TV to fire her. ABC, in its statement regarding the termination, said Lisa was fired "because she has chosen to participate publicly in partisan political activity contrary to long established ABC news policy." The fact is that she knew too much about the JFK assassination, and she was working on a book that was sure to embarrass the White House (and ABC). LBJ was aware that Celia Sánchez was telling the State Department that key LBJ associates had been involved in the JFK murder, and Lisa's closeness to Celia was also well known. Lisa Howard is recorded as committing "suicide" on July 4, 1965. Some theorists see a similarity in her death and that of Marilyn Monroe, who also is supposed to have ingested a massive overdose of Phenobarbitals — unwillingly, some say.

Celia Sánchez wrote to Nora on September 13, 1973: "Lisa visited me in Havana between her firing by ABC-TV and her death, Nora. And I spoke with her on the telephone just hours before she died. Suicide was the last thing on her mind. Her entire focus was completing her manuscript, which would have resulted in a book that tied President Johnson, the CIA, the Batistianos, and the Mafia into the conspiracy that killed Kennedy. She was not at all distressed about being fired by ABC television. In fact, she was relieved to be free of that pressure-cooker. Lisa loved America and she loved Cuba. No one worked harder to bring sanity to that relationship. She didn't give up till she realized the Johnson White House had targeted her and that there was no chance to alter that tide; in other words, no one could stand up to the anti-Cuban tsunami. But she naively believed they would give her time to finish her book, her stamp on history."

With the passage of time, historians have come to agree with Celia's account of the 1965 "suicide," and this was not the only one. Dorothy Kilgallen was another noted journalist in the 1960s who became a top celebrity. One of Kilgallen's biggest fans turned out to be Jack Ruby, the Mafia figure who killed Lee Harvey Oswald. When the jailed Ruby was allowed to be interviewed by just one newsperson, he chose Kilgallen. Kilgallen continued to interview Ruby during his 1964 trial, when Ruby knew he was dying of cancer. Ruby said many things to Kilgallen, talking about his ties to the New Orleans Mafia kingpin Carlos Marcello, one man who is known to have vowed to kill both Kennedy brothers. Kilgallen meticulously corroborated her information from Ruby and then unwisely announced that she had enough data to "break the whole JFK assassination mystery wide open." She would do so, she said, in a book. In various forums, including the television program "Nightlife," Kilgallen flashed a folder that she said contained incriminating data. Apparently, someone in the LBJ White House, in southern Florida, in the CIA or in the Mafia believed her. On Sunday, November 8, 1965, Dorothy Kilgallen was found dead in her bed, where she was known to be spending most of her time working on her manuscript. She was fully dressed, sitting up. The one thing missing was the manuscript. The results of the autopsy were released eight days later, with the coroner for the New York City Police Department stating that Dorothy had killed herself with a combination of alcohol and barbiturates. Two days later, Mrs. Earl T. Smith — Kilgallen's closest friend, who had worked with her on the manuscript — was also found dead, and the cause of Mrs. Smith's death to this day is listed as "from undetermined causes."

The number of "suspicious suicides" among persons suspected of knowing something relating to the assassination of John Kennedy runs to the dozens or more.

***

Through it all, in the 1960s and 1970s, Celia Sánchez was immersed in trying to better the lives of the Cuban peasants. All the while, Celia kept an eye over her shoulder, wondering what might be coming next from the US. She was aided by sympathizers within the US media world and within the military and intelligence establishment.

One English word — "return" — became a particular irritant. "Return! Return! The Batistianos tell the ignorant American people they are determined to RETURN freedom and democracy to Cuba! ... [What] form of freedom and democracy will [they] RETURN to Cuba..."

Setbacks such as the "suicide" of Lisa Howard and the continuing attacks from Florida inspired Celia to renew her fervor. Yet, by the mid-1970s the terrorist attacks against Cuban civilians began to take a physical and mental toll. She worked tirelessly day and night. If she managed to fall asleep, she had a recurring dream — a dream that took her back to the Sierra when she was fighting on the frontlines. Those were her glory days, her "happiest times." Only now, the quintessential guerrilla fighter could not fight back because there were no enemy soldiers to fight. No one has figured out how to fight terrorists who target innocent civilians.

"She rarely slept during this period," Marta Rojas wrote in an e-mail dated December 19, 2004. "And she had become a chain smoker. One morning...I believe it was the spring of 1974...I drove her at daybreak to visit María Ochoa's grave. But at 11:00 that morning we had to be in the little coastal town of Guanabo to attend the funeral of a 9-year-old girl killed by a machine-gun strafing from a big speed boat. Celia was still crying when we got back to Havana, and using the butt of one cigarette to light another one. 'They are winning, Marta,' she said as we sat in my parked car. 'They are winning, you know.' All I could do was lean over and hug her. Considering who she was, I wished I could do more. To this day, I can still feel her crying in my arms in my parked car, and all I could do was...hug her."

***

The Bush political dynasty has been controlled by the Batistianos in southern Florida more than any other of the last ten US presidential administrations.

It is quite possible that John Kennedy would have moved toward better relations with the island nation if time and circumstances had permitted. However, for the first two years of his administration, Kennedy was a bit in a corner with the Mafia and therefore supported Operation Mongoose and other attacks. But in the third year of his presidency, 1963, Kennedy seems to have decided that his "Camelot" popularity would enable him to shed the yoke of the Mafia. The Mafia, the Batistianos, and elements of the CIA all believed Kennedy had betrayed them in the Bay of Pigs attack, and they did not forgive him.

Since the early Kennedy years, Washington seems to be even more in the pocket of southern Florida. George H.W. Bush's alignment with the Batistianos dating back to his CIA directorship regrettably became the preamble for his presidency as well as the governorship of Jeb Bush in Florida and the presidency of George W. Bush. In regard to Cuba, only Batistianos influence the Bush administrations in Washington and in Florida.

In 2004, George W. Bush named Porter Goss CIA Director. Goss was a CIA agent in the 1960s, and Havana sees him as an anti-Cuban terrorist. He later became a successful businessman in southern Florida as well as a US congressman from Florida. Bush also put celebrated Batistianos Otto Reich and Roger Noriega in charge of Washington's Cuban and Latin American policies.

***

America's no-holds-barred approach to Revolutionary Cuba can be traced to March 4, 1960. At 3:15 P.M. that day the Belgian steamship La Coubre blew up in the Havana harbor, killing 101 people and injuring over 200 others. It was a big triumph for the CIA, which had warned Belgian not to trade with Cuba. Robert Reynolds, the head of the Miami CIA office in 1960 and 1961, attended the academic conference in Havana marking the 40th anniversary of the Bay of Pigs, in March 2001. At that time Reynolds said, regarding the bombing of the La Coubre, "We had begun to carry out acts of sabotage against Cuba." Reynolds did not mention that "sabotage" against other countries is illegal in times of peace; the CIA circumvents that not by declaring war but by declaring terrorism, the very same thing it is pledged to guard America against.

In the first two years of the Kennedy presidency and during the eight years of the G. W. Bush presidency, the CIA has encountered no restraint in its Cuban policy. Yet, through ten Batistiano-dominated presidencies, Revolutionary Cuba has somehow continued to exist, an historic fact every bit as remarkable as the revolutionary triumph over the powerful US-backed Batista dictatorship way back on January 1, 1959.

On March 1, 1998, the *Miami Herald* reported on newly declassified US government documents quoting CIA General Inspector Lyman Kirkpatrick issuing this statement: "In February, 1961, six successful amphibian operations were carried out involving weapons and materials [explosives which reduced the El Encanto store to ashes]. And on March 13, 1961, we also carried out two successful parachute drops." The destruction of the El Encanto store in Havana in February of 1961 was typical of the sabotage in Cuba leading up to the April military attack at the Bay of Pigs and the sabotage against Cuba that continues to this day.

José Basulto, a typical Cuban exile, has often bragged about being dropped off by the CIA in Cuba to commit acts of sabotage prior to 1961 and, in the 1990s, Basulto bragged about flying his Brothers to the Rescue airplanes over Havana. Most unbiased observers, including Wayne Smith (former head of the US Interests Section in Havana), believe Cuba acted correctly and even patiently in regards to the overflights, but the US media still maligns Cuba for shooting down two "private airplanes" and the provocative overflights are seldom mentioned. A US treasury check for $89 million was sent to the Florida lawyers who represented the families of the four downed Brothers to the Rescue pilots. In 2005, Basulto himself was granted a multi-million-dollar settlement by a Florida court for his "continuing stress" over the loss of his two planes. The confluence of Batistiano-controlled courtrooms with the Batistiano-controlled US treasury has created many new millionaires, at the expense of US taxpayers. Even the daughter of a CIA pilot killed in the 1961 Bay of Pigs attack on Cuba successfully sued unrepresented Cuba; daughters of Japanese pilots killed in the December 7, 1941 attack on Pearl Harbor, of course, have not sued the US.

Regarding the Bay of Pigs attack, even the hagiographic biographer of Kennedy, Arthur Schlesinger Jr., has said, "Historically, we have assumed a double role in Latin America. Sometimes we are the bully. Latin Americans feel a mixture of hate and love for the United States. They react warmly to Dr. Jekyll and fear and detest Mr. Hyde. We would feel the same way if we were Latin Americans. The Bay of Pigs was the work of Mr. Hyde."

Terrorist groups such as Alpha-66 still operate in Florida. Alpha-66 displayed its offices proudly at 2443 NW 29th Street in Miami and 1714 Flagler Street in Miami. A typical attack attributed to Alpha-66 occurred on October 12, 1971. Two heavily armed speed boats blasted the coastal village of Boca de Samá in eastern Cuba. The cabin home of Lidio Rivaflecha and Ramón Arturo Siam Portelles was strafed with machine-gun fire, killing them both. Two sisters — 15-year-old Nancy Pavón and 13-year-old Angela Pavón — were badly wounded.

Upon their return, a photograph of the jubilant shooters was released to the Miami press. Miami radio stations boasted about the successful attack, including official releases like this from Andres Nazario Sargen: "From the time of the first commando attack in 1961 the war was galvanized. Our whole purpose is to destroy everything we can inside Cuba."

But Nancy Pavón, of Boca de Samá, recalls, "That night I was sleeping when I heard gunfire. My mother began to cry because there were small children around. A bullet hit her and I was hit in both feet; one of them was cut to pieces as if I had been attacked by a machete. They amputated my right foot. I spent nineteen months in a hospital... They destroyed my life" (author interview, 2004).

The US government, asked to respond to Sargen's comment, said: "The US government will defend the law with regard to all those who attempt to violate it. US legislation, including the Neutrality Act, expressly prohibits participation in any military or naval expedition launched against a foreign nation from US territory."

Meanwhile, the Cuban government paid for the funerals of Lidio Rivaflecha and Ramón Portelles on October 14, 1971, in Boca de Samá and since

October 12, 1971, Cuba has paid for the medical care still required because of Nancy Pavón's amputated foot and the resultant nerve damage.

Always forced to watch her back, Celia Sánchez more and more was distressed by the incessant chatter in Miami that only encouraged more such inhumane attacks on Cuban civilians. Many around her urged her to strike back with terrorist attacks aimed at Miami. But she never did. "No!" Marta Rojas remembers hearing her say. "No! Most people in Miami are innocent, too. I will never permit Cuba to harm them. No! That's not the answer."

Cuba's long coastline and its proximity to Florida make it very vulnerable. Fast boats from Florida can fire on Cuban fishermen as a means to harm the Cuban economy. Ibrahim Ruiz, a fisherman trying to feed his young family, was blasted from his boat on January 28, 1973. By nightfall the commando group was announcing the attack on Miami radio stations, disregarding any government claims about the Neutrality Act.

Emboldened by what Celia Sánchez termed "their license to kill courtesy of the US government and the US taxpayers," the Batistianos gradually expanded their terrorism against Cuba to include the island's trading partners.

On September 10, 1962, the Cuban vessel San Pascual was loading sugar onto the British boat *New Lane* at the port of Cayo Frances in Sancti Spiritus, Cuba. Both ships were attacked with a barrage of artillery fire. Alpha 66 commandos took credit for the attack. Cuba and England asked the US State Department to investigate via an official statement that included pictures of the two blasted ships. The United States never responded.

On March 23, 1963, the Russian ship *Baku*, loaded with Cuban sugar, was attacked by 20mm cannon and 50-caliber machine guns in the port of Caibarién in the province of Las Villas. This was a particularly daring move at the height of the Cold War; but the Batistianos are concerned only with reclaiming Cuba and are unconcerned with collateral repercussions of their actions.

On September 12, 1964, the Spanish ship Sierra de Aranzazu was attacked off the coast of Guantánamo province because it was delivering cargo, mostly toys for children, to Cuba. The ship's Spanish captain, Pedro Ibargurengonitia, was killed. Cuba and Spain protested to the US State Department, in vain.

In January of 1993, an *Esquire* Magazine article entitled "Who Is Jorge Mas Canosa?," written by Gaeton Fonzi, implicated three prime Batistiano terrorists — Jorge Mas Canosa, Orlando Bosch, and Luis Posada Carriles — in the 1968 bombing of the Cuban ship Aracelio Iglesias in the Panama Canal as well as military operations against both Cuban and Russian ships in the Mexican port of

Veracruz. It documented money he received from the CIA in 1965 for operations against Cuba. Jorge Mas Canosa is best known to Cuba as an anti-Castro terrorist. He is best known in the US as the founder of the Cuban American National Foundation, which since the 1980s has been a richly funded anti-Cuban lobby in Washington. (After the death of Canosa, the CANF is now led by his son). Bosch and Carriles are best known in Cuba and throughout Latin America as the terrorist bombers of a Cuban airplane in 1976. They are best known in Miami and within the US government as heroes who are well protected.

Marcela Sánchez, a young Colombian-born nationally syndicated columnist for the *Washington Post*, is one of the few US journalists to denounce the US government's "shameful" protection of well known anti-Cuban terrorists such as Luis Posada Carriles and Orlando Bosch. Otherwise, the US media mostly steers clear of Cuban issues.

On October 4, 1973, the machine-gunning of a defenseless Cuban fishing boat, the Cayo Largo 17, killed Roberto Torna Mirabal. The Miami-based FNLC (National Front for the Liberation of Cuba) took credit for that murder.

On April 6, 1976, two Cuban fishing boats were attacked between Anguila and Key Sal. Two young fishermen, Mauriz Díaz and Bienvenido Mauriz Díaz, were killed. Two separate Miami terrorists groups claimed they teamed up for the attack.

Throughout the 1960s and the 1970s, CIA-funded and US government-sanctioned terrorist attacks plagued Cuba's fishing and shipping industries as well as coastal cabins and hotels.

Then, the Batistiano terrorists expanded their attacks worldwide to include Cuban embassies.

On April 22, 1976, two Cuban diplomats — Adriana Corcho Calleja and Efrén Monteagudo Rodríguez — were killed by a bomb explosion in Lisbon, Portugal. Corcho left a husband and three young children in Havana. Félix García Rodríguez, the top protocol official of the Cuban Mission to the United Nations, was shot dead as he drove his car through Queens, New York. Cuban diplomat Eulalio José Negrín Santos, assigned to work with the US and the UN to lift the US embargo against Cuba, was shot to death on a street in Union City, New Jersey, as he walked hand-in-hand with his twelve-year-old son.

On February 4, 1974, dynamite placed inside a book sent to the Cuban embassy in Lima, Peru, blinded Cuban diplomat Pilar Ramirez Vega.

The US Department of Justice and the Federal Bureau of Investigation in Miami on August 16, 1978, issued an internal report stating that: "In June, 1974,

Orlando Bosch admitted to having sent letter bombs to Cuban embassies in Lima, Peru; Madrid, Spain; Ottawa, Canada; and Buenos Aires, Argentina." That report was declassified on August 14, 1991, by the US government code 5668/SLO/JCEL and was numbered 86-0132. This is the same Orlando Bosch who has acknowledged a role in scores of terrorist acts against Cuba and who still lives freely in Miami; the same Orlando Bosch pardoned by president George H. W. Bush; and the same Orlando Bosch who is one of the shining lights at functions featuring President George W. Bush.

Throughout the 1960s and deep into the 1970s, Celia Sánchez defended Cuba against the rampant terrorism as best she could. She refused to retaliate in kind for two reasons: (1) She did not want innocent Americans to suffer; and (2) she did not want to give the US a pretext for an all-out military attack on "Cubita bella" ("beautiful little Cuba").

And through it all, Celia put in twenty-hour workdays on behalf of the Cuban peasants. "Her one and only salvation," Marta Rojas said in an e-mail dated January 7, 2005, "were the moments she could sneak away from her work to be with the children at school or at play."

At the other end of the spectrum, the saddest moments of Celia's life came on the days she buried Cuban children killed by the Cuban exile terrorists in Florida. Adriana Solár-Mendez, now seventy-seven, was a young kindergarten teacher at a school Celia often visited. "Celia loved to sit through the whole class," Adriana told me. "She always brought special snacks and drinks, and after class shared them with the children. They were so at ease with her because...she was Celia. She would hug each of them and select a little girl to sit on her lap. To the children, she was their guardian angel. They knew her legend. We told them she was our greatest heroine, and the greatest guerrilla fighter in the Sierra war. We teachers were as blessed as the children. There has never been anyone on this island to match her. She was so modest, so sincere. When we thanked her for all she did, she always apologized, wishing she could do more. She gave everything she had to Cuba. The fact she had more to give than anyone is what makes her so special. Oh, yes! She loved rainbows and she taught the children English using the words from the Wizard of Oz song. She was...she will always be...Cuba's angel."

On February 21, 1975, Luciano Nieves Mestre, a native of Cuba who had advocated dialogue between Cuba and the US, was shot six times and killed in the parking lot of Miami's Variety Children's Hospital. "There were seven Spanish angels at the altar of the sun..."

On August 9, 1976, Cuban diplomats Jesús Cejas Arias and Crescencio Galañena Hernández were tortured to death in Buenos Aires, Argentina.

An FBI report released in Argentina in 1976 concerning the infamous "Operation Condor" stated that Florida-based "Cuban exile terrorists" had "special relationships" with assassination squads throughout Latin America and "especially in Argentina, Chile, and Venezuela." "And seven Spanish angels took another angel home..."

By the 1970s, Celia's emphasis on funding and training peasant children in sports and arts had produced startlingly successful results. She purchased and refurbished two DC-8 airplanes to transport young Cuban teams to international events. Alicia Alonso's young ballet stars began to dazzle audiences in Paris, London, New York, Washington, and around the world, winning what would become a record 300-plus first-place awards against sterling competition. Then, a bomb was exploded at New York's Lincoln Center during a performance by the young ballet troupe.

In early October of 1976, Celia sent the Cuban Youth Fencing Team to compete in the Central American Championships in Caracas, Venezuela; they won. On October 6, Celia waited jubilantly at José Marti Airport in Havana for their return. But the arrival of flight CU-455 was delayed for one hour, two hours... Celia waited in the lounge. Then she was persuaded to go to the airport's second story VIP room. There, as tenderly as possible, she heard the devastating news. The Cuban airliner had been blown out of the sky at 12:23 P.M. by a suitcase bomb just off the Barbados coast; all seventy-three people aboard the plane were killed. Soon, the three governments of Cuba, Venezuela, and the United States of America identified the two prime bombers as Luis Posada Carriles and Orlando Bosch. To this day, Carriles and Bosch are protected on US soil and are hailed as heroes by the Florida-based Batistianos and by the US government, the very same US government that is spending billions of dollars and thousands of lives on what it calls "the war against terrorism."

***

Celia Sánchez never recovered from the 1976 bombing, although she continued to work as diligently as ever. Marta Rojas says, "It's easy to pinpoint the day Celia died — October 6, 1976, when that airplane went down. She just existed till January 11, 1980, when cancer, overwork, and a broken heart finally killed her."

Luis Posada Carriles and Orlando Bosch recovered quickly. Orlando Bosch said, in Miami's *El Nuevo Herald,* on October 14, 2001: "There were no innocents on that airplane. The DC-8 airplane brought down in Barbados was a war plane camouflaged with the Cuban de Aviación sign." Luis Posada Carriles, in the *Miami Herald*, said on November 10, 1991: "The sabotage was the most effective blow so far against Castro." According to Luis Posada Carriles, in the *New York Times* on July 12, 1998: "The CIA taught us everything, how to use explosives, to kill, to make bombs. They trained us in acts of sabotage."

From 1976 on, Celia blamed "the American people" more than she blamed the Batistianos or the US government. By America's own reckoning, citizens have a duty to speak out when their country strays from its high ideals. Yet, when it comes to Cuba, the only voices seem to be those calling for violence.

US hypocrisy regarding Cuba, in light of America's own justifiable "war against terrorism," hurts America's credibility around the world, especially across Latin America. That deplorable fact is repeatedly pointed out by Earl Smith, former head of the US Interest Section in Havana, Cuba. In May 2005, Earl Smith issued this statement regarding Luis Posada Carriles and Orlando Bosch in Miami: "When the US is viewed as harboring known anti-Cuban terrorists, it undermines the entire US war on terrorism."

In 2002, Ana Belén Montes, the top US government expert on Cuba at the time, said the same thing (before she was sentenced in a pro-Batistiano court to twenty-five years in federal prison). In 2005, the US government's top expert on Cuba is Fulton Armstrong, who once lived in Cuba as a US intelligence officer. Because he opposed the Batistiano positions regarding Cuba, Armstrong has been berated and transferred to an "assignment overseas," according to Nancy San Martin's May 13, 2005 article in the *Miami Herald*. Armstrong's banishment surfaced in May 2005 only because of the congressional hearings on John Bolton's UN appointment. Bolton has long been in league with Roger Noriega and Otto Reich, in terms of the Bush administration's Cuba policy.

The congressional hearings on Bolton's UN appointment became heated, in part over his propensity to hold news conferences in which he accuses Cuba of developing biochemical weapons and providing them to "other rogue nations." Bolton apparently used that as a pretext for the US to attack Cuba, which indeed went on a war footing in 2004 based on "pretexts" laid down by Bolton. Fulton Armstrong pointed out that the US government knew Cuba was not involved in biochemical weapons and that Bolton should not be suggesting it was. Fulton Armstrong was sent so far away that Nancy San Martin of the *Miami Herald* says, "efforts to reach him were unsuccessful." Efforts to reach many journalists and others who have spoken freely about US activities against Cuba would also be unsuccessful.

***

There are many illustrations today of the continuing topicality of Celia Sánchez and of the continuing harm, to both Cubans and Americans, that the US policy of purblindly supporting the Cuban exile terrorists engenders.

In 2005, Fidel Castro devoted the bulk of his May Day speech to the US government's harboring terrorists such as Luis Posada Carriles, Orlando Bosch, Gaspar Jiménez, Guillermo Novo, and Pedro Remón in Miami. Castro said, "The whole world knows that Luis Posada Carriles is the cruelest, most famous terrorist in the western hemisphere" to thunderous applause.

On March 31-2005 a major article in the Miami Herald written by Nancy San Martin began with these words: "A half a dozen terror bombings in Havana returned longtime anti-Castro activist Luis Posada Carriles to the limelight in 1997. Posada, then about 69, made front pages around the world when he admitted to masterminding the blasts and hinted the plot had been financed by Jorge Mas Canosa, the late founder of the Miami-based Cuban American National Foundation. Posada, nicknamed Bambi despite his fearsome history as a Bay of Pigs veteran, CIA explosives expert and Venezuelan political police commissioner, had been hiding in El Salvador since his escape from a Venezuelan prison while awaiting a retrial for the 1976 midair bombing of a Cuban jetliner that killed 73."

An Associated Press article from Miami on April 21, 2005 began: "Activists urged President George W. Bush to take action against a 'terrorist' accused of blowing up an airliner, bombing buildings and plotting to kill Cuba's leader, who is seeking asylum in the United States. The groups demanded that authorities arrest Cuban-born Luis Posada Carriles, who is wanted in Venezuela in connection with the death of 73 people and in Cuba for a string of bombings. 'It is not a question of ideology, it is a question of terrorism,' said Max Lesnik, leader of Alianza Martiana, who compared Posada to Osama bin Laden. 'While the US is fighting terrorism abroad, we should not be harboring terrorists at home,' Democratic representative Jim McDermott said in an open letter to the Department of Homeland Security. 'We must ask President Bush: Why have you said nothing to denounce Posada Carriles?' said Gloria la Riva, of the antiwar ANSWER group."

Meanwhile, immigration attorney Eduardo Soto has said that he plans to ask the Department of Homeland Security for asylum and parole for Luis Posada Carriles so he can live in the United States without fear of extradition.

A May 9, 2005 article by Tim Weiner for the *New York Times* noted that: "A grant of asylum could invite charges that the Bush administration is compromising its principle that no nation should harbor suspected terrorists. But to turn Mr. Posada away could provoke political wrath in the conservative Cuban-American communities of South Florida, deep sources of support and campaign money for President Bush and his brother Jeb, the state's governor."

Fidel Castro uses state television to chat almost nightly with the Cuban people, much as wily President Franklin Roosevelt used the radio for "fireside chats" to charm and instruct his electorate. The US government has been beaming anti-Castro propaganda at Cuba via Miami-based Radio Marti and Television Marti as well as a glossy website. An ABC-TV investigative report, still available on its website archives, shows that the US government has sent "hundreds of millions of dollars" to the Miami exiles to produce Radio Marti, and states that "not one word reaches Cuba because the broadcasts are easily blocked by the Cuban government."

Even if the message got through, Castro could easily overwhelm it with his avuncular televised "chats." The Cubans on the island know Castro best of all; most support him. And, even those who wish things were different are not influenced by what the US government or the Miami Mafia (as they call the Batistianos) say about him.

The US government also generously supports numerous organizations, either on the island or in the US, that so much as hint that they are "anti-Castro."

One May 16, 2005, the press noted an upswing in Cuba's economic condition. "In recent weeks, an ebullient Cuban President Fidel Castro has ... announced a doubling of the minimum wage for 1.6 million workers and an increase in pensions for the elderly while also reporting the delivery of thousands of pressure cookers and rice steamers to the poor. Diplomats and experts have been wondering where Castro is getting the cash for such initiatives. The partial answer came last month when Venezuelan Energy Minister Rafael Ramirez acknowledged the oil-rich nation has increased shipments of oil to Cuba on preferential terms.... Experts say the oil subsidies have neutralized the impact of President Bush's efforts to squeeze the Cuban economy.... De Salas said Venezuela is further bolstering the Cuban economy by purchasing hundreds of millions of dollars worth of products from Cuba and by providing financing to purchase everything from Venezuelan chocolate to sardines to work boots. The recent announcement that Cuba will increase the number of physicians and other medical personnel in Venezuela to 30,000 from 20,000 by year's end also benefits the two nations. The program has boosted Chavez's popularity because most of the Cuban medical personnel work in poor neighborhoods that are the Venezuelan leader's political base. 'The US measures have failed to achieve their purpose not because they are ineffective in and of themselves but because Fidel Castro has managed to circumvent them,' De Salas said....Castro has outmaneuvered the US president by forging closer ties to China, which recently agreed to invest $500 million in a Cuban nickel plant. Cuba has received a recent economic boost from the high price for nickel, a key Cuban export, and growth in the number of tourists, which last year topped 2 million. Yet, it is the relationship between Chavez and Castro that has blossomed in recent years, especially after the United States appeared to endorse an unsuccessful coup against Chavez in April 2002. US officials are now re-evaluating policy towards Venezuela...but experts say there are few options, given that Venezuela is among the largest sources of crude oil for the US. Experts say Castro is in a good position to outlast yet another US president as long as Chavez wins next year's presidential election, as now seems likely according to a recent poll" (Gary Marx, *Chicago Tribune*; May 16, 2005).

The 79-year-old Castro finds it ever easier to find friends when the US is alienating everyone in reach. The bungled coup attempt in Venezuela increased Chavez's power and gave him more incentive to help his neighbor. Now, all analysts seem to agree, the Castro-Chavez alliance is far stronger throughout Latin America than the US position, a fact evidenced by one election after another throughout that region. Panama was the latest to replace a pro-Bush president with a pro-Castro president.

As *USA Today* noted, the region is already "pink" and on its way to becoming "red." Thirty-four of the thirty-five countries in the Americas now hold various forms of democratic elections. In those countries, the majority of voters realize they are poor; they have no illusion that they will soon be one of the wealthy few. When poor people recognize their position, they tend to favor a pro-Castro/Chavez candidate over a pro-US candidate; concern for the little guy is clearly more in their interest than winner-take-all capitalism.

Castro may or may not live long enough to outlast the current US president. But he's done remarkably well. "The Cuban Revolution," Celia told Nora Peters in November 1979, "will not last forever. But it has lasted long enough to make a statement to history, don't you think? The best thing I ever did was go to the Sierra to fight Batista. My father was proud of me. Fidel is proud of me. I am proud of me. I hope you...are proud of me."

***

Nora Peters was back in Cuba to share the last two months of Celia's life. Marta Rojas, Celia's dear friend and fellow revolutionary heroine, wrote the front-page articles in the Cuban newspapers concerning Celia's death. In December 2004, Ms. Rojas was kind enough to send the author copies of those articles.

Celia Sánchez was a very private woman; Fidel Castro, her greatest acolyte, is a very private man. Thus, it is her life and not her death that I have chosen to emphasize. However, I believe it is important that Castro's reaction to Celia's passing is fairly documented, because that reaction is ongoing and it is to this day significant to both Cuba and America.

As the lithe Celia withered away, a distraught Fidel struggled to care for her and to console her. He consulted with the heads of the best cancer treatment centers around the world, deciding that a hospital in London was the best to treat Celia's particular illness. He arranged to fly her to London, but she refused. "No," she said. "I will not take a chance on dying anywhere but in Cuba."

There were five people in the room when she died. For days, she had been unable to speak, except the silent messages she sent with those expressive Spanish eyes. "In those last days," Nora Peters said, "Celia's eyes tried to hide the pain she suffered and tried so hard to tell us that she was fine, that she was at peace and that she would be all right. We had no choice but to accept that. But when she passed, for the first time in five days, I stepped outside. There was a light drizzle of rain, and a rumble of thunder. Then a bright rainbow dominated the skyline toward the ocean. That...was hard. Real hard."

When she died, Castro told Marta he felt "empty." And, in the hallway, he made a monumental decision that to him seemed entirely logical now that Celia was no longer there: he quit. Fifteen minutes later Fidel told his brother Raúl, "It's over for me. The island needs a new leader. Start the process now; no input from me."

For the next two days Raúl went through the motions of starting that process. He was biding his time, time that Fidel spent cloistered alone engulfed in sorrow, all alone even in rooms also occupied by others. On the fourth day, Raúl left the Palace of the Revolution for the drive to the 11th Street apartment.

Talking there with Fidel, he said, "The last thing in the world that Celia would want is for someone other than you to be the leader of Cuba."

On January 15, 1980, Fidel Castro mentally and physically returned as Cuba's leader. And with that tough decision, he made a promise to himself: As long as he lived, he would rule Cuba only in the precise manner that he perceived Celia would want him to rule it. In the many days, months, years, and decades that have followed, he has kept that promise. Such is the picture presented by the A & E biography of Fidel entitled El Comandante has actual video of him, seated with his head bowed, mourning the loss of Celia, with the voice-over explaining that this was the point when he had "quit" as leader of Cuba. Marta Rojas confirms that historical fact.

Of all the historians, I think Georgie Anne Geyer best captured Fidel's reaction to Celia's death and best projected how he has responded to it from that sad day in 1980 to the present day, with consummate ramifications, pervasive consequences, and dire fallouts for both Cuba and America. In *Guerrilla Prince*, Geyer wrote:

"But most said his turn of mood — his turn of luck — came in 1980 because of the one possibility that he had never really believed possible: the death of Celia.... Since virtually the moment they had met that damp, misty early dawn in 1956 in the Sierra, she had been his first and last and at times his only real tie to reality. Now she was suddenly gone. On those rare occasions when be bothered now to attend diplomatic receptions, he appeared strangely remote....In his office, he whiled away melancholy hours looking at designs for statues to be built to honor Celia.... More and more of the time he stalked up and down despondently in the big room next to his office, stopping to study, and restudy, the giant mock-up of the Sierra Maestra upon which he had dramatically marked all their 'battles' except this one that was his alone. More and more, he was the sole caretaker of the legend that was also singularly Celia's legend as well...." (pages 356-357).

"To this day," Marta Rojas told the author, "Fidel only speaks of Celia with a couple of us, ones he trusts as revolutionaries who knew Celia the best. When we talk about her, I think it helps him, soothes him. But at some point he says, 'No es facil' [It's not easy]. He means it's not easy living without her."

I asked Ms. Rojas how Celia impacts Fidel's rule of Cuba today. She replied: "Totally. His life, his rule of Cuba, is devoted to her. He longs to die fighting for her, for her revolution. He dreads the thought of dying in bed of old age. He remembers all the front-line fighting with Celia in the Sierra. He thinks of the front lines, of being there with Celia once again. You asked, Mr. Haney, if Celia's famous pledge that the Florida Batistianos would never reclaim Cuba as long as she lived or as long as Fidel lived impacts him today. Nothing impacts him more. [He wants] a storybook ending: fighting on the front lines for Celia."

By August 2005, Castro had reached the age of 79 and had ruled Cuba for 47 years. And Celia's voice still rang in his ears: "Fidel, I didn't promise little María Ochoa a negotiated peace settlement. I promised her a do-or-die fight. And that's the way it's gonna be."

Celia Sánchez beat Batista, a phenomenon of history. Celia Sánchez has kept the Batistianos from reclaiming Cuba for forty-seven years and counting, another phenomenon of history.

"The greatest maker of Cuban history," to quote Pedro Alvarez Tabío, gave everything she had to "mi Cubita bella."

If the counterrevolutions that swept through Eastern Europe make their way to Cuba, all this will end. Celia would understand that. And if the Batistianos flock back to Cuba, the monuments and shrines to Celia will likely be torn down. But in the annals of history, Celia Sánchez will never be forgotten.

Odds are, those Spanish eyes are keeping a close watch over "mi Cubita bella," her beautiful little Cuba. She deserved those rainbows to brighten her darkest days, and Cuba deserved her.

Printed in the United States
70398LV00003B/136

9 780875 863955